PLAINS INDIAN RAIDERS

Plains Indian Raiders

THE FINAL PHASES OF WARFARE FROM THE ARKANSAS TO
THE RED RIVER *With Original Photographs by William S. Soule*

By Wilbur Sturtevant Nye

University of Oklahoma Press : Norman and London

By Wilbur Sturtevant Nye

Carbine and Lance: The Story of Old Fort Sill (Norman, 1937, 1951)

(with Jason Betzinez) *I Fought with Geronimo* (Harrisburg, 1959)

(with Edward J. Stackpole) *The Battle of Gettysburg: A Guided Tour* (Harrisburg, 1960)

Bad Medicine & Good: Tales of the Kiowas (Norman, 1962)

Here Came the Rebels (Baton Rouge, 1965)

Plains Indian Raiders (Norman, 1968)

Library of Congress Catalog Card Number: 67-24624

ISBN: 0-8061-1175-5

6   7   8   9   10   11   12   13   14   15   16   17   18   19   20   21   22

To the memory of

GEORGE HUNT

Kiowa historian, guide, interpreter,

and my esteemed friend

FOREWORD

The nomadic Indians of the central and southwestern Plains were untamed, frequently hostile to the whites, and of uncertain temper, even as late as 1875. A man had to be constantly alert to danger when dealing with them, as with any feral, predatory creature. Chief Satanta of the Kiowas was typical. He would enter a military post for a friendly visit with the commanding officer, whom he would greet with a bear hug and a hearty handshake. The next day, at the head of two hundred warriors, he would dash in close to the post, whooping and shooting, to run off the grazing herd of horses. If the few soldier-herders tried to resist, they would be speared, shot, scalped, and mutilated.

It is surprising, therefore, that a single cameraman—a tenderfoot fresh from the East—could get portraits of these Indians when they were almost continually on the warpath. Nearly all of the tribal chiefs and many lesser warriors, together with women and children, came to the studio of William S. Soule and, despite their superstitious fear of the black box, sat for their photographs. The Indians were mostly Kiowas, Kiowa-Apaches, Comanches, Cheyennes, and Arapahoes, with a few from the minor tribes. Soule also obtained views of their camps, and of several white men who lived with the Indians and acted as guides and interpreters for the army.

Mr. Savoie Lottinville, former director of the University of Oklahoma Press, knowing that some thirty-two years ago I had obtained what is probably the complete collection of Soule's Indian photographs, suggested that I prepare a book presenting them to the reading public. A number had been published from time to time, but they were not always correctly identified either by photographer or by subject. And the whole collection had not been assembled in one volume. This project appealed to me because I have long felt that the graphic arts should be more thoroughly exploited as an aid to historical writing. The Soule photographs show exactly how the Plains Indians looked a century ago—how they dressed, what ornaments they wore, and how they lived.

Not enough is known about Soule to devote more than a few pages to him. Therefore, this book, the text of which serves as a background for his photographs, is confined to the activities of these Indians during the period in which they were seen and photographed by Soule. It is the story of how they were moved south from the Arkansas River, which had been the general area of their hunting (and raiding) grounds, and how they were established on their assigned reservations in Indian Territory. This in turn makes necessary an account of their chief opponents—the military forces.

The soldiers first attempted to control the Indians by defensive measures, building army posts and substations along the overland routes in Kansas, but finally they found it expedient to conduct offensive operations in the field. Brief accounts are given of the setting up of several posts along the Arkansas route; one post, Fort Wallace, on the Smoky Hill Road; and another Camp Supply, on the North Canadian River. Fort Sill was established at the east end of the Wichita Mountains to control the Kiowas and Comanches, but that story is told in my earlier *Carbine and Lance: The Story of Old Fort Sill*, first published in 1937 by the University of Oklahoma Press and still in print. *Carbine and Lance* and *Plains Indian Raiders* are companion volumes, but *Plains Indian Raiders* precedes the other in the flow of events.

WILLIAM S. SOULE

William Stinson Soule was born at Turner, Maine, on August 28, 1836, of Yankee parentage and English ancestry. Miss Lucia A. Soule, his daughter, lives in Boston and has done much research into the family genealogy. She has told me that her family arrived on one of the voyages of the *Mayflower*, and that there are two chief branches of the Soule family in the United States today. Most members spell the name without an accent over the "e" and pronounce it "Sool" or "Sole" rather than "Soo-lay," which would be French. William S. Soule signed his name without the accent.

Other than that he was brought up on a New England farm, little is known of Soule's early years. He must have had a good schooling, however, for the photographer of those days had to be versed in chemistry, optics, and art—and Soule gave his occupation as "photographer" when he enlisted in the army in 1861. It is believed that prior to the Civil War he was associated with his older brother John in a photography studio in the Boston suburb of Melrose, Massachusetts.

At the outbreak of the Civil War, Soule enlisted in Company A, Thirteenth Massachusetts Volunteer Infantry Regiment. This unit served during the first year in the major campaigns in Virginia, but its most severe test came at the Battle of Antietam. As a part of Rickett's division of

Hooker's corps, the Thirteenth Massachusetts charged south through D. R. Miller's cornfield, where the dead afterwards lay in rows. Near the Dunker church the opposing lines almost tore each other to shreds. Soule's regiment alone lost six hundred men, nearly its entire strength, in less than twenty minutes.

Soule was struck in the hip by a Minié ball and was evacuated to a field hospital at Keedysville. From there he was moved via the old Cumberland Valley Railroad to a base hospital at Harrisburg, Pennsylvania. His recovery was slow and incomplete, retarded no doubt by one of the epidemics, such as measles and typhoid, that swept those hospitals. When his regiment was mustered out in September, 1864, by expiration of term of service, Soule re-enlisted in the Invalid Corps, which consisted of men incapacitated for field service but used for administrative work. The commander was Major General William S. Hancock, who had been badly wounded at Gettysburg.

In 1865, Soule set up a photographic studio in Chambersburg, Pennsylvania. No one except professionals owned cameras in those days, yet there was a great demand from soldiers and veterans for small portraits, called *cartes de visite*, to be given to their relatives or sweethearts. Soule did a good business in these photographs, a few of which may still be found in farmhouse attics in central Pennsylvania.

In 1866 or early 1867 an accidental fire damaged his studio. In spite of his wound, which still bothered him, and the lingering weakness caused by his long stay in the hospital, Soule decided to take the popular advice of Horace Greeley to "go west, young man." He sold his photographic business and with the proceeds bought a new camera and accessories, including darkroom supplies. He then took the "steam cars" for St. Louis. From there he went to Fort Leavenworth, where his former general, Hancock, had his headquarters of the Department of the Missouri. Nearby was Leavenworth City, the outfitting point for people going farther west, especially to Colorado. Soule heard that there was a job vacancy at Fort Dodge, a new post on the Arkansas River route (the old Santa Fe Trail). John Tappan, recently the adjutant of the District of the Upper Arkansas and now a civilian, needed a chief clerk in the sutler's store that he operated at Dodge. Soule applied for and got the job. He went by rail to Salina, where he bought a ticket on a stagecoach leaving the next day for Fort Dodge. His journey is described in Chapter VI.

In his off-duty time at Fort Dodge, Soule resumed his photographic work. He also took up horseback riding. This exercise combined with the better climate soon brought him back to health.

Few of Soule's photographs can be definitely identified as having been made at Fort Dodge. It may be presumed that many if not most of the photographs of Cheyennes and Arapahoes were made there, for later, when he was at Camp Supply, the Cheyennes rarely visited the post, and their agency was soon moved one hundred miles to the east. Still later, while he was at Fort Sill, he would have had little if any opportunity to photograph Cheyennes and Arapahoes, because their agency was then one hundred miles to the north.

Early in 1869 or possibly even when the troops first went to Camp Supply in November, 1868, Tappan and Soule went there as traders. Tappan had lost his franchise at Fort Dodge, and he never secured a formal permit to trade at Camp Supply, although he remained there several months.

It is not clear when Soule first went to Fort Sill. He may have accompanied General Grierson in the reconnaissance of December, 1868. There are several Soule photographs of Grierson and his staff at Medicine Bluffs, and these are believed to have been made at that time. However, it is certain that in 1869 Soule obtained a position with the Engineer Corps as official post photographer at Fort Sill. He was employed to take pictures of the successive steps in the construction of the post. These prints, a few of which are included in this book and all of which I obtained through official channels in 1935, are now on file at Fort Sill.

When the post trader's store was erected by Neal and John Evans at Fort Sill, Soule obtained a concession for a photographic studio in their main building. He maintained this studio for six years, during which time his income came chiefly from taking and selling photographs of the officers and their families and of the soldiers and civilians who were stationed at the post. From time to time he would persuade Indians to sit for portraits.

Soule was one of the best photographers of his day, although he never became famous. His pictures are in sharp focus, and are well composed. His contrast and tone values are as good as those of the photographs attributed to Matthew Brady or to Brady's two assistants, Alex Gardner and Timothy O'Sullivan.

Cameras of his day had a fairly good lens mounted in a brass barrel and fitted to a leather bellows on slides. The assembly permitted sharp focusing, but the lens was slow, with little or none of the versatility of modern equipment. The lens and bellows were fitted into a black box having the proper focal length, with a lid at the back for insertion of a plate of ground glass on which the image was focused and the picture composed. There was no rectifying lens, hence the image was seen reversed—upside down. Because the lens and the photographic emulsion were slow, requiring a time exposure of about twenty seconds, the camera had to be attached to a heavy tripod while the picture was being taken.

The operator draped a black cloth over his head and the rear of the camera to exclude all light except that which came through the lens. When the subject was properly composed and in good focus, the photographer substituted a loaded plate holder for the ground glass, and made the exposure. This was accomplished by quickly slipping off the lens cover, counting the number of seconds estimated as necessary for the exposure, and replacing the lens cap. Shortly after the exposure was made, the photographer went to a darkroom and developed and fixed the negative.

The necessity for focusing on ground glass caused the English scientist William A. Bell, who crossed the plains with a group of surveyors in 1867, a bit of embarrassment. He was photographing several Indian women, who were members of a tribe similar to the Cheyennes, whose women were excessively modest. One of them indicated by signs that she would like to look through the camera at her friends. When she saw them inverted on the ground glass she was incensed that the photographer would stare at them with their legs in the air. The women refused to let Bell make the exposures.

Soule's early work antedated the development of photographic film and fast emulsion, and he had to prepare his own plates in a darkroom. The first step was to pour a coating of collodion over the plate and allow it to dry. This was usually done the night before the pictures were to be made. Then, just prior to making the exposures, he again went to a darkroom and immersed the plate in a bath of silver nitrate. This sensitized plate was exposed in the camera while still wet and was developed and fixed as soon as possible after making the exposure. Baths containing iron sulfate and acetic acid were used in these processes. In all cases the photographer mixed his own solutions; although during the time Soule was making photographs in the West, it was possible to purchase the collodion and perhaps the iron sulfate solution from supply houses in Philadelphia.

The developed plate was fixed, washed, dried, and varnished. Prints were made by clamping sensitized paper to the negative and exposing the sandwich to sunlight for a time estimated to give good results. The paper, purchased in Philadelphia, came coated with albumen, but it, like the negative, had to be sensitized before it was used. Furthermore, it was developed in the same manner as the negative. Soule's negatives seem to have been 8x10 inches, but many of his prints are smaller, about 5x7.

With this equipment Soule was unable to obtain action "shots." It is noticeable that if dogs or horses are in outdoor scenes or if people are in motion, their images are badly blurred. But in his posed portraits of the Indians, even the children are perfectly still—there are no blinking eyes or twitching mouths.

For his field work, Soule used an enclosed buckboard to carry his supplies and to serve as a darkroom. He also had a small tent for the latter purpose, similar to the umbrella type used by campers today. Modern-day amateurs and professionals can appreciate the difficulties under which he worked, for he lacked both running water and temperature control.

Soule's studio props were simple and few in number. The furniture consisted of a couch, on which he sometimes had the women and children recline, a stump or pedestal with a buffalo robe or shawl over it, perhaps a chair or a stool, and the inevitable backdrop of painted canvas. The background scenes were usually ancient Roman or Greek, which contrasted strangely with the straw thrown on the floor to suggest the great outdoors and the impassive savages seated in front of the camera. It is noteworthy, too, that nearly all the studio portraits show the Indians dressed in their best finery. It is only in some of the camp scenes that old men may be seen in slovenly dress. The half-nude Wichita women whom Soule photographed were in their customary attire, not stripped to stimulate sales of the pictures to soldiers on the post—though Soule may have enjoyed increased revenue in this instance. Several of the early commissioners who visited Wichita villages commented that both men and women wore little clothing.

Soule mounted his Indian photographs individually on cardboard for sale to people who visited the trader's store. He also sent negatives to his brother, who had established an art store in Boston, and prints from some of these negatives were sold in the East, especially to schools and students in the Boston area. At Fort Sill, Soule mounted prints of all or nearly all of his photographs in large albums. He labeled many of his prints with a pen, using white ink. I know of several such albums. The post trader Neal Evans had one, which is now, I believe, in the collection of Mr. Claude Hensley of Oklahoma City; Charles Cleveland, an employee of the Evans brothers had one, and it was his widow, Mrs. Charles Cleveland of Anadarko, who graciously permitted me to make copies in 1934. Captain Robert G. Carter, Fourth Cavalry, writes in one of his books of purchasing Soule photographs at Fort Sill. One or two of the Indian agents at Sill either had albums or individual prints, for it was from this source that James Mooney of the Smithsonian Institution obtained a few pictures about 1895. Miss Lucia Soule presented her album to the Smithsonian, Bureau of American Ethnology in 1955, and Mr. Henry G. Peabody sold a partial collection to that agency in the same year. Doubtless, other albums of prints are in existence, but it is unlikely that Soule made many, since it was all handwork.

In conversation with Miss Soule, I endeavored to learn what had become of the negatives. She said that her mother had told her that someone, probably a former business associate, had sold them to some unknown person in the West. Sixty-nine negatives have recently been found in the Los Angeles County Museum, and the fifteen contact prints that have been published by officials of that agency show the amazing quality of the negatives, with even finer tone and texture than have been seen on the older prints, though the latter have stood up well over the years.

Many of the prints in the three albums I have examined are untitled. For years I endeavored to fill in these gaps by showing the prints to old Indians, many of them sons or daughters of the subjects. Gillett Griswold, director of the Fort Sill Museum, is still engaged in this work. Claude Hensley obtained considerable information from the papers and photograph collection of Neal Evans, who had made notes and inscriptions on the backs of his prints. Mrs. Margaret Blaker of the Bureau of American Ethnology has pieced out considerable data from Indians who visit her office frequently to look through the extensive collection there. Some of the Soule pictures, unfortunately, will never be identified, and there are a few that we are not even certain were made by Soule. These are generally prints made in Kansas, where Soule did not have a monopoly. Occasionally it is difficult to be sure of the tribe to which a particular Indian belonged. George Hunt told me that sometimes the only way to identify the tribe was by the beadwork on the Indian's clothing or moccasins.

General Benjamin Grierson, first commander at Fort Sill, mentions in letters to his wife (collection in the University of Illinois Library) that he had Soule to dinner on Christmas Day in 1874 and tried to dissuade him from his announced intention to return to the East. A few months later Soule did go to Washington with a delegation of Indians who were conducted there to shake hands with the Great White Father and to be impressed with the works and power of the white man. While there he met and fell in love with Miss Ella Augusta Blackman. Soon they were betrothed and making plans for an early marriage. Soule hastened back to Fort Sill to wind up his affairs and bring his equipment and other assets to Washington. To his dismay he found that a business associate, or partner, whose name is not known to me, had gone to California with everything except, perhaps, one of the albums and the negatives of the Indian collection.

This meant that Soule would have to begin his marriage and his profession on a shoestring. He took his bride to Philadelphia, where he had found employment, and later they moved to Vermont. In 1882 they went to Boston, where Soule again went into business with his brother. Their firm was called The Soule Art Company, but William Soule soon purchased his brother's interest. He continued the enterprise until he retired in 1900. From then until his death in 1908, he lived with his family in Brookline, Massachusetts. He was active in veterans' and philanthropic work during his later years. His daughter closed the old family home several years ago and sent me his collection of Indian artifacts. With her permission, I have since deposited this collection in the Fort Sill Museum.

Except when otherwise noted, all photographs in this book are believed to have been made by Soule (a few are doubtful), and were taken at Fort Dodge, Camp Supply, and Fort Sill. It has been customary in other publications to credit them to "Soule, about 1870." They were made, however, during the period 1867–75. Unless otherwise stated, the drawings are by Theodore R. Davis.

The maps are all based on the modern U.S. Geological Survey maps, with roads, towns, and other features taken from old maps in the National Archives or the map collections of Ernest Archambeau and Edward Beougher and from a big, authoritative study on the Santa Fe Trail in the headquarters of the National Park Service.

I wish to acknowledge gratefully the assistance of the late George Hunt, Hunting Horse, and many other Indian friends in identifying photographs. I am also grateful to Miss Lucia A. Soule, Gillett Griswold, Claude Hensley, and Mrs. Margaret Blaker. Mr. Griswold, director of the Fort Sill Museum, has carried on the work of identification, assisted especially by the Kiowa Gourd Society and Sarah Pohocsucut. I am indebted to Hugh D. Corwin, of the Southwestern Oklahoma Historical Society, for the rare photograph of Maman-ti's son. I am deeply indebted to my friend Ernest R. Archambeau of Amarillo, Texas, editor of the *Panhandle-Plains Historical Review*, and Edward M. Beougher, Grinnell, Kansas, president of the Fort Wallace Memorial Association, for much valuable information. Most important, they helped me place exactly certain historical sites and routes and supplied rare data on events. Above all, I wish to thank my wife, Elleane, for helping with the research and for typing the manuscript.

Wormleysburg, Pennsylvania   WILBUR STURTEVANT NYE

CONTENTS

ILLUSTRATIONS

MAPS

PLAINS INDIAN RAIDERS

1. DISTRESS ALONG THE ARKANSAS

Nomadic wild Indians created such an uproar along the overland routes through Kansas in the post–Civil War years that the government at length had to move them south into Indian Territory. Before this logical solution was adopted, the army sought to protect travelers and settlers by building a chain of military posts along the two main roads leading west and operating from them. This was ineffective. The Great White Father attempted, again ineffectively, to solve the problem by appeasing the Indians with talk, presents, and annuities.

In 1864 there were only three "forts" of any consequence on the roads across the central Plains—Fort Riley at the eastern fringe of the Indian country; Fort Lyon, Colorado, at its western edge; and Fort Larned, Kansas, in the center and on the Santa Fe or Arkansas River route. Fort Larned was the site of the Indian agency and, because of its central location, was initially the most important of the three forts. During the succeeding four or five years the focus of interest shifted gradually to more westerly stations and eventually to posts in Indian Territory.

The defensive features of the terrain surrounding Fort Larned were excellent, for the post was situated in a tight bend of the Pawnee Fork of the Arkansas River. The steep banks of the Pawnee protected the fort on three sides. The Kiowa Indians who had ranged over this area, called the small, tortuous stream "Red Sleeves River" because one of their more noted war chiefs had been killed there during a fight with the Pawnees.[1] However, by 1864 the Kiowas' range tended to be centered farther south—from the Arkansas River to the Washita.

A great rolling prairie of scanty vegetation surrounded Fort Larned, becoming more arid nearer the eastern slopes of the Rocky Mountains two hundred miles to the west. South of the post the grass grew more luxuriantly, especially in the bottom lands of the Arkansas River, six miles away, where a civilian contractor cut hay in the summertime. Along the banks of the

[1] James Mooney, "Calendar History of the Kiowa Indians," *Seventeenth Annual Report of the Bureau of American Ethnology*, 286 (hereinafter referred to as Mooney, "Calendar History").

3

stream were a few native elms and box elders, but by 1864 the best timber had been cut for firewood.[2] This practice always angered the Indians, who felt that the trees belonged to them.

The site had first been occupied by troops in September, 1859, when a detachment of the First U.S. Cavalry camped there to protect wagon trains and stagecoaches on the Santa Fe Trail. Eight months later, in May, 1860, two companies of the Second U.S. Infantry supplanted the cavalry and began building a permanent post.[3] Stone could be quarried three miles from the post, but the commander chose to construct the buildings of adobe. Since the soil contained sand and prairie sod was not used, the sun-dried bricks began to crumble as soon as they were attacked by heavy rains. Nevertheless, the troops persisted. They first erected two company-size barracks, a small hospital, a storehouse for quartermaster and commissary supplies, a guardhouse, and two sets of laundress quarters. At first the horses, mules, and officers were on low priority. The horses and mules were tied to picket lines in the open, and the officers were quartered in tents or dugouts.[4] Additional buildings were constructed in 1862 and 1863; these included a large stone store for the sutler—Crane and Weichselbaum Company.[5]

From the outset, Kiowas, Kiowa-Apaches, Comanches, and Arapahoes frequented the area. They were nominally friendly to the United States, their white enemies being the Texans, but this was at best an uncertain peace, often violated by eager warriors on both sides. The Comanches were mostly of the northern band, commonly called Yamparikas or Yapparikas (Yam-eaters), with occasionally a fewer number of Kotchatekas (Buffalo-eaters). The southern bands, called Penatekas, rarely came so far north. The fourth large group of Comanches, called the Quohada or Kwahadi, roamed the Staked Plains and had no peaceful contact with white Americans.[6]

The Arapahoes, who were associated with the Cheyennes, had only recently arrived in the central and southern Plains, and they were inclined, under the influence of Little Raven and several other chiefs, to be friendly.

2 "Medical History, Fort Larned," Book 164, 1, 9, 13.

3 *Ibid.*, 1, 2; *War of the Rebellion: Official Records of the Union and Confederate Armies*, Series I (hereinafter referred to as *OR*), Vol. XXXIV, Pt. IV, 403.

4 "Medical History, Fort Larned," Book 164, 2.

5 *Ibid.*

6 Comanche tribal names used herein are popular forms which seem to me, when listening to old Comanches, to correspond closely to the sounds. For scientific renditions used by ethnologists and more precise breakdowns of the tribe into bands, see Ernest Wallace and E. Adamson Hoebel, *The Comanches: Lords of the South Plains*, 25–31.

The Cheyennes, however, were generally hostile, although Black Kettle's band was friendly and often camped south of the Arkansas with the Arapahoes, Kiowas, and northern Comanches. The more warlike Cheyenne bands, especially the "Dog Soldiers" under Medicine Arrow, Tall Bull, Bull Bear, and Roman Nose, usually camped on the headwaters of the two forks of the Republican River, where they were often joined by a small number of Brûlé Sioux.[7]

The Kiowas and Arapahoes were the tribes most frequently seen at Fort Larned, where the agent usually made his headquarters and issued rations and annuities granted under earlier treaties. As a consequence, several of their chiefs were familiar sights to the post personnel, and one or two became well liked—notably Kicking Bird of the Kiowas and Little Raven of the Arapahoes. Satanta and Satank of the Kiowa tribe were equally well known, but chiefly for their bloodthirsty reputations, and no warmth of affection on the part of the military personnel was extended to them. Even the most consistently friendly bands contained young men who would depredate whenever they felt in the mood, and the chiefs exercised little or no control over them. Of all the high-level officials who came in contact with the untamed Indians during this troubled period, only General William T. Sherman seemed to realize clearly that the Indians lived in a true democracy—that every man did exactly as he pleased, and that it was absurd to expect the tribes to observe treaties made by their chiefs.[8]

In the summer of 1860, the Second Infantry contingent at Fort Larned was augmented by two companies of the Second U.S. Dragoons, but in November the entire garrison was ordered to Fort Riley, leaving the post in the hands of a caretaking detachment. A year later, with the Civil War in progress and the Regular Army units needed elsewhere, the post was reoccupied by Volunteer units from Kansas, Colorado, and Wisconsin. There were frequent changes, but most of the time the garrison consisted of the Ninth Wisconsin Battery, Light Artillery, commanded by Lieutenant W. D. Crocker.[9]

Nothing of great interest appears in the post records until April, 1864, when several parties of Indian raiders attacked wagon trains on the Santa Fe Road west of Fort Larned while others stole stock from settlers in eastern Colorado. During one of the latter affairs a family of four whites was butchered by Indians, who were at first thought to have been Chey-

[7] Donald J. Berthrong, *The Southern Cheyennes,* Chaps. IV–VI.
[8] Report of General W. T. Sherman, July 1, 1867, 40 Cong., 2 sess., *House Exec. Doc. 1324,* 67.
[9] "Medical History, Fort Larned," Book 164, 1.

ennes, but who may have been Arapahoes. Most of the outrages during the Indian "war" of 1864 occurred north of the Smoky Hill Road, generally along the Platte and Republican rivers.[10] The area most affected was the Military District of Colorado, commanded by Colonel John M. Chivington, who, together with the governor of Colorado Territory, John Evans, favored a policy of harsh reprisals against the Indians. Chivington was outspoken in his desire to exterminate all Indians, whether innocent or guilty.[11]

During April, Colonel Chivington sent out several expeditions to run down and punish the Indians. A few skirmishes occurred, generally well to the northwest of Fort Larned. In one such skirmish, four soldiers were killed and three wounded—one mortally.[12]

Although Fort Larned was not threatened directly, Lieutenant Crocker, in his isolated post and far from support, began to feel apprehensive. His next higher commander was Brigadier General Thomas J. Kean, Headquarters District of South Kansas, at Paola. Crocker applied to Kean for more troops, stating that the Kiowas in his area were becoming more troublesome. Without specifying incidents, he said they were attacking trains and stealing stock. Part of his communication follows:

> With the garrison I have, it is impossible to do more than post duty. I have been at this post nearly two years and during that time I have never known the Indians to be so insolent as they are at present, and I believe that unless this post is re-enforced with cavalry soon, there will be serious difficulty.[13]

Kean, instead of sending Crocker additional troops, forwarded the request to the next higher headquarters, recommending approval.[14] Thus, the request was sent to the Headquarters Department of the Missouri at Fort Leavenworth, Kansas, commanded by Major General Samuel R. Curtis. Curtis, of course, had sufficient military resources to buttress the defenses of the posts along the Arkansas River route, but his department was under far more serious threats from the Confederate forces in Missouri and Arkansas, and his troops in the District of South Kansas were fully occupied with Quantrill and other guerrillas. Therefore, he told Chivington to send a detachment from Denver to reinforce Fort Larned. Then, satisfied that Larned was indeed exposed to imminent attack, Curtis had Kean send

---

[10] *Ibid.*, 2. The reports of the Indian raids during this period are in *OR*, XXXIV, Pts. I–IV; XLI, Pt. 1. See particularly XXXIV, Pt. I, 881; Pt. III, 113; and Pt. IV, 595.

[11] Berthrong, *The Southern Cheyennes*, 220.

[12] *OR*, XXXIV, Pt. I, 881; Pt. III, 113.

[13] *OR*, XXXIV, Pt. III, 241.

[14] *Ibid.*

Captain James Parmetar with Company H, Twelfth Kansas Volunteer Infantry.

Parmetar must have been an officer wanted by no one, for he was an alcoholic who within two months was to be dismissed from the service. When he was not drunk in quarters, he had the garrison at Larned out on what he called "scouts" but which were actually buffalo hunts.[15]

Having thus "solved" the Fort Larned problem, General Curtis turned his attention to other matters. Then, on June 3, he received two letters he could not ignore. One, from the Governor of Colorado, stated that Indian forays had interrupted the lines of supply to the extent that the Denver area was running short of food. Freighters were afraid to cross the plains, and his people faced disaster unless greater military protection was furnished.[16] On the same day, Curtis was informed by a representative of the Post Office Department that the U.S. mail service to Fort Larned, Fort Lyon, Fort Union (New Mexico), and Santa Fe had been stopped because stagecoaches and stations had been attacked. Mail contractors were unwilling to continue service unless they were afforded protection.[17]

Curtis was politically sophisticated, having been mayor of a city and three times a congressman. He appreciated the folly of brushing off the pleas of a governor and the Post Office Department. He knew that, whereas "political generals" were derided in some quarters, the most successful high-level commanders were those who enjoyed political support. Therefore, he at once directed Forts Riley and Larned to give all possible protection to the mails, and sent his inspector general, Major Thomas I. McKenny, to Fort Larned to investigate, effect remedies on the spot, and return with a full report.[18]

McKenny moved from Salina with forty men on June 9. That evening he reached the point where the Santa Fe Road crossed the Smoky Hill River. Here he found the stage station and "ranch" deserted, and commenced to build a blockhouse out of square-hewn logs he found there. On the thirteenth, having one story completed, he left Lieutenant Allen Ellsworth, Seventh Iowa Cavalry, with a detachment to complete the structure. This was the beginning of Fort Ellsworth, later named Fort Harker, the establishment of which is usually credited to General Curtis. The post was thus founded about June 10, 1864.[19]

---

[15] *OR*, XXXIV, Pt. IV, 402–405; "Roster of the Twelfth Kansas Volunteer Infantry," *Volunteer Army Register 1861–65*, 112.

[16] *OR*, XXXIV, Pt. IV, 206.

[17] *Ibid.*, 205.

[18] *Ibid.*   [19] *Ibid.*, 402.

Major McKenny arrived at Fort Larned on June 14. Captain Parmetar was absent on one of his scouts, but there was much more to criticize. The post was a fort in name only, for the side not protected by the river was fortified by a breastwork less than two feet high. The adobe huts were inferior in quality, and the storehouses were virtually in ruins. Rain water, which had been streaming down through grass-and-dirt roofs, was spoiling the corn, flour, beans, and other perishable supplies and over $5,000 worth of grain for the animals. "I think the men's time could be much better employed in the erection of stone buildings," commented the Inspector, "instead of going every few days on fruitless scouts that wear out the horses without prospect of meeting Indians."[20]

The next day McKenny received a visit from Do-hauson, principal chief of the Kiowas. Once a mighty warrior, the old man had held his position for over thirty years, and although his immediate following now consisted of only a dozen lodges of old people and children, he still had great influence in the tribe.[21] Major McKenny felt that the chief was sincere in expressing friendship for the whites. "He asked me many questions as to where I came from and what was my business. I told him, through an interpreter, that the great general commanding all this country was much pleased with him, and that he was known far and wide as a great chief."[22]

Do-hauson was in mourning for a close relative. He had cut off one of his fingers, killed three of his horses, and burned his fine lodge containing nineteen robes and all his favorite things. He had also burned his wagon, an object of much interest to the other Indians because none of them possessed a wheeled vehicle. It was a light spring wagon with a canvas top, known in the army as an ambulance but used in peacetime more as a personal conveyance for high-ranking officers who were too portly to mount their horses than for the sick. In 1859, Major John Sedgwick, who was later a corps commander in the Army of the Potomac, had formed a friendship with Do-hauson when Sedgwick was camped with his battalion on the Arkansas River. He had ordered a decrepit ambulance condemned, and he presented it to the chief, who was very proud of it.[23]

McKenny also talked to Little Raven, principal chief of the Arapahoes, a plump, elderly Indian who knew a little English and had the reputation of being consistently friendly.

While at Fort Larned, Major McKenny established a system for guard-

[20] *Ibid.*, 402–405.
[21] Mooney, "Calendar History," 164.
[22] *OR*, XXXIV, Pt. IV, 403.
[23] Mildred P. Mayhall, *The Kiowas*, 204.

8

ing the mail coaches more effectively. Twenty men from the post at Salina would escort the stage to the Smoky Hill crossing and remain there to accompany it on the return trip. In a similar manner a detachment would go with it to the Walnut Creek crossing, where McKenny planned to establish another post, and a third detachment would take it to Fort Larned. West of Fort Larned the responsibility for guarding the coach had been assigned to Fort Lyon. As an added protection for traffic, McKenny directed that westbound trains wait at Salina until a sufficient number were collected to ensure a stout defense against Indian attack.

He completed his visit at Fort Larned by forbidding further running of buffalo and by directing that a stone hospital and another commissary and quartermaster storehouse be started at once. Then, on his return trip, McKenny camped on or about June 18 at the Walnut Creek crossing, where he dropped off Captain O. T. Dunlap and forty-five men of the Fifteenth Kansas Cavalry to build a "stone fort." This was the founding of Fort Zarah, also credited to General Curtis, who later passed through the fort.[24]

When he returned to Fort Leavenworth, Major McKenny urged General Curtis to replace the drunken Parmetar as commander at Fort Larned. Curtis passed this suggestion on to Kean at Paola, who made the usual reply that he had no officer "available." Nevertheless, Parmetar was later ousted from the army and replaced by Captain William T. Backus, First Colorado Cavalry.[25]

In July a bit of excitement occurred at Fort Larned that was blown up in the reports far more than was justified—the post lost all its horses. This was among the first of many such occurrences; before the Indian troubles were settled, nearly every post along the Arkansas and Smoky Hill routes was to have a similar embarrassing experience. Here is how it happened. The Kiowas in June had celebrated their annual medicine dance, called the sun dance. Each annual dance had a name. The dance in 1864 was called the "Ragweed Sun Dance" because it was held in a field at the junction of Medicine Lodge Creek and the Salt Fork of the Arkansas where a quantity of ragweed grew. At the conclusion of the dance the entire tribe moved to the vicinity of Fort Larned to draw rations and annuities.[26]

On June 17 several chiefs entered the post, to which they had always been given free access for a visit with the post commander. Back at the camp a scalp dance was in progress.[27] The Kiowas called it a victory dance, for it was staged by the women to honor their successful warriors—it was never

[24] *OR*, XXXIV, Pt. IV, 575.
[25] *Ibid.*
[26] Mooney, "Calendar History," 177.
[27] Statement of An-pay-kau-te (Satank's son) to author, 1935.

held if some member of the party had been killed. In the dance the women clasp hands and form a circle around a tall pole from which trophies dangle. They move around sideways in a stately sort of two-step while several old men provide music by beating on a piece of rawhide and singing, "Hi-yah, He-yah," and other meaningless phrases to mark the rhythm.

The soldiers at the post called this a "squaw dance," not knowing its significance and possibly thinking it was staged for their benefit. But on this occasion the officers were alarmed. They had heard rumors circulated by civilians that the Indians were plotting to attack the post and massacre the entire garrison. When they heard that a squaw dance was about to be held in the Indian camps, they thought it was part of a scheme to lure the soldiers away from the barracks where their arms were kept in racks. Meanwhile, they conjectured, the Indians might be planning to infiltrate the post and attack at a given signal.[28]

An-pay-kau-te, son of Satank, told me what happened:

> It was the first raid I went on. After the Ragweed Sun Dance the Kiowas and Kiowa-Apaches went to the Black Timber River near Fort Larned. Some old colonel [J. H. Leavenworth, the Kiowa and Comanche agent] was there. We were having a Victory War Dance. The chiefs were going to post head-quarters to see the commanding officer. My father [Satank] and another fellow wanted to go there too. They didn't understand about the guard— tried to cross the line. The guard said, "No, no, no!" The Indians wouldn't listen. The guard raised his rifle. Satank shot three arrows at him, the other fellow two, and hit the guard. The excitement started. Everybody ran out. They didn't know what it meant. They chased the soldiers' horses off. Herded them. They helped themselves from the herd. In the evening we broke camp. The excitement had spoiled everything.
>
> Some of the Indians wanted to go on a raid. I joined them. Toward day-break we came to an Arapaho village, then went to a place where there were freighters. A big wagon train. We attacked them. I was there. On their return the Indians made another raid, which I joined. We killed another soldier close to some fort. He was a herd guard. Lots of wagons there. It was a black timbered place.[29]

The attack on the wagon train occurred near where the new post was being built at Walnut Creek crossing. Ten men, probably teamsters, were killed in the attack. The Indians ran off all the horses of the cavalry detachment stationed there, and the troops withdrew to Fort Larned.

[28] "Medical History, Fort Larned," Book 164, 3.
[29] Statement of An-pay-kau-te to author, 1935.

The Kiowas camped near Fort Larned had been peaceable until the affair of July 17, although a party under Satanta had attacked a ranch near Fort Lyon, one hundred miles to the west, and had killed four men at the stage station at Cimarron Crossing.[30] But An-pay-kau-te said that, when the Kiowas whooped away with the horse herd at Fort Larned, they threw away all the restraint that old Do-hauson had imposed. The affair touched off raiding all along the Arkansas route.

Even the Arapahoes joined in the raiding. Chief Left Hand and several of his men rode up to the post a day or two after the Kiowas had captured the horse herd, to offer assistance to the soldiers in tracking down the Kiowas and recovering the stock. When they approached the post, they were fired upon. The Arapahoes galloped away, convinced that the whites had decided to make war.[31]

Like a prairie fire racing before the wind, the troubles ran eastward along the Arkansas, and at the same time the Cheyennes stepped up their attacks at various points on the South Platte and the near settlements in Colorado.

Traffic on the overland routes stopped. As no mail came through from the west, General Curtis at Fort Leavenworth did not hear about the episodes at Fort Larned and Walnut Creek crossing for several days. Then the reports began to pour in, and he believed the situation had become serious.[32] But because of the threat presented by Confederate General Sterling Price in Missouri, he had no troops to take the field against the Indians. Therefore, he appealed to local officials in Kansas to call out the state militia or home guards. He had not waited to take this matter up with Governor Thomas Carney,[33] but the latter, when informed, made no objection.

On July 23, General Curtis began organizing a punitive expedition at Fort Riley; the bulk of the troops were to consist of militia cavalry reinforced by a Volunteer cavalry company and a section of artillery from Council Grove.[34] That night two teamsters came to Council Grove to report that four government wagon trains were surrounded by Indians at the Cow Creek crossing of the Santa Fe Road, one hundred miles to the west. Two men had already been killed, and the others would soon abandon the train and flee individually unless help arrived.[35]

---

[30] *OR*, XLI, Pt. I, 231–32.
[31] *Ibid.*, 964–68.
[32] *Ibid.*, Pt. II, 368.
[33] *Ibid.*, 445–46.
[34] *Ibid.*, 54–55, 369, 428, 445.
[35] *Ibid.*, 378.

Captain James H. Dodge, the commander at Council Grove, set out early the next morning with a relief column consisting of half of the Ninth Wisconsin Battery and one hundred home-guard cavalry.[36] When they arrived at Cow Creek, they found the wagon train safe, for the Indians had been frightened away by the troops of the Eleventh Kansas under Captain Henry Booth. However, the Indians had succeeded in running off 150 oxen.[37]

General Curtis assembled four hundred men, which he thought were enough to handle the Indians. He was satisfied that the purpose of the attacks was to steal stock and that they would not make a stand to oppose his expedition. He was correct. The Indians melted away before his advance; even friendly Indians were afraid to approach his command. On his march to Fort Larned he camped successively at the Smoky Hill and Walnut Creek crossings and directed that the posts which Major McKenny had started be reoccupied and the construction continued.[38] He was at the Walnut Creek site on July 28 and issued an order naming the new post Fort Zarah, in memory of his son Zarah M. Curtis, who had been killed by guerrillas in eastern Kansas.[39]

Curtis arrived at Fort Larned on July 29, simultaneously with four companies of the First Colorado Cavalry, which he had ordered Colonel Chivington to send two months earlier. He at once wrote Chivington an unfriendly letter which he signed, "Truly, your friend," but which contained some plain words. He chided Chivington for his tardiness in sending the reinforcements to Larned and advised him to pay more attention to his military duties and not to concern himself so much with politics. He told the Colonel that his Colorado troops made a fine appearance though their minds were mostly on their imminent mustering-out.[40]

Although Curtis had not yet seen an Indian, he saw the results of their attacks while at Fort Larned. A wagon train from New Mexico had been attacked at Cimarron Crossing. When it arrived at Fort Larned after a harrowing experience, the wagon train brought with it two wounded young men, both of whom had been scalped alive. One youth's scalp had been flayed off down to his ears, and he had eighteen other wounds. The post surgeon thought, however, that both boys would recover.[41]

[36] *Ibid.*

[37] *Ibid.*, 445.

[38] *Ibid.*

[39] *Ibid.* Henry M. Stanley, in *My Early Travels and Adventures in America and Asia*, 11 (hereinafter referred to as Stanley, *My Early Travels and Adventures*), says that Zarah Curtis was killed in "Blunt's Massacre," at Buckster's (Baxter's?) Spring, near Fort Scott, Kansas.

[40] *OR*, XLI, Pt. II, 483–84.

[41] *Ibid.*

General Curtis, realizing that Cimarron Crossing was a favorite target for the Indians and that it was too distant from Fort Larned to receive protection either from there or from Fort Lyon, directed the commander at Larned to establish a new post at Cimarron Crossing. A detachment of one company accordingly was sent out—and shortly lost all their horses to a band of raiding Indians. They had to be brought back to Larned. This was the first abortive attempt to establish what later became Fort Dodge.[42]

Meanwhile, at the end of July Curtis organized a big Indian hunt using Fort Larned as a base. The main column, which the General accompanied in person, consisted of the best horses and men of the Fifteenth Kansas Militia plus a company of Colorado cavalry. They crossed the Arkansas River and headed toward the Salt Fork, where the Kiowas and Comanches were supposed to be hiding. They did not go far before turning back to the northeast. Apparently they simply marched along the south side of the Arkansas to the great bend, for Curtis was issuing orders at Cow Creek crossing on August 4. A second column under Colonel D. W. Scott, Fourteenth Kansas Militia, was directed to scout along the north bank of the Arkansas and rendezvous with the main column at Little Arkansas Station, due east of Fort Zarah.[43] It would have been more logical for both columns to travel up the Arkansas instead of down, for the Indians had been reported to the southwest; but the route followed toward home for the militia, who had been fretting to return to their homes from the very day they were called out. As might be expected, the expedition encountered no Indians.

Curtis had ordered Captain Henry Booth with a battalion of the Eleventh Kansas Cavalry to march north from Fort Larned to the Smoky Hill, thence east along that stream to Fort Ellsworth and on to his home station at Salina. He was to drop off Lieutenant Ellsworth with his company of Iowa cavalry to continue building Fort Ellsworth. Captain William T. Backus, also at Larned, was told to occupy Fort Zarah.[44] The General then returned to Fort Leavenworth and sent a telegram to Chief of Staff Henry W. Halleck stating that everything was now quiet along the Arkansas and that traffic on the Santa Fe Road was moving normally again. The recent mischief, he said, was attributable to the Kiowas, Comanches, and Big Mouth's Arapahoes.[45]

He spoke too soon. On August 7, the Indians ran off all the horses at Fort Ellsworth, leaving the garrison of that embryo fort dismounted for three

[42] *Ibid.*, 692.
[43] *Ibid.*, 491.
[44] *Ibid.*
[45] *Ibid.*, 545, 610.

13

weeks until remounts could be procured and shipped to them. Captain Booth sallied forth from Salina once more to chastise the delinquent Indians but failed to bag a single one.[46]

And so ended the war of 1864 along the Arkansas and the Smoky Hill. The Indians had profited considerably, having stolen virtually all the horses at all the posts west of Salina. The monetary loss was considerable, and the distress was felt all the way back to Washington.

[46] *OR*, XLI, Pt. I, 189–90, 233–34.

2. A VILLAGE IS DESTROYED

When the July outbreak occurred in Kansas, General Curtis realized that the district commanded by General Kean was too unwieldy. He therefore issued an order on July 23, just before he started on his expedition from Fort Riley, creating a separate District of the Upper Arkansas. Major General James G. Blunt was designated as the commander, and the district limits were established, extending from Council Grove on the east to Fort Lyon on the west and from the District of the Platte on the north to the southern border of Kansas.[1]

Blunt arrived at Fort Riley on August 4 and established his headquarters there. First Lieutenant John E. Tappan, Second Colorado Cavalry, was appointed assistant adjutant general.[2] This was the key staff position, for the incumbent was *the* adjutant, not an assistant, and he had many of the responsibilities of a chief of staff as well. Another important slot, that of inspector general, was filled by the able and active Captain Henry Booth, who was made post commander in addition to his other duties.[3]

Blunt was ready to take over the responsibilities of protecting the overland routes in his district, and it was not long before the Indians proved that this was indeed necessary. They had faded away before the advance of Curtis' militia, but soon after his withdrawal, Indians were again striking various points along the Santa Fe Trail. There were also raids on new settlements or farms north and northwest of Fort Riley, and people in several northern counties began clamoring for protection.[4] The continuation of attacks on wagon trains and stages at Cimarron Crossing made it increasingly clear that another military post would have to be established in that vicinity.

At first General Blunt and his quartermaster were fully occupied in obtaining horses to replace the several hundred taken by the Indians from the posts west of Fort Riley. Blunt also hoped to mount another body of militia so that he could move about in his district and keep the Indians

[1] *OR*, XLI, Pt. II, 396.
[2] *Ibid.*, 775.
[3] *Ibid.*
[4] *Ibid.*, 641–43.

15

intimidated, but this would require still more horses.[5] Added to these difficulties was the prospect of troop shortages. Many Volunteers looked forward to the pending expiration of their terms of service. Also, there were supply deficiencies, for freight contractors feared sending their wagon trains into Indian country.

By the middle of August, Fort Larned was nearly out of ammunition. Fortunately, the new commander there, Major Scott J. Anthony, had brought some from Colorado, and he took immediate steps to secure more. The supply of ammunition was complicated by the many types of small arms used by the troops, who were armed with Sharps, Merrill, and Starr carbines and with army and navy models of Colt's revolvers.[6]

General Blunt cautioned the commanders at Forts Ellsworth, Zarah, and Larned to be on the lookout for Indians who had been raiding to the northwest of Fort Riley. They were thought to be moving southwest across the Arkansas, and Blunt had no force with which to pursue them. The several post commanders had troops, but they were still dismounted. On August 16, when seven Iowa cavalrymen were attacked near Fort Ellsworth, with four killed, the post commander was powerless to take action. Fort Larned was not in trouble, but there were two more tragedies near Cimarron Crossing. On August 19 a wagon train was destroyed there; the repulsive details were described by Major Anthony:

> The ten white men with it were killed and their bodies horribly mutilated, heads cut off, hearts cut out, and evidently placed in the center of their dance circle while they [the Indians] held their fiendish war dance around them and kicked the mutilated bodies about the prairies. The Mexicans with this train were permitted to take one wagon, with subsistence to last them back to Mexico, and sent back.[7]

Passengers on a stage arriving at Fort Larned from Fort Lyon said that on August 23 they had seen two dead men lying beside the road. Apparently they were victims of an attack that had been made near Cimarron Crossing on the twenty-first in which a wagon master and one or more teamsters had been killed and all the stock taken. Teams were sent out from Larned to haul the abandoned and looted wagons back to the post.[8]

Major Anthony considered the situation to be so critical that he called in his detachment at Fort Zarah and another he had sent to the future site of

5 *Ibid.*, 670–71.
6 *Ibid.*, 693.
7 *Ibid.*, 827, 926.
8 *Ibid.*, 926.

Fort Dodge—a stage station twenty miles east of Cimarron Crossing. This gave him a force of 420 men, but this was reduced by the 125 troopers who were constantly escorting stages. His civilian employees—teamsters, herdsmen, carpenters, and stonemasons—had prudently departed for the "states" and had to be replaced by soldiers. The Colorado troops were due to be mustered out in November. Anthony, remarking that all he was able to do was guard his post, asked for reinforcements.[9]

Major Edward W. Wynkoop, like Anthony a member of Chivington's First Colorado Cavalry, was in command at Fort Lyon. He too was concerned for the safety of his post. On August 16 he had appealed for more troops, but was told that none were available. He was advised to throw up earthworks around his post and be prepared to withstand a siege.[10]

On September 19, General Curtis again declared that the Indian troubles had abated.[11] This was the second time he had made such an announcement, and for the second time the raiding broke out afresh. As before, an expedition was being made ready to go out and give the Indians a whipping. General Blunt had scraped together three hundred militia; enough, he thought—with one hundred more he could obtain at Fort Larned—to handle anything he might encounter. He marched to Fort Larned, where he completed his force by taking with him Major Anthony and two troops of the First Colorado Cavalry.[12]

The column left Larned at 4:00 A.M. on September 22 and reached Cimarron Crossing at dark on the twenty-third. At 3:00 A.M. on the twenty-fifth they were again in the saddle and marching north toward the Smoky Hill River, where Blunt had heard there was a large Indian encampment. At daylight, when the troops were approaching Pawnee Fork, Blunt sent out a small detachment to locate a ford. On their return they reported finding Indian signs. Major Anthony and his two cavalry companies rode forward to locate the Indians. An hour passed. Blunt decided to follow Anthony. After marching over a mile, he saw Anthony's squadron ahead, surrounded by circling Indians. The cavalrymen were trying to fight their way back to the main body.[13]

At the sight of Blunt's column the Indians rode away. Anthony had lost two men killed and seven wounded. The command followed the Indian trail for two days, but when it turned upstream and crossed over toward the

[9] *Ibid.*, 827.
[10] *Ibid.*, 881.
[11] *Ibid.*, Pt. IV, 260.
[12] *Ibid.*, Pt. I, 818.
[13] *Ibid.*

17

Smoky Hill, Blunt decided to turn back. It was evident that the Indians' horses were faster than those of the cavalry so that there was no hope of overtaking the hostiles. Indian war parties always rode with spare mounts, sometimes as many as five or seven for each brave; and they changed mounts frequently. The soldiers had only one mount apiece, and when one gave out, the trooper had to walk. Blunt thought that the Indians they had been following were Cheyennes and Arapahoes, and this was probably the case, for the Dog Soldiers frequented this area.[14]

It now seemed likely that the Indian troubles were really slackening. Nevertheless, a few attacks took place late in the fall before the Indians went into their winter camps. Just after dark on November 13, 1864, thirty Indians attacked a teamsters' camp on Ash Creek twelve miles east of Fort Larned, where five wagons loaded with corn for the post had stopped for the night. One man was killed and four others fled to Fort Zarah, abandoning their stock to the Indians. In the morning Captain Theodore Conkey, Third Wisconsin Cavalry, then in command of Fort Zarah, sent a detachment after the raiders. Although they rode thirty miles up Walnut Creek, they failed to find Indians.[15]

On November 20, Captain Henry Booth and Lieutenant Albert Helliwell of General Blunt's headquarters were on an inspection tour of the posts along the Arkansas route. On leaving Fort Zarah they allowed their escort to precede them by two hours, thinking they could easily overtake it. On the way to Larned, and five miles from Zarah, they ran into an ambush. Twenty or more red warriors dashed at them from a gully. The two officers wheeled and galloped back toward Fort Zarah, closely pursued by the yipping braves. An arrow thudded into Booth's back but was deflected by his shoulder blade and passed through his arm. Helliwell was hit twice in the head, once in the back, and once in the arm. Three miles from the post the Indians gave up the chase. The officers continued on to the post, where they were treated for injuries that miraculously were not fatal.[16]

Just after nightfall on December 4, four soldiers of the Seventh Iowa Cavalry who were escorting an ammunition wagon to Fort Larned were attacked in their camp at the Cow Creek crossing. Three fled into the darkness and made their way to their home station, Fort Ellsworth. The other

---

[14] *Ibid.* Dog soldiers were members of warrior societies charged with "policing" the tribe, i.e., maintaining order on certain occasions such as large buffalo hunts. They constituted the more hostile portion of the Cheyenne tribe. With their families they had become virtually a separate band of the tribe.

[15] *OR*, XLI, Pt. I, 919.

[16] *Ibid.*, 934.

man hid in the brush until, two hours later, he was rescued by the escort of a stagecoach traveling toward Fort Zarah.[17]

At daybreak Captain Conkey sent an officer with sixteen men to discover what had happened to the ammunition wagon. They found the wreck of the wagon, and in the grass nearby, the naked corpse of the teamster, bristling with arrows. The Indians had captured all the teams and the soldiers' mounts except for one wounded animal which the Indians had left behind. The Indians had vanished.[18]

By mid-November nearly all the Indians were in their winter camps. The Kiowas and Comanches had gone to the Staked Plains, either to Palo Duro Canyon or to other deep gulches. There they spent the winter making lodge poles. The main Kiowa camp near Bent's old trading post—Adobe Walls—was attacked on November 24 by a force of three hundred New Mexico troops and one hundred Utes and Jicarilla Apaches under Colonel Christopher (Kit) Carson. The Indians were scattered but suffered few losses.[19]

The hostile bands of Cheyenne and Arapaho tribes were at the head-waters of the Republican River. The more friendly bands—Cheyennes under Black Kettle and Arapahoes under Little Raven, Left Hand, and Neva—tried to camp just outside Fort Lyon, where they hoped to receive protection from the post commander. They realized that otherwise they were apt to be attacked by any troops making a winter campaign.

Major Anthony was now the commander at Fort Lyon. He had replaced Wynkoop, who had been relieved by Chivington because of his soft atti-tude toward the Indians.[20] Anthony, though considerably less sympathetic toward the Indians than Wynkoop, was nevertheless moved by the destitute condition of Little Raven's village. He checked with his department head-quarters to see if there had been any modification of an order published by Curtis after the July raid on Fort Larned, which prohibited any post com-mander from allowing Indians to enter a military installation except as prisoners of war. Anthony accordingly advised the Arapahoes that they could camp near the post only if they surrendered their arms and animals and became prisoners. They even agreed to this. Black Kettle's Cheyennes also asked permission to come to the vicinity of the post, but when Anthony referred this request to Fort Leavenworth, permission was refused.[21]

17 *Ibid.*, 981–82.
18 *Ibid.*
19 Mooney, "Calendar History," 283; W. S. Nye, *Carbine and Lance: The Story of Old Fort Sill*, 36–37 (hereinafter referred to as Nye, *Carbine and Lance*).
20 *OR*, XLI, Pt. I, 959, 962, 963–69.   21 *Ibid.*, 912, 914.

19

This was the beginning of a chain of events that culminated in the notorious Sand Creek Massacre on November 29. Prior to this, Wynkoop had persuaded these friendly bands of Cheyennes and Arapahoes to attend a conference in Camp Weld, on the outskirts of Denver. Governor Evans and Colonel Chivington were present but showed a hard attitude toward the Indians.[22] Nevertheless, the Indians agreed to secure the release of several captives.

Chivington apparently used the conference to learn where the Indians were camped. He attacked Black Kettle's village on Sand Creek while the Indians thought they were under government protection. The details of this well-known affair will not be repeated here except to remark that it rivaled, if it did not surpass, in barbarity and savagery, any outrage committed by the Indians.[23] General Sherman called it one of the blackest pages in American history. Chivington boasted that he had killed several hundred Indians, but bodies counted later by Wynkoop totaled sixty-nine—mostly women and children. There were a considerable number of mutilations, including scalpings and worse. The troops even shot the half-blood son of old "Uncle John" Smith, an interpreter who usually lived with the Cheyennes.

Chivington and the men who perpetrated the massacre were not in the service of the United States, having been mustered out of the army earlier in the fall.[24] However, they had been recalled by the territorial governor as state militia for a limited period. When the details of the affair became known in the East and it was evident that public horror was growing, General Curtis advised Governor Evans to get Chivington out of his service quickly, before the lid blew off. This was done.[25] There was an investigation, but Chivington was never punished.

Black Kettle and the members of his village who survived the attack fled to a place called Big Timbers, a large cottonwood grove near the Smoky Hill Road some twenty-five miles west of where Fort Wallace was later built. The Smoky Hill River was said to have been given its name because of this grove, which, when seen in the distance, looked in a certain light to be a cloud of smoke. The grove was an old Indian camping ground, with numerous burial platforms in the trees. This was the Cheyenne method of disposing of their dead (the Kiowas and Comanches always buried theirs in the ground).[26]

---

[22] *Ibid.*, 960. [23] *Ibid.*, 948–72.

[24] Dates of service of the Volunteer Army regiments are given in the *Volunteer Army Register, :1864–65*.

[25] *OR*, XLVIII, Pt. I, 416.

[26] Mrs. Frank C. Montgomery, "Fort Wallace and its Relation to the Frontier," *Kansas*

Black Kettle, Little Raven, and their followers later moved south of the Arkansas River and tried to obtain help from the other tribes in that region. A band of Indians whose village had been destroyed was in a pitiable condition, especially in the winter, for they had lost the necessities of life, and could not readily replace them. A tipi consisted of fifteen or more buffalo hides, the tanning of which required many hours of backbreaking work on the part of the women, who fleshed and scraped the hides with short elk-horn tools. The lodge poles were scraped down from cedar logs obtained in the western mountains or in Palo Duro Canyon. The Indians' bedding and their outer winter garments were of buffalo hides tanned with the fur on. They could not be readily replaced in the winter, for the weakness of the ponies inhibited buffalo hunts. Their parfleches were packed with jerky and pemmican, and this constituted their winter food supply. Their brass buckets and other utensils were handed down from mother to daughter, and their loss was felt keenly.

The Kiowas, having been attacked by Kit Carson, were unable to give Black Kettle's people much help, but Colonel J. H. Leavenworth, the agent for the Kiowas and Comanches, issued the supplies that were supposed to go to the Kiowas to Black Kettle. For this he later incurred much ill will, for the Kiowas thought Leavenworth had stolen their goods.

The Sand Creek Massacre influenced governmental policy for several years. The nation suffered pangs of conscience that dictated a policy of appeasement based on deeply humanitarian motives. Unfortunately, it did not solve the problem of what to do with the Plains Indians. It only postponed the day when they had to be disciplined, their old way of life ended forever, and their people reduced to poverty and hopelessness.

Historical Collections, Vol. XVII (1926–30), 198–99 (hereinafter referred to as Montgomery, "Fort Wallace").

3. "PEACE COULD BE PURCHASED"

In the winter the Indians customarily remained quietly in their camps, for their ponies, then subsisting chiefly on the bark of the cottonwood trees, were too poor to travel. The winter of 1864–65 was no exception. Raiding ceased except for one isolated attack on a squad of soldiers chopping wood near Fort Zarah on February 1. One soldier was killed in that attack, but the others ran to the safety of the post.[1]

A small detachment of cavalry scouts under Sergeant David Nettleton rode out from Fort Larned several times each month, even when the snow was a foot deep and the temperature down to thirty degrees below zero. They confirmed that Indian trails and camp sites were old, and that the buffalo between the Arkansas and the Smoky Hill were unusually tame, indicating that they were not being hunted.[2]

Troop morale in the posts was low. The soldiers were nearing the end of their enlistments and were becoming increasingly anxious to go home. There were even symptoms of mutiny.[3] The Volunteer officers, uninterested in the future of their posts, did little to improve living conditions beyond effecting temporary repairs.

Changes were occurring in the command and troop lists at all levels. Major General John Pope was now commander of the principal headquarters in the West—the Military Division of the Missouri at St. Louis. Generals Curtis and Blunt were superseded by Major General Grenville M. Dodge and Colonel (Brevet Brigadier General) James H. Ford respectively.[4] The Confederate menace in northern Missouri had been largely disposed of by the Union victory at Westport and the subsequent pursuit of Sterling Price's battered army; however, there were still hostile Indians in Kansas who were expected to resume their attacks when the grass came up in the spring.

In addition there was the possibility of an invasion of Kansas from the south. In 1859 an agency for the Kiowas, Comanches, and several minor

[1] *OR*, XLVIII, Pt. I, 75.
[2] *Ibid.*, 25, 47–48, 99, 117.
[3] *Ibid.*, 74.
[4] *Ibid.*, 686, 780.

22

tribes had been established at Fort Cobb, some two hundred miles south of Fort Larned. This post had been abandoned by the federal troops, officials, and those Indians who maintained allegiance to the Union (Delawares, chiefly); and Confederate militia had taken over the fort. Now, early in 1865, certain Southern officers, notably Douglas Cooper, were advocating that an Indian force commanded by the Indian brigadier, Stand Watie, be organized to invade southern Kansas.[5]

Intelligence of this project reached the federal commander at Fort Gibson, Indian Territory, who transmitted it to General Pope, who in turn apprised General Dodge. Since the Volunteers in the District of the Upper Arkansas were becoming undependable and reinforcements would be needed to repel either the wild Northern Indians or the tame Southern ones, General Dodge secured several regiments of former Confederate soldiers who had been captured during the Civil War and released to fight for the Union, especially on the frontier, where they had proved their fighting ability against the Sioux. These men were officially designated United States Volunteers but were popularly called "Galvanized Yankees." The Second U.S. Volunteer Infantry was distributed along the Arkansas route, one company each at Riley, Salina, and Ellsworth, two at Zarah, and three at Larned.[6]

On March 9, General Ford sent a scouting party under Lieutenant Richard Jenkins south of the Arkansas to learn the location of the Indian camps and to gauge their temper. Jenkins visited no camps, but from an Arapaho belonging to Little Raven's village, known to be friendly, he learned that fifteen hundred Comanches were on the Cimarron and that some of the Kiowas and Kiowa-Apaches were on Crooked Creek. All seemed quiet.[7]

General Ford now revived the plan to establish a new post between Forts Larned and Lyon. He notified General Dodge that he intended to build it near the site of old Fort Atkinson, which had been abandoned many years before.[8] A delay occurred, during which Colonel Jesse H. Leavenworth, an Indian agent who had no fixed headquarters but was generally at Fort Larned, went south of the Arkansas to visit the Indian villages and try to persuade the chiefs to meet him for a series of peace talks.[9] Leavenworth had seen all the preparations for a military expedition, and thought that

[5] *Ibid.*, Pt. II, 72, 73, 83, 85, 91, 1009, 1144.
[6] *Ibid.*, 277, 1117.
[7] *Ibid.*, Pt. I, 136–38.
[8] *Ibid.*, 131, 1211.
[9] *Ibid.*, 933, 936, 1012; Pt. II, 59.

peace could be obtained more elegantly by negotiating with the Indians than by attacking them.

Leavenworth was a strange, even mysterious man. His earlier history was known, but his character and his motives were subject to speculation.[10] A West Point graduate, he should have been thoroughly indoctrinated in the creed of "Duty, Honor, Country." But he had been dismissed from the army during the war, after showing promise as a fine combat leader. General Dodge knew this, and was influenced by it, not knowing, perhaps, that the offense that had brought about Leavenworth's downfall was one of ignorance or misplaced enthusiasm and that he had been reinstated and later honorably discharged at the end of his term of service as a Volunteer. Colonel Leavenworth had subsequently been appointed an Indian agent, and from that time he seemed to have the interest of his charges fully in his heart. However, the Kiowas accused him of graft, and his opposition to the military caused him trouble. Within two or three years he left the government service and disappeared from public notice. There is no evidence that he obtained money illegally from his position as agent, and personally I think he was innocent. But he did make mistakes in judgment, and undoubtedly he was an impractical idealist with respect to the Indians.

Leavenworth tried to persuade General Ford to postpone his warlike preparations, and failing in this effort, he went to Washington in March to obtain support for his cause. There he interviewed army Chief of Staff Henry W. Halleck and the Secretary of the Interior.[11]

Meanwhile, with General Dodge's approval, Ford sent out an expedition to establish the new post in the Cimarron Crossing area. Captain Henry Pearce, Eleventh Kansas Cavalry, commanded this force, which consisted of Companies F and G, Second U.S. Volunteer Infantry; Company C, Eleventh Kansas Cavalry; and Company K, Second Colorado Cavalry. They arrived at Adkins' ranch, two miles above the head of the Dry Route, on April 10, 1865.[12] This date may therefore be cited as the date of the establishment of Fort Dodge—the name apparently was pre-selected. General Dodge has been credited with the founding of Fort Dodge, one history even putting the date in 1864 when Dodge was in Georgia, and he had nothing to do with it in April, 1865, except to give his approval.

Henry D. Janes, chief of scouts at Ford's headquarters, who accompanied the force, wrote to headquarters:

[10] For a profile of Leavenworth see "Col. Jesse Henry Leavenworth," by Carolyn Thomas Foreman, *Chronicles of Oklahoma*, Vol. XIII (March, 1935), 14–29.

[11] *OR*, XLVIII, Pt. I, 1162; Berthrong, *The Southern Cheyennes*, 233.

[12] *OR*, XLVIII, Pt. II, 74, 277; "Medical History, Fort Dodge," Book 79, 1–2.

Adkins' ranch . . . offered many natural advantages over either Five-Mile Point or Old Fort Adkinson. I directed Bradley, the guide, to remain at Fort Dodge for the present to show them where to obtain wood, etc. Good wood can be found about eight miles from Fort Dodge on the south bank of Pawnee or Cordwood Creek.[13]

During his trip south of the Arkansas in March, Colonel Leavenworth was able to find only a few Comanches and an Arapaho. Leavenworth must have learned from the Arapaho that the tribes, except for the hostile elements of the Cheyennes and Arapahoes, were moving south. Before he left for Washington, he sent his Negro servant, George Ransom, south to find the Indians and let them know that he wanted the chiefs to come to the mouth of the Little Arkansas for a peace talk.[14] Leavenworth had been collecting goods for issue to the Indians, and doubtless he held it out as bait.

General Dodge soon had evidence that Leavenworth was having some success in Washington. A telegram came from Halleck directing that Ford's expedition against the Indians be held up pending the outcome of Leavenworth's conference with other officials. Ford at this time was at Fort Zarah, assembling troops and supplies. On April 23 the Indians attacked a wagon train fifteen miles east of Fort Zarah, killed and scalped four Mexicans who were with the train, and ran off the stock.[15]

In Washington, Leavenworth talked to the Commissioner of Indian Affairs and the Secretary of the Interior and believed he had persuaded them of the wisdom of holding a peace council with the Indians as soon as he could assemble the chiefs. He hastened back to Cow Creek Station, where he had left some of his mules, for he was eager to start assembling the chiefs.

It was not as simple as Leavenworth had supposed. Although he had been the originator and moving spirit in the proposal to make a treaty with the Indians, the officials in Washington, who were, after all, politically oriented, did not intend to give him the leading role and the credit. A commission was to be appointed, comprised of statesmen with authority to act for the government. This turned out to be a Senate investigating committee, consisting of Senators James R. Doolittle of Wisconsin, L. S. Foster of Connecticut, and E. J. Ross of Kansas.

General Pope received a telegram from Secretary of War Stanton stating that the Secretary of the Interior had informed him that Colonel Leavenworth had no authority whatever to make a treaty with the Indians and

[13] *Ibid.*
[14] *OR*, XLVIII, Pt. II, 687.   [15] *Ibid.*, Pt. I, 201.

that there was no reason why General Dodge should not proceed with his expeditions. Dodge, appraised of this, wired Ford: "I want those Indians punished."[16]

Leavenworth did not learn of this immediately. He had returned on April 26 just after the Indians had attacked Cow Creek Station where they collected seventeen head of stock, including his own four mules.[17] He investigated the incident and was satisfied at first that the guilty tribesmen were not *his* Indians but Cheyennes. Later he thought they were Kicking Bird's Kiowas.

Ford did not move immediately; he was not ready. His hesitancy gave Leavenworth a chance to complain by wire to the Commissioner of Indian Affairs, W. P. Dole. He had at last succeeded in assembling the Indians, but he was mortified and discouraged that he must now tell the Indians that the conference could not be held—that it would be dangerous for them to congregate where the troops could find them.[18]

This message lacked accuracy. The agent had not assembled any Indians. They were all in the vicinity of Fort Cobb, deep in Indian Territory, and Leavenworth knew this from Ransom's report. Ransom had not reached the Indians' camps, but had talked with the well-known frontiersman Jesse Chisholm, who was part Cherokee and who, since he lived in southern Indian Territory, was well posted on the situation there. Chisholm had said that the Indian gathering at Fort Cobb had been addressed by a Confederate officer who had told them that the Civil War was over, that the Union had won, and that the Indians had better make peace with the United States.[19] All this made little or no difference to the Kiowas and Comanches, who had gone to Fort Cobb solely to get free food. Furthermore, the Kiowas planned to hold their annual sun dance on the Washita River.[20]

The senatorial investigating committee arrived at Fort Leavenworth, where they were joined by General A. McD. McCook, whom Pope had designated to be their military aide and adviser. On their way to Fort Larned they picked up Colonel Leavenworth, who persuaded them that he could bring the Indians in for a conference and that peace could be secured. Consequently, when they reached Fort Larned, General McCook told Ford to suspend his expedition.[21] When Dodge was notified of this order, he com-

[16] *Ibid.*, Pt. II, 637.
[17] *Ibid.*, 245.
[18] *Ibid.*
[19] *Ibid.*, 1009.
[20] Mooney, "Calendar History," 317.
[21] *OR*, XLVIII, Pt. II, 707, 708.

plained to Pope, who wired back: "Do what you think best about Ford. McCook had no authority from me to interfere in any manner with your troops."[22] Ford, however, was still held up by high water, for the streams were at flood stage.

Senator Doolittle reported this to Secretary of the Interior Harlan, expressing his satisfaction in this blocking of military plans. He said that, in his opinion, if Ford had gotten across the river, he would have been beaten by the Indians and forced to retreat. In this letter the Senator disclosed the basic reason for his mission, which was to give the Indians reparations to atone for the Sand Creek Massacre and thus to attain peace.[23] There was no mention of requiring the Indians to give up white captives held by them or to return the hundreds of horses, mules, and cattle they had taken from the government and from private individuals. Nor were they to be asked to pay damages to the relatives of persons murdered by them.

Doolittle also declared that peace could be purchased more inexpensively through negotiation and presents than by sending out a military expedition that would cost from $25,000,000 to $50,000,000.[24] Since $150,000 would have been ample for Ford's expedition, it seems apparent that the Senator's extravagant statement was politically inspired and made for the effect it would have both in Congress and in the press.

Within two or three days of the arrival of the peace commission at Fort Larned, the Indians began to cast doubt on the validity of Leavenworth's predictions by attacking all along the Santa Fe Road. By this time the Kiowas, Kiowa-Apaches, and Comanches must have been assembling for the Kiowa sun dance on the Washita. The dance was almost always celebrated in June when the down appeared on the cottonwoods, and it was now June. This year the dance was called the Peninsular Sun Dance, because it was held in the bend of the Washita just east of the present site of Mountain View, Oklahoma.[25] All Kiowas were required to be present, and none were allowed to leave until the dance was concluded. The dance itself lasted only four days, but was preceded by two or three weeks of assembly, initiation of candidates into warrior clubs, the making of medicine, and much socializing. As usual, the northern and middle Comanches were present. They had no medicine dance of their own, but usually watched that of the Kiowas.

Because of the absence of these tribes along the Arkansas River during June, the raids made there must be attributed to the hostile elements of the Cheyennes and Arapahoes, chiefly the former.

22 *Ibid.*, 708.
24 *Ibid.*

23 *Ibid.*, 868.
25 Mooney, "Calendar History," 317.

Possibly because it was new, Fort Dodge was the first place to be struck. Since it was rarely possible to ship sufficient forage, especially grain, to posts where it was needed, the post animals were grazed on the prairie. Each day the herds had to be grazed farther from the post. With so many men escorting stages, guarding stage stations, and, as they were in June, 1865, assembling at some other point in preparation for an expedition, only a few were available to tend the grazing herds. The incident at Fort Dodge on June 8 was typical of the Indian strikes.

That afternoon the animals were being grazed near the river half a mile from the post. Since they were so close and plainly in view of the garrison, no anxiety was felt for their safety, not even when the herders saw fifteen or twenty riders approaching from a ravine in the hills to the west. The strangers, who were clad in blue uniforms, rode quietly to the river and watered their mounts, which were not Indian ponies but big "American" horses of the type used by the army. The guards were still not alarmed when the strangers approached the herd at an easy canter. When they reached the herd, they suddenly began yipping and shooting their pistols. The herd stampeded and was being run off.[26]

The herdsmen dashed in and managed to turn several horses back. They guided these to the post, where they were quickly saddled and mounted by the few men not on other duties. This small party rode after the Indians and recovered nearly two-thirds of the stolen animals.

Three days later a thick fog hung along the river bottoms. Under this cover the Indians approached unobserved. Suddenly they burst upon the herd and this time succeeded in running off virtually all the horses at Fort Dodge. They killed two soldiers and wounded three in that raid.[27]

On June 9 a war party attacked four wagon trains two and one-half miles east of Chavis Creek, capturing 101 mules, 75 oxen, and 3 horses. One teamster was killed. Lieutenant Jenkins and sixty men rode from Cow Creek Station in pursuit of the raiders. They followed the Indian tracks to the Arkansas River, but the Indians escaped by swimming across.[28]

On the evening of June 10, two messengers, Corporal George W. Hicks and Private Samuel J. Huestis, both Second Colorado Cavalry, arrived at Fort Larned after having been chased by Indians for twelve miles. The post commander, Captain Theodore Conkey, declined to go after the Indians, declaring that all his men were needed to guard the large amount of stock

[26] *OR*, XLVIII, Pt. I, 311.
[27] *Ibid.*, 308, 311.
[28] *Ibid.*, 308.

accumulated at the post because of the arrival of the peace commission and its escort. Colonel Leavenworth's transportation was also there. He had brought several wagonloads of goods to give to the Indians at the projected peace council. There were also several stages and wagon trains whose drivers were afraid to move.[29]

Although standing orders required couriers to travel only at night, when Indians were supposed to be inactive, Hicks and Huestis left the fort at 9:00 A.M. on the eleventh.

A few hours later Captain Conkey received a report that a wagon train was under attack near Pawnee Rock, sixteen miles east of Fort Larned, and he set out with a cavalry squadron to rescue it. Four miles west of Ash Creek he came upon a body lying near the road. It was Private Huestis—shot, scalped, stripped, and mutilated. At the creek crossing, the remains of Corporal Hicks were lying in the road. He was naked and beheaded, with his hands and feet chopped off and his body sliced up fearfully.[30]

The mule train Conkey had come to rescue was safe. Lieutenant Martin Hennion and his twenty-man escort had driven off the Indians, but the Lieutenant told Conkey that another train eight miles down the Arkansas, on the lower road, was also under attack. Conkey sent Captain John D. Walker, Eleventh Kansas Cavalry, with seventy-five men to its relief, but they found the train corralled and safe. The Indians had disappeared.[31]

On June 12, Sergeant M. P. Doud, Seventh Iowa Cavalry, was returning to Larned with twenty men who had escorted a wagon train to Fort Zarah. On his way he met Sergeant George Cronk, Second Colorado Cavalry, who was escorting another train eastward. They were attacked by one hundred Indians near Plum Buttes, and one soldier was killed, but Doud drove the Indians across the Arkansas.[32]

At the same time, Lieutenant Jenkins and six men were attacked while escorting a stage four miles west of Fort Zarah. The soldiers were following in a separate coach when suddenly they were surrounded by mounted Indians. They opened fire through the windows of the coach, and drove the Indians back out of range. The Indians then withdrew a mile toward Fort Zarah, where they came upon a wagon train which had just left the post. The Indians closed in again, and in the hand-to-hand fighting, one Indian was knocked from his horse and two soldiers received lance thrusts in the head.[33]

29 *Ibid.*, 315–16.
30 *Ibid.*
31 *Ibid.*, 315.
32 *Ibid.*, 314.
33 *Ibid.*, 313–14.

Captain Elisha Hammer, seeing the fighting from the roof of a building at Fort Zarah, rode out with fifty-five troopers, and the party drove the Indians away. The pursuit continued to the river, where the redskins again escaped by swimming.[34]

During this excitement the senatorial committee crouched at Fort Larned, persuaded that the Indians were not in the mood for a powwow. Senator Doolittle did not demur when Ford received a message from General Dodge to get his expedition under way.

Ford, though greatly embarrassed, was unable to move. The river was still at flood stage, and, besides, some of the required supplies had not arrived from Fort Leavenworth. When this was reported to Dodge, he was not pleased. He had begun to have doubts about Ford, but in sending explanations to higher headquarters he blamed the supply agencies for the delay. He also recommended that future expeditions be equipped with pontoon bridges.[35] He pointed out that a mounted expedition would then be independent of fords and high water, and could take more direct routes across the Plains. Since the army had become proficient in the art of throwing a pontoon bridge across even a wide stream, Dodge's suggestion had merit. In June, 1865, however, no pontoon train was available in the District of the Upper Arkansas.

Ford attempted to make up for the deficiency by requisitioning a pack train. One was sent to him, but the Indians made off with many of the mules, and Ford had to ask for replacements.[36] This, together with the extra grain and hay being requested, caused raised eyebrows in Washington. As invariably happens after a major war, military expenses were being cut to the bone, and economy had become the watchword. General Grant wired Pope: "The cost of keeping the amount of cavalry called for on the prairies is so enormous I wish you would cut down the expenditures all you can and direct that animals be grazed as far as possible."[37]

General Grant, who perhaps knew as much about horses as any man in the army, must have been bemused. He certainly knew that, though the large horses used as army mounts could live on prairie grass, they would gradually lose flesh and become unfit for the rigors of campaigning unless they were fed grain nearly every day. And he must have known that hay would have to be purchased unless the Indians were to be given free access

[34] *Ibid.*
[35] *Ibid.*, 333; Pt. II, 949–50.
[36] *Ibid.*
[37] *Ibid.*, Pt. II, 933.

to the grazing herds at each isolated post. Hay and grain were expensive, not at the source, but because of freighting them across the Plains.

The Indians were unaffected by these handicaps. Their mustangs kept well on prairie grass during the raiding season. The Indians usually sold in New Mexico the horses they captured from the army. They traveled light when on the warpath, requiring no food other than the jerky they carried in saddlebags or what game they could kill. In emergencies they would kill and eat horses or mules, and the Cheyennes ate their camp dogs, a practice which disgusted the Comanches. Deep streams constituted no obstacle. When a war party came to an unfordable river, they stopped briefly to make floats of hides or canvas wrapped around bundles of brush. On these they ferried their firearms and powder, or sacred objects such as the Kiowa *Tai-me*, if they had been so foolish as to carry tribal medicine on a raid.

All through June the senators remained at Fort Larned hoping for a break in the situation that would permit Leavenworth to assemble the chiefs for the promised peace conference.

4. TREATY OF THE LITTLE ARKANSAS

The policy of retrenchment at government level was to have a perceptible effect on the operation of military posts and in the dealings with the Indians. The Indian Bureau's argument that it was more economical to make treaties with the Indians than to fight them was sympathetically received by Congress and by the country. The military point of view—that the Indians ought to be punished for the outrages they had committed in the past and were still committing—received scant favorable notice outside the army. Both parties to the controversy had, however, the same eventual object—peace. And both agreed that the southern Plains tribes should be moved well south of the Arkansas River while the Cheyennes and their Sioux allies should be moved north of the Platte. This would leave a corridor through which the wagon roads, and eventually the railroads, could penetrate without peril.

For some reason the Indian raids slackened in July. Perhaps the hostile bands had acquired enough horses and other loot to satisfy them for a while, or they were fully occupied in buffalo hunts. They may have become aware that Ford had assembled some 1,500 soldiers and could move against them at any time. At any rate, by mid-July Ford knew that Leavenworth expected to meet Indian representatives at some point eighty miles south of the mouth of the Little Arkansas. The Indians—Kiowas, Comanches, and the less hostile portions of the Cheyennes and Arapahoes—had heard of Doolittle's commission from Washington and were eager to hear what its members had to say. Doubtless they were also eager to receive the goods promised by their agent.

Ford assessed the situation in his correspondence with Dodge: "I therefore think that Colonel Leavenworth will succeed in making peace with the Indians. All trains, coaches, etc., are now passing safely through the district."[1]

It sounded as though Ford had joined the peace party, but this did not matter. Dodge had already decided to relieve him and appoint a more aggressive district commander, one who would get the much-delayed puni-

[1] *OR*, XLVIII, Pt. II, 1044–45.

32

tive expedition under way. He issued an order on July 1 relieving Ford "at his own request" and appointing Brevet Major General John B. Sanborn in his place.[2]

Ford heard nothing of this development for a week. Then he expressed surprise and asked what was to become of him. Dodge explained that Ford's regiment was being mustered out of the service and that there was no vacancy for him.[3] This was a time-honored army maneuver—dispose of an individual who is no longer desired by declaring his slot no longer authorized.

Dodge now thought that everything was clear for him to launch his expedition against the Indians. He told Sanborn to get busy.[4]

Sanborn was cagey. He sent an emissary south of the Arkansas to locate Leavenworth and learn just what he was doing, not what he said he was doing. Sanborn was not a regular army man. A Yankee lawyer who had gone west before the war and who had come into the service from Minnesota, he had done well as a brigadier during Price's raid and had been brevetted major general. He was thirty-nine years old and had a stern visage that probably was at variance with his inner feelings, for he did not prove to be the warlike fellow General Dodge desired.

He arrived at district headquarters on July 12, but despite Dodge's urging, he showed no inclination to take the field. Instead, he set up the old refrain about supplies not coming through. As late as the twenty-third he had not even visited Fort Larned to get firsthand impressions concerning the supposed Indian menace.[5]

On the twenty-third General Sanborn received an optimistic report from Leavenworth that a delegation from the five tribes of southern Plains Indians had come in and asked for a general council. Sanborn was a little cautious in taking action. He wrote to Dodge that he did not know Leavenworth or how much faith to place in him. He asked Dodge for advice but received none.[6]

Two days later Sanborn did receive a copy of a paper from the Department of the Interior spelling out the department's policy for dealing with the Indians. One surprising provision, showing commendable co-ordination among the departments, specified that in treating with hostile Indians, agents should conform to the policy, orders, and actions of the War Depart-

[2] *Ibid.*, 1038.
[3] *Ibid.*, 1071.
[4] *Ibid.*, 1117.
[5] *Ibid.*, 1086.
[6] *Ibid.*, 1115.

33

ment. On the other hand, said the directive, with respect to Indians "in amity with the United States," military officers should subordinate their actions to those of officials of the Indian Bureau.[7]

This seemed fair enough, but who was to decide which Indians were peaceful and which were hostile? The question was left unanswered, which was just as well, for it was impracticable to hold a plebiscite and the Indians seemed variable.

Sanborn forwarded the document to Colonel Leavenworth, commenting that all the southern Plains Indians were, in his opinion, hostile. He directed Leavenworth, who was not his subordinate, to terminate his interviews with the Indians at once. In the next sentence he told the agent to find out when he, Sanborn, could confer with the Indians and where.

"I will meet them in person," he said, "and satisfy myself what the results of the conference will be." He added that he was sending Leavenworth two squadrons of cavalry, a statement that seemed unrelated to his previous remarks.[8]

General Dodge, meanwhile, was vigorously thumping his war drums. There was no doubt in his mind that *all* Indians were hostile. He wired Sanborn: "Push out your columns into the Indian country as soon as possible. Not a day is to be lost. When you get there you can determine whether you can make peace safely before whipping them [the Indians]. If not, fight them, then make the agreement."[9] But on the same day, July 25, Secretary of War Stanton telegraphed Senator Doolittle to go ahead and make a treaty with the Indians, including those south of the Arkansas River.[10]

General Sanborn informed Dodge that he was about to accompany his expedition down into the Indian country, but included an escape clause by saying that tremendous rains had flooded the entire country.[11]

There were other troubles, too, of which General Dodge was well aware. The Volunteer units were being demobilized so rapidly, now that the war was over, that only five regiments remained in Kansas—not enough to guard all posts on both routes and at the same time form punitive expeditions. Furthermore, streams were over their banks, supplies could not be moved, teamsters were bitter, and settlers were frightened.

At the end of July, General Grant was again calling on Pope to curtail

[7] *Ibid.*, 1115–17.
[8] *Ibid.*, 1116.
[9] *Ibid.*, 1117–18.
[10] *Ibid.*, 1117–18, 1122.
[11] *Ibid.*, 1122, 1124.

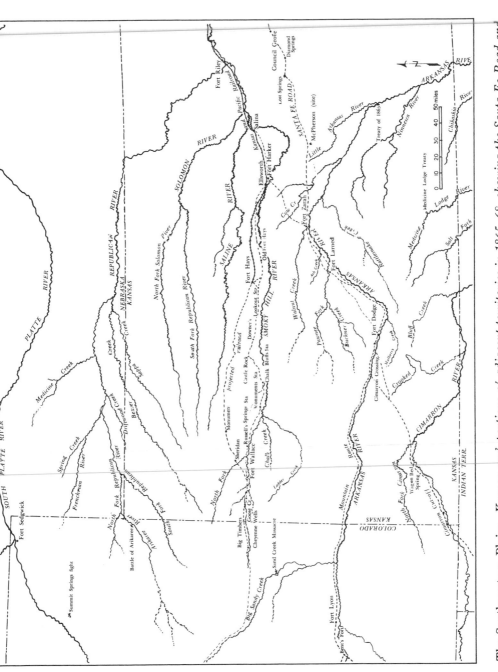

The Southwestern Plains. Kansas and portions of adjacent territories in 1865–68, showing the Santa Fe Road and the stage line (Smoky Hill route) to Denver.

requisitions for supplies and to study the possibility of reducing the number of cavalry regiments in his command.[12] In compliance Pope notified Dodge that when field expeditions returned to their stations, the troop basis would be reduced to the minimum needed for the protection of the overland routes. All other units would be mustered out, whether the expeditions were successful or not. Pope said he had applied for regular army units to replace the Volunteers. Later Pope informed Dodge that "the pressure on me about expenses on the plains is tremendous. Whether reasonable or not, the demands of the government must be complied with."[13]

Meanwhile, Dodge had allowed Sanborn's column to cross the Arkansas and proceed toward the mouth of the Little Arkansas. Sanborn was told that he could attack the Indians or arrange for them to meet for a peace party, according to the situation. In his own opinion, Dodge added, the straightest road to permanent settlement of the Indian problem was to deal the Indians a crushing blow before offering them a treaty.[14]

With this paper in hand, Sanborn might well have descended on the Indian camps with fire and sword. But he exercised restraint, and it is impossible to say what the eventual outcome would have been had he acted otherwise. At least he dealt with the Indians in the Christian tradition, and his memory is clear of stain.

He waited at Fort Larned until he heard from Leavenworth. On August 4, General Pope sent him a telegram directing him to suspend his movement south, place his troops in camp, and await further orders. He was to send messengers to the Indians to propose that a council be held with them on or about October 1.[15]

Sanborn sent the courageous and experienced Lieutenant Jenkins accompanied by two civilian scouts. They learned that Do-hauson and a party of Kiowas had come to Leavenworth's camp, and that Jesse Chisholm was on the way with Comanches.[16] With this assurance, General Sanborn went to Leavenworth's camp. He arrived on August 15 and was greeted cordially by the Indians. A preliminary agreement was made, in which both sides promised to meet on October 4 at Bluff Creek, forty miles south of the Little Arkansas. At that time the government commissioners would be present, and a formal treaty would be made. In the interim the Indians agreed to refrain from attacking the frontier settlements and travelers on

[12] *Ibid.*, 1128.
[13] *Ibid.*, 1154; Pt. I, 350, 351, 355.
[14] *Ibid.*, Pt. I, 359, 360.
[15] *Ibid.*, 361; Pt. II, 1172.
[16] *Ibid.*, Pt. II, 1175, 1176.

the Santa Fe Road. Sanborn promised that no military action would be taken against the Indians during the period of truce.[17]

This preliminary agreement was reduced to writing and signed. The chiefs making their *X*'s were: Do-hauson, Lone Wolf, Satanta, Kicking Bird, Heap of Bears, and Stumbling Bear for the Kiowas; Lean Bear for the Kiowa-Apaches; Big Mouth for the Arapahoes; and Over the Buttes for the Comanches. The Cheyennes were not represented, but when their chiefs—Black Kettle, Little Robe, and Storm, and the Arapaho chief Little Raven—learned of the meeting on the sixteenth, they came to Leavenworth's camp on the eighteenth. Both parties signed a paper in which Sanborn and Leavenworth acknowledged that the Sand Creek Massacre had been the cause of the Indians' subsequent hostility. The chiefs in return expressed a hope of peace and a willingness to meet the peace commissioners in October.[18]

Sanborn, elated over this happy outcome, notified his superiors, adding that he thought his command could now be reduced by 2,000 men, with a further reduction after the October peace council. He was safe in making this suggestion, for the War Department was going to do it anyway. The troop strength in Kansas would drop from 15,000 men to 1,500, and Sanborn's field force of 1,500 would shrink to 500.[19]

The chances for successful negotiations with the Indians south of the Arkansas had improved markedly, but they were not the bands who had been making trouble. The troop situation, on the other hand, was deteriorating. The Colorado and Kansas Volunteer regiments that had defended the frontier in Kansas up to early summer had been returned to civilian life and replaced by other Volunteers from the Army of the Tennessee and elsewhere in the Middle West. Some of the units used to form Ford's (later Sanborn's) force had come from north of the Platte, and these men, who were generally from outside the district, were disgruntled over being shipped outside their own states and held in the service while others had gone home. Some of the men were actually mutinous, and in this they were encouraged by their home-town newspapers and some state officials. Already the desertion rate had climbed to 25 per cent. General Pope admitted that the only troops on which he could now depend were the Galvanized Yankees—former Confederates.[20]

[17] *Ibid.*, Pt. I, 361; Pt. II, 1197; *Report* of the Commissioner of Indian Affairs for 1865, 394–95.

[18] Mooney, "Calendar History," 178–80.

[19] *OR*, XLVIII, Pt. I, 362.

[20] *Ibid.*, Pt. II, 1157, 1165.

Pope and Dodge were beset by other worries. On August 6, Quartermaster General Montgomery C. Meigs had reported to the Secretary of War that the cost of quartermaster's stores and rations delivered to the 22,000 troops on the plains cost $10,000,000, and this sum did not include wagons, animals, clothing, and equipment. "It remains to be seen," he observed sharply, "whether there will be results commensurate with the expense."[21]

Because of the cutback in forces, General Pope again reorganized the Department of the Missouri. Among other changes, the Districts of the Upper Arkansas and of Kansas were consolidated under Brevet Major General William L. Elliott, thus throwing Sanborn and Mitchell out of their jobs. Elliott was instructed to close out a number of posts, retaining along the Arkansas only Forts Riley, Larned, and Dodge and the detachment at Cow Creek Station. It seemed likely, however, that one or two new posts might have to be built on the Smoky Hill route because David A. Butterfield had just opened a stage line which traveled that road.[22]

In spite of the shortage of funds, the Quartermaster General promised to send lumber to build better storehouses at Fort Larned. This post was still an advance supply depot for the other garrisons in the western part of the state, and was to continue in this capacity until railroads were built. Two such lines were soon to be under construction.

The treaty-making in October came off according to schedule, though the council was held at the mouth of the Little Arkansas instead of farther south as planned. The government was represented by General Sanborn, Major General William S. Harney, known to the Indians since before the Civil War, Thomas Murphy of the Central Superintendency at Atchison, and James Steele from the Office of the Commissioner of Indian Affairs. Old plainsmen William Bent and Kit Carson were there, and of course Jesse Leavenworth.[23]

A week's delay occurred while the Indians were brought up from Bluff Creek, where they had been told to assemble. During this time several bands of Cheyennes and Arapahoes also came in. The talks, which began on October 11, were concluded on the fourteenth, when a treaty was signed. Its purpose, so far as the United States was concerned, was to move the Indians south of the Arkansas River and keep them away from the overland routes.[24] The Indians were indemnified by grants of land and goods.

[21] *Ibid.*, 1167.
[22] *Ibid.*, 1203–1204, 1208; Montgomery, "Fort Wallace," 189.
[23] *Report* of the Commissioner of Indian Affairs for 1865, 47.
[24] Mooney, "Calendar History," 180.

Kiowa chief Do-hauson, though he signed the treaty, strongly protested against being confined on a reservation. He said his tribe owned the prairies from the North Platte to Texas, and had always owned them. He did not want his lands cut up and given to the white man. His people wanted a large country in which to roam. They did not want to stay in one place but wanted to move about. His warriors would leave the Santa Fe Road open, and would not disturb people on it, but he wanted the rest of the country left alone.[25] None of the old chief's hopes or demands were realized.

One of the major weaknesses of the Treaty of the Little Arkansas was that the Indians who signed it represented only a fraction of their several tribes, and even all the warriors in their own bands did not feel bound by it. What was worse, the more warlike portions of the Cheyennes, notably the Dog Soldiers, were not even at the council.

Few persons present at the signing of the treaty felt any great optimism that a permanent peace had been achieved. Nevertheless, the Indians who signed the treaty generally remained south of the Arkansas, and with the exception of Satanta and a few others, gave little trouble in Kansas during the next fourteen months. They simply transferred their depredations to Texas and Mexico. Once or twice a large war party went out against the Utes or Navahos in New Mexico.

A respite was sorely needed by the army units on the plains. During 1866 the last of the troops that had formed the great armies of the Civil War were phased out and replaced by green Regular Army regiments. The adjustments required, the hardships encountered, and the low state of morale that resulted would make this period the most unhappy one in the whole history of the United States Army.

---

[25] *Ibid.*

5. THE REGULAR ARMY TAKES OVER

$\mathbf{F}$ollowing the treaty of October, 1865, and continuing into the summer of 1866, there were few, if any, Indian raids south of the Smoky Hill route. Except for two handicaps, the troops had an uninterrupted opportunity to complete the construction of permanent facilities at the new posts. The first drawback was the lack of appropriations to buy materials and to hire key artisans. The second was the turnover in personnel occasioned by the replacement of the Volunteers by Regular Army soldiers. The latter had to be recruited in the East and shipped to the frontier, and this procedure took time.

Because of political resistance and the fear that certain localities were still menaced by the Indians, only the camps at Cow Creek crossing and Fort Zarah were phased out. Two new posts were authorized on the newly reopened Smoky Hill Road.

Fort Larned, still the hub of military activity along the Arkansas, was the first station to receive Regular Army troops. In December, 1865, three companies of the Thirteenth Infantry and one of the Second Cavalry, all under Major Hiram Dryer, arrived.[1] Winter was too far advanced to begin replacing the "dobeys" with stone quarters. The only carpenter work attempted was the repair of the leaking roofs—the deficiencies noted by Major McKenny and by subsequent inspectors had apparently not been corrected. Although the new soldiers badly needed military training, they spent most of their time cutting necessary firewood. Since the post had been occupied for eight years, all usable wood had been cut within a radius of thirty miles. Consequently, although there was always the danger of Indian attacks, outlying woodcutters' camps had to be established. The winter was unusually severe, and firewood was essential.

There had been talk of establishing the permanent post at a new location. A site on the bluff five miles down the Pawnee Fork had been under consideration. Nevertheless, Colonel (Brevet Major General) Cuvier Grover, who arrived in May with two companies of the Third Infantry, decided to build the permanent post at the same spot where the old, mud buildings then

[1] "Medical History, Fort Larned," Book 164, 4.

stood. In June, construction began on the first building—a stone commissary warehouse.[2] It was not completed until the fall of 1866, and no other buildings were erected until June, 1867. In August, 1866, Grover was superseded by Captain Henry Asbury, Third Infantry.[3]

Fort Dodge, the new post west of Larned, had been under consideration for abandonment, but it was finally decided that such a station was needed to protect the long stretch between Larned and Lyon.[4] In the summer of 1865, Fort Dodge had been only a tent camp, but when Regular Army units came (in January, 1866), they burrowed like muskrats into dugouts along the top of the river banks.[5]

The typical dugout was an open-cut pit with the entrance facing the river. It was four or five feet deep with a roof raised two feet above the level ground. It was ten feet wide and twelve feet long and accommodated three or four men. The bunks were straw-filled ticks laid on mounds raised a foot or two above the dirt floor. The men would have preferred wooden bunks, but no lumber was furnished by the government. Because the temperature dropped to twenty or thirty degrees below zero at times, any timber cut locally was needed for firewood.

The roof of a dugout was made of a frame of poles covered with brush and a layer of earth. The door at the front and a small window at the rear, the only openings, were covered by gunny sacks. A sod fireplace and chimney in one corner provided some heat and much smoke.[6]

The early Fort Dodge consisted of seventy such dugouts. Although the river rose menacingly after heavy rains, it never quite reached the floor of the shelters. On dark nights, when the water could be heard swirling by, or even lapping just below the door, the inhabitants must have shivered in their blankets.

Three sets of officers "quarters" were built of sod just behind the line of dugouts. They were two-room affairs measuring 14x20 feet.[7] Within each dwelling huddled the officer and his wife and children, happy to be together after the lonely years of separation during the war.

During the late summer of 1865, the Volunteers had built a sod hospital having three small rooms—an infirmary, a sick ward (four beds), and a

2 *Ibid.*
3 *Ibid.*, 5.
4 *OR*, XLVIII, Pt. II, 1212.
5 "Medical History, Fort Dodge," Book 79, 9.
6 *Ibid.*
7 *Ibid.*, 10.

"dead" room or morgue. The last two rooms were taken over by the officers as a club and mess—the sick and dead being relegated to tents. Because the winter was so cold, the post commander transferred the sick back inside. Post Surgeon C. S. McGraw was critical of these medical facilities:

> The snow beat in in many places. The roof was almost flat and covered with dirt, and whenever it rained, muddy water leaked through into the rooms below. There was a dirt floor, damp most of the time. The wood furnished was barely sufficient to keep fires half the time. The ceiling and walls of the dispensary were covered with condemned canvas. Snakes, gophers, and mice infested the roof and walls.[8]

On the western edge of the post a storehouse measuring 20x180 feet was built from pit-sawed lumber for the use of the quartermaster and a commissary of subsistence. Like the other edifices, it had a sod roof, and, just as at Fort Larned, mud and water spoiled the forage, rations, and clothing.[9]

One might expect any funds allocated by the quartermaster generals at Washington, St. Louis, and Fort Leavenworth would be earmarked for the construction of adequate storage facilities and stables for the mules, but this was not so. Captain (Brevet Lieutenant Colonel) G. A. Gordon, one of a succession of post commanders at Fort Dodge, complained to department headquarters in the spring of 1866 that his mules had been standing in the open during the winter and urged that stables be erected immediately. He was told that he could build them himself, using troop labor and locally-available materials. In looking about for construction material, Gordon saw only sod. He had a stable built of turf, with walls eight feet high. Gordon and his tenderfoot troops used sod still wet from recent rains. When the last rectangle of turf was patted into place, the whole structure collapsed like a too-juicy mud pie.[10] The mules hailed this with an outburst of their customary uncouth noises.

Not long after this experience, a stone quarry was discovered five miles from the post. Gordon sheepishly admitted the failure of his sod experiment and asked his department headquarters for funds to hire civilian stone cutters. General Pope approved, and work was begun in July.[11] But Gordon did not remain to witness the fruition of his building program. He departed on recruiting duty and was superseded by Lieutenant G. A. Wallace. During the next five months, the post command was changed as many times.

8 *Ibid.*, 4–6.
9 *Ibid.*, 9.
10 *Ibid.*, 10.
11 *Ibid.*, 10–11.

The continual changes in command did not foster continuity of plans and effort, for each new commander assigned a different priority to the work. As a result, by October nothing had been finished, though in November, the threat of winter storms brought about a spurt that resulted in the completion of the warehouse and bakery. With the onset of winter, all work ceased.[12]

Cow Creek Station was given up as a military post, though the stage company retained it as one of their relay points. Fort Zarah was also given up as a military installation, but the buildings were used for other purposes, and a small troop detachment camped there. Fort Ellsworth was retained, for it was at the point where the Smoky Hill Road forked from the Santa Fe Trail. It would eventually become a station on the railroad, and it was even destined to be, for a time, the site of the district headquarters. The records of the post are scanty and suggest that Fort Ellsworth was unoccupied from the time the Volunteers left, about the end of 1865, until November 17, 1866, when Major Alfred M. Gibbs arrived with two companies of the newly organized Seventh Cavalry and one each of the Third and Thirty-seventh Infantry.[13] Gibbs was a roly-poly, droop-eyed officer who had been a brigadier during the war and was brevetted major general. A graduate of West Point, 1846, he had served with distinction in the Mexican and Civil wars.[14] He was well liked at Fort Ellsworth, but soon began to show symptoms of the brain tumor that was to cause his death in 1868.

On his arrival at Ellsworth, General Gibbs received an order to replace the camp with a permanent post to be named Fort Harker in honor of Brigadier General Charles Garrison Harker, who had been killed on June 27, 1864, at the Battle of Kennesaw Mountain.[15]

Gibbs's first care was to get his men out of tents and dugouts and into more comfortable and healthful quarters. He gave first priority to the construction of the new post, although he was well aware that his recruits needed military training. In January, 1867, he reported:

> All hands being employed in building stables, etc., there is little military duty except guard mounting and Sunday inspection. The 7th Cavalry is particularly deficient, many of them never having been taught to mount. All are ignorant of the manual of arms, the cavalry never having drawn their sabers

[12] *Ibid.*, 11.

[13] "Post Returns, Fort Harker" (Ellsworth), 1866.

[14] Francis B. Heitman, *Historical Register and Dictionary of the United States Army, 1789–1903*, I, 452–53 (hereinafter referred to as Heitman, *Historical Register*).

[15] "Medical History, Fort Harker," Book 128, 2.

from the boxes. They would make a very sorry figure in a conflict with the Indians. The men are quiet and well-behaved, with but few in the guard house . . . . The band of Sioux camped on the Forks of the Saline are a small band called the "Cut-off-band," who made a separate treaty last year at Fort Laramie, and who, having heard of the massacre at that place, came down the country, fearing to be attacked by the whites. They have since moved up the Smokey Hill about 150 miles from here, where they are trading with the Cheyennes for skins, etc.[16]

Further emphasizing the substandard living conditions at his post, Gibbs wrote, early in February, 1867, that his officers were still living in tents, though the weather was severe. "Those who are in houses are in hovels too poor to dignify by the appellation of shelters," he added.[17]

The Indians were quiet and remained in their winter camps at a considerable distance from Fort Harker. Gibbs wanted to arrest Roman Nose, a chief of the Dog Soldiers whom he regarded as a trouble maker, but was restrained by a directive from Lieutenant General William T. Sherman, now commanding the Division of the Missouri.[18] Sherman had written all commanders to refrain from taking action that would stir up the Indians.

Meanwhile, in 1865, the Smoky Hill route had been reopened by the establishment of David Butterfield's Overland Dispatch stage line. Two new posts were established to protect it. The most easterly, Fort Hays, was founded October 18, 1865, to guard construction crews on the railroad, which was then being pushed westward.[19]

On October 26, a more distant post on the Smoky Hill route was begun by the military escort of a survey party, initially as a temporary camp. Named Camp Pond Creek for Major James B. Pond, Third Wisconsin Volunteers, this installation was near the stage station on Pond Creek.

The first garrison was Company A, Thirteenth Missouri Volunteers, commanded by Captain DeWitt McMichael. The mission was to protect the stage station and furnish escorts along the line.[20]

During the first winter nothing happened to disturb the peace except that the post surgeon, a Dr. Whipple, who held sick call for the detachment at Monument Station, fifty-seven miles to the east, was robbed by Indians

[16] Gibbs to Noyes, January 25, 1867, "Letters Sent, Fort Harker."

[17] Gibbs to Easton, February 3, 1867, "Letters Sent, Fort Harker."

[18] Gibbs to Easton, November 19, 1866, "Letter Book, Fort Harker."

[19] Francis Paul Prucha, *Guide to the Military Posts of the United States*, 78 (hereinafter referred to as Prucha, *Guide to Military Posts*).

[20] "Medical History, Fort Wallace," Book 343, 1; Montgomery, "Fort Wallace," 189–203.

while returning to the Pond Creek camp. This same gentleman had another adventure that winter. One dark night while he was sleeping quietly in his sod hut, a buffalo bull came lumbering along a game trail across which the camp had been built, plunged through the roof of the good doctor's quarters, and landed snorting in the interior.[21]

Whipple found the episode "disagreeable." The bull was wild-eyed; perhaps he was unnerved by the unaccustomed sight of an apparition in a white nightshirt erupting from a hole in the ground.

During the winter of 1865–66, Captain McMichael and his men consumed nearly all the rations in stock at Camp Pond Creek. When no new suppies had come in by February 14, McMichael suddenly saw the specter of starvation. He marched his command eastward toward civilization and muster-out, abandoning the post and its tents and other equipment.[22] A few days later a wagon train loaded with rations and other supplies arrived at Camp Pond Creek, but the tents were standing empty with their untied flaps waving idly in the breeze.

The Regular Army took over. On April 1 the post was reoccupied by Captain Edward Ball and Company H, Second Cavalry. Rather than clean up the vacated camp. Ball moved it to a point near the present site of Pond City.[23] On April 18, by authority of General Orders Fifty, Headquarters Department of the Missouri, the new post was named Fort Wallace, in honor of Brigadier General W. H. L. Wallace, who had been killed in 1862 at the Battle of Shiloh. On April 30, Ball submitted plans for a permanent post to hold two companies of cavalry and one of infantry.[24] This plan was standard—the military theorized that the cavalry would chase Indians while the infantry guarded the post and escorted wagons supplying troops in the field. However, the theory did not always work—the cavalrymen were often on foot because the Indians had run off their horses.

Ball received his additional mounted unit, Company M, Second Cavalry, within a week. On June 6 a company of the Sixth U.S. Volunteer Infantry, commanded by Captain James J. Gordon, reported. Since Ball had departed on recruiting duty, Gordon fell heir to command of the post.[25]

Gordon enjoyed the arrival of spring at Fort Wallace. The redbud blooms and the fluffy, white wild-plum blossoms had blown away, but the air was still crisp and the creeks were running clear and cold. No Indians had been

21 "Medical History, Fort Wallace," Book 343, 1.
22 *Ibid.*
23 *Ibid.*
24 Ball to AAG District of Kansas, April 10, April 30, 1866; "Letter Book, Fort Wallace."
25 "Medical History, Fort Wallace," Book 343, 1.

seen, and it was rumored that their agents had extracted promises from them to leave the Smoky Hill route alone. In a letter to Colonel Innis N. Palmer, district commander, Gordon grew lyrical over the sweet, healthful water in the streams, the luxuriant hay in the meadows, and the heavy timber, suitable for lumber, to be found in the nearby canyons and along the bluffs within two or three miles of the post.[26]

Gordon was not far wrong in his estimate of the Indian situation. Major Edward W. Wynkoop, still in the military service though on loan to the Interior Department, had been assigned as a special agent to the Indians with the mission of following up the Treaty of the Little Arkansas and securing participation in its provisions by the bands that had not been present at the council. In February, he had sought out several leading chiefs and persuaded them to abide by the treaty. In effect they thus gave up the Smoky Hill route to the whites. It allowed Indians to hunt in the area, but they were to keep away from the traveled roads. In discussing this with the Indians, Wynkoop found that those who had signed the treaty had construed their signatures to mean only that they were declaring their friendship for the whites but not that they were surrendering the Smoky Hill country. Later in the summer they would yield this point. Again not all the bands were present at the talk with Wynkoop. The Dog Soldier chiefs in particular were not there. And even the chiefs who did agree admitted that they could not answer for their braves when some influential war leader carried the pipe—that is, recruited a raiding party.[27]

Despite these weaknesses in the agreement Wynkoop had secured, chiefly from the Cheyennes and Arapahoes, he reported to the Central Superintendency that he had talked to all the Indians and had made peace, and "consequently the different routes of travel across the plains are perfectly safe." Among the chiefs from whom he had obtained pledges were "Black Kettle, Little Wolf, White [Gray] Beard, Setting Bear, Little Black Kettle, and Man Who Shot the Rea [Arickaree?]."[28]

Gordon, a Volunteer officer, was mustered out of the service on July 1 and was succeeded in command of Fort Wallace by Lieutenant Albert E. Bates.[29] One would scarcely believe, from Bates's initial report on conditions at Fort Wallace, that he and Gordon were describing the same locality.[30] Bates thought the site very poor, and proposed to district head-

---

[26] Gordon to Palmer, May 23, 1866, "Letters Sent, Fort Wallace."
[27] *Report* of Edward W. Wynkoop to Commissioner of Indian Affairs, 1866, 54.
[28] *Ibid.*
[29] Bates to Easton, July 12, 1866, "Letter Book, Fort Wallace."
[30] *Ibid.*

quarters that the post be moved two miles eastward to a nice tableland.[31] Although Gordon had regarded the water from nearby springs and streams to be sweet and pure, Bates was suspicious of it. He started digging a well in the center of his chosen site for the post, but after his men had cut through solid rock for thirty feet, they still had a dry hole. He persisted; by July 23, the men had descended to sixty feet, where they found shale and an oily substance that smelled like coal oil. Bates decided to haul water in barrels from the creek.[32]

Bates thought Gordon must have been drawing on his imagination when he reported tall hay in the meadows. Bates said the grass had been cropped off for miles in all directions. The fine timber described by Bates's predecessor did not exist. Bates declared that not even saplings could be found within ten miles, except for a few old cottonwoods along the streams. These were too soft and brittle to be used for lumber.[33] Bates was a realist.

On July 11, Bates moved Fort Wallace, still a tent camp, to the site he had chosen.[34] Near the line of tents he had a picket line stretched for the animals. The officers, instead of organizing a mess, rode three miles to the stage station, where meals were served to travelers and the woolly characters who began to congregate about the military encampment seeking wood contracts and hoping to start small stock ranches.[35]

Three miles southeast of the site, Bates found sandstone soft enough to be cut with axes and picks and trimmed with saws. By July 12, the men had quarried forty cords of this building material. Bates, who was not handicapped by undue modesty, wrote, "In two or three days I shall commence laying up the stone, as I am the only man in the command who knows how a stone wall should be built."[36] (In December, Captain Myles W. Keogh commented on Bates's superior handiwork: "The walls that were erected are so badly built it is doubtful if they will support the roof.")

Since Fort Wallace was at the apex of a double line of military posts that were thrust like a lance into the very heart of their hunting ground, it offered a challenge to the Indians. An older, more experienced officer than Bates should have been placed in command. Bates was only a year out of West Point and as green as his troops. But when he departed on a staff assignment on September 1, the command devolved on Second Lieutenant

---

[31] Bates to Palmer, July 1, 1866, "Medical History, Fort Wallace," 2.

[32] Bates to Palmer, July 13, 1866, "Medical History, Fort Wallace," 2.

[33] Bates to Easton, July 12, 1866, "Letter Book, Fort Wallace."

[34] George A. Armes, *Ups and Downs of an Army Officer*, 167.

[35] *Ibid.*

[36] Bates to Easton, July 12, 1866, "Letter Book, Fort Wallace."

George A. Armes, who had just been commissioned from civil life and who, when he shaved for the first time in his life shortly after his arrival at Fort Wallace, was able to scrape only a little fine down from his chin.[37] Yet neither Bates nor Armes seem to have been overawed by their responsibilities or by fear of the Indians. Their writings at this critical time reflect only a confident and lighthearted attitude and a concern chiefly for chasing wolves, buffalo, and antelope and for killing dozens of rattlesnakes with their pistols.

The more senior officers of the Regular Army, who had been colonels and generals but were now captains and majors, were mostly serving on staffs, courts, boards, and recruiting duty and enjoying a taste of civilized living that had been denied them for four years.

Young and inexperienced as Bates was, and with no older hand to guide him, he did well during his short tenure as post commander. For example, he realized that his men would get whisky somewhere, so instead of issuing orders restricting the men to coffee and water, he established "whisky calls." Three times daily an officer marched the companies to the sutler's store, where each man was permitted to buy one drink and consume it at once.[38]

Partly because of the tight control imposed and because the men had not yet undergone a winter on the Plains, discipline and morale were reasonably good at Fort Wallace. When Colonel Innis N. Palmer, District Commander, visited the post with his inspector and the paymaster, the men made a creditable appearance at muster parade. That night, as was to be expected on payday, the men were "quite jolly," but most of them were in ranks at reveille. One soldier who was still drunk and hard to handle was given the cruel treatment of being spread-eagled on the ground for five hours under the burning sun.[39]

Bates and Armes met the Indians for the first time on the afternoon of August 24. When one of the sentries reported that a group of mounted men, apparently Indians, was approaching the post, Bates sent his guide-interpreter to see what was wanted.[40] This young man, whom Bates had hired at $125 per month, was William Comstock, a former Pony Express rider and a friend of William "Buffalo Bill" Cody and "Wild Bill" Hickok. He spoke Cheyenne and was known favorably by the Indians. Furthermore he

[37] Armes, *Up and Downs of an Army Officer*, 166.
[38] *Ibid.*, 170.
[39] *Ibid.*, 168, 169.
[40] *Ibid.*, 170; Bates to Harrison, August 28, 1866, "Letter Book, Fort Wallace."

was reported to be one of the most experienced and resourceful men on the Plains.

The Indians, Spotted Horse and two or three dozen other Dog Soldiers, explained to Comstock that they were men of peace and desired to visit the white chief for a friendly talk. Although Comstock suspected that they really came to scout the post and see how well the horses were guarded, he took them to the headquarters tent, where there were many handshakes and grunts of pleasure. Then the blanketed guests and their host—all with tongues in cheek—sat down for a formal smoke and protestations of warm regard. After an hour of these formalities, Bates gave the Indians the run of the camp so that the soldiers could obtain souvenirs by trading tobacco and personal articles for buffalo robes, moccasins, and beadwork.[41]

At sundown the Indians bivouacked three miles away, and in the morning they were gone. Comstock, with the foresight born of experience, went twenty miles west to the next stage station to keep an eye on the Indians. Soon they burst into the building, helped themselves to whatever suited their fancy, and ordered the proprietor to cook food for them. Eight other white men were present, two of whom were inclined to resist. Comstock dissuaded them by pointing out the disparity of numbers. After three hours of swaggering, bragging, and bullying the Cheyennes departed, carrying off saddles, bridles, and rations. As they climbed on their ponies, the chief told the stationmen they had fifteen days to clear out of the country. At the end of that period of grace, the Indians would return and destroy the station and any white people still there.[42]

Comstock followed the Indians to their camp and asked them to return the goods they had seized. They refused. The chief said that they had not told the post commander the truth, for they had no intention of giving up the Smoky Hill Road. On the contrary they expected to return within fifteen days and dispatch any soldiers and other white men who remained.[43]

The next day Messrs. Favor and Thompson and other settlers from the vicinity of the Big Timbers Station brought their families to Fort Wallace for safety. Then some of the men, including Thompson and Favor, returned to their ranches, saying that they would not be intimidated.[44]

The Indian threat was reported to higher headquarters, where it created a sensation and was taken seriously by Major General Winfield S. Hancock,

[41] *Ibid.*
[42] Bates to Harrison, August 28, 1866.
[43] *Ibid.*
[44] *Ibid.*

the newly appointed department commander. The Cheyennes, however, acted on their ultimatum to only a minor extent. On October 13 they attacked Chalk Bluff Station, seventy-five miles east of Fort Wallace, killing two stock herders and burning the buildings. A third attendant escaped, and later caught several loose Indian ponies. The Indians impudently insisted that Wynkoop secure the return of these animals, and he actually did so. While the stationman was in the Indian camp returning their horses, he recognized several Indians whom he had seen drawing rations from the agent at Fort Zarah.[45]

Also on October 13, Indians entered another station east of Fort Wallace and demanded that the attendant turn over all the stock in the corral. When he refused, they beat him nearly to death and took the stock.

Fort Wallace itself was raided on September 19, 1866. Armes, temporarily in command, was absent chasing buffalo and deserters, leaving Lieutenant R. B. Flood in charge. When Comstock came in to tell him that 150 Indians had stampeded the quartermaster herd, Flood ordered eighteen cavalry horses saddled and set forth in pursuit. Lowering clouds soon loosed a heavy snow storm, unusually early for the season. After riding eleven miles, Flood lost the trail. The Indians, however, succeeded in capturing only fourteen horses.[46]

Flood was soon replaced by Lieutenant Joseph C. Hale, Third Infantry, who continued building the new quarters, hoping to complete them before winter set in. He had to send wagons ninety miles to obtain timber for the floors, roof beams, and window and door frames.

Captain Myles W. Keogh, a brevet lieutenant colonel, took command at Fort Wallace on November 30, bringing with him Company I, Seventh Cavalry. Lieutenant Frederic W. Beecher, a nephew of the famous cleric, Henry Ward Beecher, became post quartermaster. He walked with a limp, having been wounded at the Battle of Gettysburg, but was active and vigorous and greatly interested in scouting and Indian fighting.

Keogh was disturbed by the shortage of firewood. The men were still under canvas, although work on the stone barracks had been pressed. The temperature was falling steadily, and there was a succession of heavy snow falls. Only three cords of wood were on hand, and it was evident that the contractor, impeded by the weather and an inadequate sense of urgency, would not fill his obligations. The situation was so critical that Keogh would have sent out the post quartermaster's wagons, but Captain (Brevet

---

[45] Hale to Harrison, October 14, 1866; Keogh to Harrison, December 20, 1866.
[46] Flood to Harrison, September 20, 1866.

50

Colonel) Michael V. Sheridan, brother of the potent general, had come through on a trip west and had taken many of the wagons with him. Keogh, in reporting this to district headquarters, added resignedly,

> There are stoves here but not a foot of pipe, so that even if we had the wood to heat the tents we have no means of burning it. Lieutenant Beecher, the AAAQ Master, has presented this matter before, but there seems to be very little hope of getting them until the men will have suffered.[47]

His final remark was unappreciated at district headquarters.

By the end of 1866, Keogh had completed one company barracks, into which he was able to move all his men, for he had only thirty-seven cavalrymen and twenty-three infantry. He reported that the men were comfortable, but said that the horses were not. The stables were without roofs and, Keogh complained, his repeated requisitions for nails with which to construct roofs had met with no response from higher headquarters. This remark caused an unfriendly reaction and failed to speed the shipment of nails.[48]

The cold weather and frequent snows were having one beneficial effect—they were keeping the Indians within their tents when they might otherwise have been whooping it up along the Smoky Hill. Spotted Tail's Sioux, who had been helping the Cheyennes make war in 1865, were on Beaver Creek 60 miles north of Fort Wallace; Spotted Horse's and Dull Knife's Cheyennes were 120 miles north; and another village under Cut Nose was 75 miles distant. Though aggrieved over the reopening of the Smoky Hill route, they had not recently threatened war according to Comstock.[49]

Nevertheless, General Hancock was aroused to an extent considerably out of proportion to the seriousness of the few episodes which had occurred that fall. Already he was considering plans for a big expedition into the Indian country in the spring of 1867.

[47] Keogh to Harrison, December 4, 1866.
[48] *Ibid.*, January 1, 1867.
[49] *Ibid.*

6. SOULE GOES TO FORT DODGE

Early in 1867, General Hancock completed his plans for leading a military expedition into the plains, but he held back until Major Wynkoop, the newly appointed agent for the Cheyennes and Arapahoes, had determined which band was guilty of the depredations committed near Fort Wallace and at Chalk Bluffs. Hancock went to St. Louis to lay his plans before General Sherman, who gave his approval and even went to Washington to explain the situation to government leaders and to secure an appropriation. These actions alerted the big newspapers of the country to the imminence of a campaign; they arranged for correspondents to accompany Hancock when he went into the field.

One of the most famous of these correspondents was Theodore R. Davis, whose on-the-spot illustrations of the Civil War had appeared in *Harper's Weekly* and who still represented *Harper's* after the war. Another reporter, not then well known nationally, but who was to gain even greater notice than Davis, was the young Welshman known as Henry M. Stanley, who had been in the Confederate Army, was captured, and had served as a Galvanized Yankee.

Unfortunately, there were no news photographers. The photoengraving process was not known, and consequently, the illustrated periodicals could not directly reproduce photographs. Furthermore, lenses and emulsions were too slow to record action. One of the finest photographers of his day, William S. Soule, whose portraits of the Indians of the southern Plains are unsurpassed, was at Fort Dodge in 1867.[1] However, Soule did not photograph any of the well-known army officers—Sherman, Sheridan, Custer, Hancock—who visited Fort Dodge while he was there. Perhaps, like some other former enlisted men, he was uneasy in the presence of rank or had an aversion to officers. Similarly, he avoided taking pictures of famous scouts

[1] Soule left no papers. Data concerning him were obtained from: (a) correspondence between the author and Miss Lucia A. Soule, W. S. Soule's daughter; (b) an interview between Miss Soule and author in 1965; (c) a biographical sketch furnished by Henry G. Peabody to Matthew Stirling, Bureau of American Ethnology; (d) an abstract of Soule's military record in National Archives; (e) a history of Soule's military unit written by Charles E. Davis, Jr., *Three Years in the Army, The Story of the Thirteenth Massachusetts Volunteers,* 135, 137, 457.

like Comstock, Cody, Hickok, and Beecher, though he did take pictures of more retiring civilian plainsmen like Ben Clark, Ed Guerrier, and Phil McCusker. Soule did make pictures of nearly all the famous Indian chiefs and many lesser warriors. But he neither captured on his plates any of the big events like the Medicine Lodge Treaty, nor did he photograph what was to be seen after a bloody atrocity, though several occurred within his immediate vicinity. He took only one picture of a dead man—Ralph Morrison—and apparently he took that picture only to prove it could be done.

In spite of all the interesting people and events Soule did not photograph, his album of Indian pictures is a fine contribution to graphic history, and, because of it, we know exactly what these primitive people looked like

When Soule went west in 1867 he stopped at Leavenworth and obtained employment with John Tappan, sutler at Fort Dodge. From Leavenworth he went via the Kansas Pacific Railroad to its terminus at Salina, Kansas, where he engaged passage by stagecoach to Fort Dodge. He heard from experienced travelers that it would be a rough and possibly dangerous journey, but the winter storms were abating, spring was just breaking through, and Soule was anxious to reach his destination.[2]

While waiting for the stage to depart, Soule saw wagon trains assembling on the outskirts of Salina. For decades wagons drawn by oxen had carried freight across the plains to Santa Fe. They were still the chief means of supplying army posts and settlements in Kansas and Colorado, and in the Southwest.

The prairie schooners comprising these trains were large and durable, but cumbersome, and were capable of transporting three or four tons each. Eight to ten yoke of oxen or big steers were hitched to each wagon; usually the wagonmaster connected two wagons in tandem. In this way he economized on "bullwhackers," as the teamsters were called. These loud-mouthed characters doubtless derived their names from the manner in which they urged their phlegmatic teams forward, for they wielded twenty-four-foot bull whips with which they could rip the hide from man or beast. They also employed epithets of awesome wickedness.

One traveler claimed that most bullwhackers, and an occasional stage driver, were men of culture and refinement who had sought such employment in order to recover from incipient "consumption." The outdoor

---

[2] Soule's trip to Fort Dodge is reconstructed from accounts by others who made the trip about the same time: Theodore R. Davis, "A Stage Ride to Colorado," *Harper's New Monthly Magazine*, Vol. XXXV (July, 1867), 137–50; and Stanley, *My Early Travels and Adventures*, I, 11–60.

exercise in the pure, bracing air of the plains reputedly had a curative effect. If there were such gentlemen among the teamsters, they were not noticeable. Virtually every bullwhacker, Mexican or Nordic, was a grimy, bearded specimen who could fairly describe himself in the words of the old army jingle:

> *I'm wild and woolly and full of fleas,*
> *I've never been curried below the knees.*
> *Yee-ow! I'm wild!*

Commercial ox trains usually contained eighty or more wagons, which should have given them sufficient fire power to withstand an Indian attack —a rifle was strapped to the side of each wagon where it was quickly available. But the defensive qualities of each train depended more on the courage and determination of the men than on their armament. When Indians appeared, the weak and timid did not show their panic by fleeing, but by becoming apathetic and unresisting.

Trains belonging to army regiments were smaller than the commercial trains and were drawn by horses or mules. When in Indian country, they had escorts of infantry, who walked in single file on the flanks, close in, and out to the front and rear.

The western sky was already dull red and the billowing prairie grass in shadow when, at the end of the second day, Soule's stagecoach reached Ellsworth. Overhead flew large flocks of crows on their way northeast to roost in the cottonwoods bordering a stream. The hamlet, situated near Fort Ellsworth, consisted of a stage station, two dugouts, and two long cabins made of small logs thrust upright into the ground and chinked with mud. A few weeks later, when the new railroad would reach the spot, Ellsworth would become, overnight, a roaring, mushrooming town. But when Soule went through, in early March, whisky was the only accommodation. It was sold at both huts.

This was one of a chain of stage stations located every fifteen miles or so for the changing of teams. When the weather was good a stage could make eighty miles a day, but it would be a very long day, and the teams had to be in prime condition. Each station was operated by two or three men whose chief duty was to tend the stock, but in some cases there was a small restaurant. This convenience could not be depended upon, especially if Indian raiders were active; therefore, experienced travelers carried their own food and blankets.

At Ellsworth the road forked and the Santa Fe Road branched off to the southwest while the Smoky Hill Road continued straight ahead. At this important junction, a lunch counter had been established in the stage station. Soule and the other passengers were able to climb out and go to the station for their supper.

While at supper, Soule had a short conversation with a lieutenant from the fort, who came to the station with his young wife to collect the mail. Fort Ellsworth, they said, was falling apart and would soon be replaced by Fort Harker, which was under construction a mile or so to the east. Most of the officers still lived at the old post waiting for their new quarters to be completed.

Soule, supposing he would live at Fort Dodge under the same conditions, asked what sort of houses were at these frontier posts. The officer's wife replied,

We are living in a hovel. It is twelve feet square and made of rough logs set upright, palisade style, and plastered with mud, sticks, straw, and boughs. The mud persists in falling to the inside at all hours of the day and night. It drops on our plates at dinner time, and into our mouths if we are so careless as to sleep with our mouths open—otherwise into our faces. Recently we had the bright idea of stretching a piece of canvas above our bed, and thus defy the mud. Unfortunately the first night we were under this canopy it snowed, and the tent cloth caught several bushels of snow that drifted through cracks in the roof and walls. Towards morning a thaw released a stream of water on to us. As we wrung out the tent, the mud resumed its steady clop, clop on our heads.[3]

When Soule remarked with some anxiety that these conditions seemed a little austere, even for the frontier, the lady responded,

Oh, that wasn't all. When you add the overpowering aroma of some skunk concealed in the brush roof, you have the Black Hole of Calcutta. Mice ran riot through the roof, too. A week before we moved in the previous occupant of our quarters killed three rattlesnakes that were warming themselves before the fire.

Soule privately told himself she was exaggerating for the benefit of a tenderfoot. But she was not. He asked if there were any Indians about.

"Yes," said the officer, "mostly the so-called friendlies, Kaws and Omahas, who live on a small reservation east of here. Cheyennes and

[3] *Army and Navy Journal*, Vol. IV (February 16, 1867), 414.

Arapahoes are believed to be camped not far to the west. The Cheyennes are a bold, saucy people, who will surely give us trouble this summer."[4]

His wife, who obviously wanted to talk, spoke feelingly of the high cost of living, stating that all supplies came by wagon train. She said that prices increased in proportion to the distance from civilization. A can of sardines marked twenty-three cents in Boston sold for sixty cents at Fort Harker and for one dollar and a half in New Mexico.[5]

"One thing you can always buy on the plains," she concluded, "is sardines—and whisky."

After an hour's halt, the stage resumed its journey into the night.

When dawn broke, Soule saw that the appearance of the country was gradually changing.[6] The black, gumbo soil of eastern Kansas had given way to a thinner loam mixed with granitic sand. The streams had cut deep channels, in places small canyons, and there were areas of dunes, hills, and bluffs. Along the tributaries of the Arkansas River were cottonwoods, elms, and hackberries, with some elders and other low bushes that seemed to be mostly wild plums. Even the prairie grass was getting thinner and there were large black areas where fire had swept the plains. A heavy, wet snow had blanketed the prairie a few days earlier but was now melted. There were still patches in the shade made by a bluff or stream bank. The buffalo grass had been cropped off close to the ground, especially where new sprouts were coming up through the ashes.

The buffalo had passed recently. Over the surface of the prairie as far as the eye could see, there was a network of buffalo trails, and the ever-present chips (droppings) were everywhere.

"We'll see buffalo today, sure," said the stage driver, "and likely antelope. Injuns tomorrow, or signs of 'em."

The sun was shining on the distant low hills when the stage reached Cow Creek Station. Mules replaced horses here and thereafter would alternate with them. Animals were selected for their speed and endurance and the stage company paid fancy prices for them. It was no wonder the Indians made so many raids on the stations.

The human inhabitants of the station must have been less choice, for they cost the company only twelve dollars a month apiece—and keep. Soule could not understand why a man would stay in such a perilous post for so

---

[4] *Ibid.*

[5] *Ibid.*

[6] The description of the remainder of the trip is based chiefly on the accounts of Davis and Stanley, cited in the foregoing, with added descriptions of the terrain, weather, and army posts given in the military medical histories.

little money. He did not appreciate that the work was easy, and that there were good opportunities for selling liquor, trading with buffalo hunters and even, sometimes, with friendly Indians; and that the profits were often substantial. Also, the prairie had an allure which was hard to explain.

Cow Creek Station had been a favorite target for Indian attacks because ox trains camped there; they were especially vulnerable while crossing a stream. Stock tenders, teamsters, and even soldiers could be found in the vicinity from time to time—lying in the grass with dozens of arrows sticking in them and their scalps missing. Since the last attack, made in the fall when the buildings had been destroyed, the customary troop detachment had been withdrawn. It would soon be re-established, but in the meantime, the attendants were living in a hole in the ground, or a cave and were obtaining water for themselves and for the stock from another depression into which rain water seeped.

While the grazing mules were brought in and harnessed, the passengers climbed out of the coach to cook breakfast over a fire made of buffalo chips. They roasted venison from a haunch obtained the day before when one of the men killed a mule deer. Baked potatoes and corn dodgers completed the meal. Soule filled his lungs with the bracing air and felt some of the mysterious spell of the prairie. Presently the driver cried "Yip! Yip!" and they were on their way.

True to the driver's prediction, buffalo began to appear, at first singly or in small groups. The travelers, seeing several on a distant ridge, hazy in the early light, were not sure whether they were hummocks or clumps of bushes. Then a number of the great, shaggy beasts were seen nearer the road, grazing unconcernedly and seemingly unafraid of the stagecoach, which was now moving slowly.

Everyone wanted to shoot a buffalo. The driver, who had gone through this many times, pulled up and pointed to a lone bison some two hundred yards distant. He suggested that a few of the men stalk him by slipping up a draw. The quarry was a venerable bull, stiff in the joints and slow to react. He only looked up in bewilderment when several shots were fired and then dropped to his knees, flopped over, and expired. The exultant hunters cut out the tongue and a chunk of the hump—said to be the choicest parts—and brought the meat back to the coach where it was stowed carelessly with the baggage.

Other buffalo were aroused by the shooting and the sight of men on foot. As they began to run, it became evident that there were greater numbers in the immediate vicinity than had been realized. By the time the coach moved

57

on, a fair-sized herd was racing parallel to the road. The driver whipped his team and shouted to the passengers to take shots at the animals through the window. The buffalo increased their speed until they succeeded in cutting across in front of the careening vehicle; then the buffalo went off in a wide curve that soon left the coach in the rear.

Since the buffalo could easily have turned away at the outset, their action in racing to cut across the front of the coach seems silly. It was explained by an authority on plains life:

> The principle under which the bison act is the same as that of cattle when cowboys are trying to cut one or more out of a herd. Each animal "knows" it is the one you are after. It can see you only out of the side, and only from one eye; and is afraid to take its eye from anything dangerous.
>
> Hence the buffalo, running parallel to a vehicle, try to escape by means of speed rather than by dodging off to the side. As a buffalo gets ahead of its pursuer, it loses sight of him, so it swerves over in front, in a curve, and thus attempts to cross in front. Antelope and many other animals do the same.[7]

The next station beyond Cow Creek was Fort Zarah, where the travelers would again see human habitation. Along the way, buffalo were continually in sight, and an occasional antelope bounded away. Wolves and coyotes skulked on the fringes of the herds, watching for a weak or aged animal or a newly dropped calf. The driver remarked that Indians might be nearby, as Fort Zarah was now the place where they drew rations.

About noon they saw an Indian trail that the driver thought was less than one day old. It had been made by a small band with women and children, he said, pointing out the travois marks on the ground. This trail consisted of three parallel traces a few feet apart. The center was made by the ponies walking in single file, while the outer marks were made by the lodge poles fastened to the sides of the horses and dragging the ground. On such a rig the women packed some of their gear and even transported feeble persons or children too small to ride. Most infants were carried in papoose carriers strapped to their mothers' backs.

The driver assured the passengers that there was no cause for alarm, for it was too early in the season for raiding parties. This, he said, was probably a small village either hunting buffalo or going to Fort Zarah or Fort Larned. Soule hoped he was right.

Fort Zarah, though it had been recently abandoned as a military post,

[7] General Hugh L. Scott, manuscript on Indian sign language, Division of Manuscripts, Library of Congress.

was still guarded by a small detachment of soldiers who acted as scouts for the stages when the Indians seemed threatening. They were also guarding Colonel Leavenworth's Kiowa and Comanche agency, which he was at the moment maintaining at Fort Zarah where he had the use of one of two completed stone buildings. The other building, at the opposite end of the post, was being used by a trader and freight contractor named Charles Rath.

Soule's stage stopped overnight at Fort Zarah. This was not unusual. Drivers often waited there for a report on whether Indians were attacking localities farther west and whether it was necessary to ask for an escort. In the morning it was learned from an eastbound stage that no escort was necessary.

The next lap of twenty-three miles, from Fort Zarah to Fort Larned, could be made in half a day, but they made a late start because they had waited for a road report. The road now ran roughly parallel to and at no great distance from the Arkansas River. The country was wilder; the vastness of the plains made the travelers feel more remote from the settled parts of the country, and they began to sense the loneliness and isolation of the land.

Though they had passed the great buffalo herds, there was still much wild life. The travelers were entertained by the inhabitants of prairie dog towns, fat little marmots that sat on the edges of their burrows and chirped and jerked their tails at the passing coach. Soule also saw small owls sitting beside prairie dog holes in which they had apparently nested. Soule, riding on the seat beside the driver, asked why they stared so fixedly at passersby. The driver didn't know, but he solemnly assured Soule that if he dismounted and walked in a circle around one of these owls, it would keep turning its head in order to keep him in view. If he completed several continuous revolutions he could cause the bird to twist off its head. Soule didn't know whether to believe this story or not.

The sunset was gorgeous as they came over a hill and saw the rectangle of low, whitewashed buildings that constituted Fort Larned. Overhead, the sky was a porcelain-like blue, but closer to the edge of the prairie the sky became gold with fleecy clouds, then crimson with bright gold again on the far edge of the clouds. Through the bare branches of trees along Pawnee Fork the sun was a great orange ball rolling into the distant purple hills.

To the tired wayfarers, the military post was an oasis with its neat, well-kept appearance. They were pleased to learn that they would spend the night in Dave Butterfield's trading camp—rude accommodations but far preferable to the crowded coach. There would be a plentiful supper of buffalo steak, potatoes, bread, and coffee, with whisky and cigars afterwards. The meal would be worth the two dollars it cost.

In the morning, the stage left for Fort Dodge, sixty miles to the southwest. Ordinarily it was a fourteen-hour trip, but bad weather caused an overnight stop at one of the intervening stations.

At first the trip was merely monotonous. The terrain was again a rolling prairie with sparse brown grass, then a series of bleak, barren, sandy hills. The scenery became more pleasing when the road dipped toward the river, where the willows were already in timid leaf and the hackberries were powdered with a reddish mist. In the river occasional small islands sprouting early grass and shrubbery broke the shimmering surface of the water.

As the day wore on, the clouds darkened, and the north wind increased. The driver, who was well acquainted with the weather on the central Plains, knew they were being stalked by a late spring blizzard. Big flakes were already driving across their faces when they came to the next station, and they were relieved when the driver turned everyone out, shouting that they would hole up for the night.

This station had been burned by the Indians in 1864 but had been rebuilt. It consisted of a frame house, a corral, and a shed for the stock. A tunnel led from the house to the shed and to a sort of underground redoubt; the roof of the redoubt was only a foot above the ground and the walls were loopholed on all sides. On the parapet inside were loaded rifles, extra ammunition, and casks of water. In this miniature fort the stationmen could endure a siege of two or three days, if they didn't lose their nerve and try to run for it. By stretching out on the floor in the house and on the ground in the dugout, the stage passengers managed a somewhat fitful night's sleep.

In the morning the sun was glittering on a foot of driven snow. But the wind had died down, and the driver decided to push on before a thaw converted the road into a quagmire. It was rough going at first, but before noon they passed a stage going east. It had broken a trail for them, and they reached Fort Dodge well before dark.

Soule found the place to be a well-fortified post surrounded by stone and earthen embankments and then by a wide ditch. There were sallyports on two sides, sandbagged, provided with wooden drawbridges, and commanded by Parrott three-inch rifles.

John Tappan, after buying articles for his store, had left Leavenworth before Soule and was waiting for him at Fort Dodge. He had spent over $1,000.00 in erecting his sutler's store, which was a long, one-story frame building with nice windows and stout, well fitting doors. Tappan considered the cost exorbitant, but he had had to freight the lumber and other materials for a long distance, and the carpenters had demanded $5.00 a day, over twice the rate paid in the East. Stonemasons and bricklayers were paid $7.00 a day. Ordinary laborers were overpaid at $2.00 a day, but Tappan had not needed many.

Tappan's merchandise was expensive by the time it was freighted out to Fort Dodge, but he had a monopoly and did a thriving business—not only with the military but also with the squatters, civilian employees, and Indians.

Soule was immediately busy in his new job of keeping the books, supervising the other employees, and helping wait on customers during rush periods. He set up sleeping quarters and a photographic studio in the two-room apartment Tappan had assigned him at the end of the building. He had brought a canvas backdrop on which was painted a Grecian scene for his studio, and on the floor he incongruously scattered some straw to give an outdoor effect. His photographic subjects either sat on or stood with an elbow resting on a stump, over which he draped a buffalo robe.

If the stage effects were amateurish, the photographer was not. He began to develop a good trade among people at the post who wanted pictures of themselves and their families. And it was not long before he found a growing interest in persuading Indians, who began to visit the post, to sit for photographs. They were suspicious and superstitious at first, but Soule induced them to come into the studio to watch sleight-of-hand tricks, in which he had some skill. The one that delighted and fascinated them most was a fire-eating stunt in which he stuffed his mouth with cotton impregnated with some secret chemical and soon began to blow smoke and sparks from his mouth.[8] While at Fort Dodge, Soule took a number of his best Indian portraits, but with a few exceptions he did not mark them; it generally is not possible to determine which pictures he took there.

[8] Statement of Lucia A. Soule to author, October 3, 1965.

7. TALK OF WAR

William Soule probably had little op-
portunity to photograph Cheyennes and Arapahoes until the fall of 1867,
for until then, with one exception, none came near Fort Dodge. The exception was a large village of Dog Soldiers. Hancock had visited the village
while they were camped on Pawnee Fork, two days' trip north of Fort
Dodge, but that was too far for Soule to venture without an escort, especially since that band was probably hostile.

But he was able to take pictures of Kiowas and Kiowa-Apaches, for they
visited the post repeatedly during the spring. He may have gone out to one
of their camps, since at this time, or a little later, he rigged up a buckboard
to be used as a dark room. He also had a small tent in which he loaded his
plates into the holders, and where he may have developed them.

Major Henry Douglass, post commander at Fort Dodge, rode south to
the Kiowa and Comanche camps on the Cimarron early in the year.[1] His
purpose was to keep track of the Indians and to determine their attitude.
Douglass had served on the frontier for five years before the war and thus
had had previous experience in dealing with Indians. Although they seemed
quiet and friendly, Douglass was somewhat disturbed to note how well
armed they were. He knew that all five tribes had been issued firearms and
ammunition at Fort Zarah in fulfillment of the promises made by the Treaty
of the Little Arkansas. But now they were buying additional weapons from
clandestine traders. Although this was common knowledge, Douglass could
see no reason for them to possess pistols, for these certainly were not
needed for hunting. Every brave had at least one revolver thrust in his belt
and some had two or three.[2]

Kicking Bird, the most consistently friendly chief, visited Fort Dodge in
January to complain about the Kiowa and Comanche agent, Jesse Leavenworth. He said the Kiowas were "mad" at Leavenworth because he withheld
the presents due them by treaty. According to Kicking Bird, the Kiowas

[1] There is some question as to whether the name is spelled "Douglass" or "Douglas."
Whether the final "s" is a letter or a flourish in the signature is not clear. I use the spelling
given in the Register of Graduates, USMA.
[2] Douglass to AAG Hq. Div. of the Mo., January 13, 1867, "Letter Book, Fort Dodge."

had received no presents whatsoever in 1866 and none until then in 1867. The Kiowas thought that the agent had given the goods to other tribes or had sold them and pocketed the proceeds. He admitted that they had not yet gone to Fort Zarah for issue day that winter, but said he had sent Leavenworth a request to hold the presents until spring, when their horses would be strong enough to make the trip.[3] Douglass had some doubts about the story, and thought that perhaps the trouble lay in bad management rather than dishonesty.

Kicking Bird also informed Douglass that there was much indignation among the Kiowas, for they felt they had been treated unjustly by the agent. The chief said that it required all his influence to prevent an outbreak, and he feared that the tribe would commence hostilities in the spring. Satanta, he added, was forever talking of war, and a council had already been held at the Kiowa camp, where representatives from the Cheyennes, Arapahoes, Comanches, and Sioux had met. At that time they had agreed that when the grass was an inch high they would commence war. Kicking Bird emphasized that he was telling these things not in defiance or as a challenge to the white man, but because he had always been treated kindly at Fort Dodge and he wanted to put the people there on guard.[4]

Throughout the late sixties and early seventies, Kicking Bird was as active as Leavenworth, and possibly more so, in keeping the Kiowas from embarking on a general war. Kicking Bird's endeavors to avert war injured him in the eyes of many of his tribesmen. When old Do-hauson died in the winter of 1866, Kicking Bird, Lone Wolf, and Satanta were the leading candidates for the position of principal chief. Although Do-hauson had a nephew who was a fairly prominent warrior, he had designated Lone Wolf as his successor. But both Kicking Bird and Satanta were men of great ability. As it turned out, Kicking Bird increased his influence until, by 1874, from one-half to two-thirds of the tribe followed his lead.

Over thirty years ago a venerable Kiowa said to me, "Kicking Bird must have been appointed by God to lead his people during those years, the most difficult ever faced by us."

During those troubled years, William Soule took at least two photographs of Kicking Bird, but it is uncertain whether they were made at Fort Dodge or Fort Sill.

In February, John Dodge, one of Charley Rath's traders, visited the Kiowa camps. Through him, the Indians notified Colonel Leavenworth that

[3] *Ibid.*
[4] *Ibid.*

their horses were too poor to make the trip to Fort Zarah to draw rations and annuities and that it was too cold to travel.

"Squaws making robes, grass covered with snow, and it would kill more horses than it is worth," they declared. They urged the agent to haul the supplies to them, as he had plenty of corn to feed his mules, and the trip would not hurt them.[5] Leavenworth declined.

Little Raven's Arapahoes crossed the Arkansas late in January and went south into the Kiowa-Comanche country. The chief stopped at Fort Dodge to tell Major Douglass that they were nearly starving and were going south to hunt buffalo. Douglass, in his report of this to district headquarters, confirmed that Little Raven's band was in wretched condition.[6] Soon after this, Douglass sent Captain John H. Page with F. F. Smith (an interpreter) and sutler John Tappan to visit the Indian camps to check their attitude. On the way they met Satanta, who with his wife was going to Fort Dodge for food. But when the men said they were bringing provisions, Satanta accompanied them back to the village. Evidently the buffalo were already growing scarce, and the Indians, especially in the winter, were only slightly removed from starvation.[7]

Satanta echoed Kicking Bird's complaint that the Kiowas were being poorly treated by their agent. Other Kiowas in the camp asked Page when the Great White Father in Washington was going to give them an honest agent. Before Page departed, Satanta told him that he must inform the commanding officer that all soldiers must leave the country, that the Santa Fe Road was to be closed as far east as Council Grove, and that no travel was to be permitted on it.[8]

"He will be allowed to use it to haul provisions and other supplies to us, however," Satanta hastened to add.

Page next went to Black Kettle's Cheyenne village, where the chief asked him, somewhat piteously, if his village would be safe from the soldiers if they moved three hundred miles farther south. He said that the Sioux had commenced war [north of Kansas] and that they were drawing all the Indians into it.

Page replied, "In case of war no place in the Indian country will be safe."[9]

Satanta rode into Fort Dodge on February 11, tied his horse in front of

---

[5] John Dodge to Leavenworth, January 18, 1867, "Letter Book, Fort Dodge."

[6] Douglass to AAG, District of the Upper Arkansas, February 2, 1867, "Letter Book, Fort Dodge."

[7] Page to Douglass, February 13, 1867, "Letter Book, Fort Dodge."

[8] *Ibid.*

[9] *Ibid.*

post headquarters, and strode in to see his brother, the white chief. He gave Douglass a hug and sat down to exchange the latest news.[10]

Satanta was better known to the whites along the Arkansas than any other Indian. This was partly because of his reputation as a killer and kidnapper and partly because of his formidable appearance and colorful personality. He was changeable—one moment arrogant and boastful, the next humble and begging. He claimed to be a friend to Americans, and it is true that most of his raiding was done in Texas and Mexico, though he did not entirely neglect the Arkansas line. He insisted that Texas was an enemy nation and that, therefore, its citizens were fair game.

Far from concealing his misdeeds, Satanta bragged about them. Everything about this Indian was big—his barrel chest, his booming voice, and his love of whisky. Even his tipi stood out, for it was painted bright red—the only red tipi in the tribe.

Satanta told Douglass that his tribe favored war, for they had not received their annuities, but he was doing all he could to keep his young men quiet. He was the great chief, he said, not only of his own tribe but of the Cheyennes, Arapahoes, and Kiowa-Apaches. He led them all and presided at their councils. Even the Sioux had beseeched him to join them in making war, but he had not yet accepted the pipe. Now he had come to learn what the white men were going to do.

While the interpreter was putting this into English, Satanta suddenly forked off on another trail. He said the buffalo were scarce and his people were hungry. If Douglass would give them enough food, they would refrain from "getting mad." He had spoken. But he would have more to say in the morning.

On the following day Satanta returned to Fort Dodge accompanied by several other Indians. He again demanded that the soldiers clear out of the country as far east as Council Grove. Otherwise there would be war. Douglass was to stop building houses at Fort Dodge.[11]

"All the country with wood and water and grass, belongs to the Indians," Satanta said, "and the Government has not paid for it. You have no right to it, and must leave."

At this point several of the other Indians interrupted Satanta and told him he was going too far. "Be still," they ordered him. Satanta sat down.

Douglass made a mild response, saying he was friendly to the Indians but that it would be foolish of them to start a war, for the result would be

[10] Dodge to Mitchell, February 13, 1867, "Letter Book, Fort Dodge."
[11] *Ibid.*

65

their complete ruin. He offered to give them a meal, but refused to furnish a wagonload of provisions. When Douglass reported these talks to district headquarters, he asked for more troops at Fort Dodge.

On February 24, Dodge had another visit from Satanta, Stumbling Bear, and other Kiowa chiefs. As usual, Satanta did most of the talking. He covered the same ground as on his previous visit but added that some Cheyennes had stolen mules belonging to white men who were hunting wolves on the Cimarron. As before, Satanta was interrupted by his companions, whereupon he changed his tune and begged for food.[12] When Douglass offered Satanta peace or war, the chief's only reply was to repeat his request for food.

Douglass informed district headquarters that Little Raven, normally friendly and complaisant, had sent him a message directing that no more wood be cut on Pawnee Fork and that the soldiers must move out of the country. Satanta also sent an impudent message telling Douglass to fatten his horses, as he, Satanta, was coming to get them.[13]

On March 18, Satanta again visited Fort Dodge, but this time he was quite humble. The Cheyennes, he said, were making fools of themselves by running off stock. He would have nothing more to do with them. He also said that he would say nothing further about the road; the whites could use it as much as they pleased. Douglass was unable to guess the reason for Satanta's change in attitude.[14]

By March 26, a two-hundred-lodge village of Cheyennes under Bull Bear was camped on Pawnee Fork, within thirty miles of Fort Larned. More bands were joining this camp, and the Cheyennes were said to be preparing to hold one of their medicine ceremonies. Bull Bear told an interpreter sent out to investigate, that the Cheyennes had been talking war, but that these manifestations of restlessness came only from some of the younger men. The Sioux who were camped with him favored peace. They had obeyed government commissioners who had visited them in the north and told them to move south of the Platte if they wished to stay out of the troubles brewing in the north. The interpreter told the Cheyenne leaders that General Hancock was coming to the plains with a military expedition and was planning to meet with the Indians and give them the choice of peace or war. Bull Bear expressed pleasure at the prospect of the visit, and said he would come to Fort Larned for the council when notified to do so.[15]

---

[12] Douglass to McKeever, February 24, 1867, "Letter Book, Fort Dodge."
[13] Douglass to Noyes, March 14, 1867, "Letter Book, Fort Dodge."
[14] Douglass to Noyes, March 19, 1867, "Letter Book, Fort Dodge."
[15] Douglass to McKeever, March 31, 1867, "Letter Book, Fort Dodge."

The interpreter reported that Bull Bear's horses were in miserable condition, with several dying each day. He did not think the Cheyennes would be in any condition to make war before summer even if they wanted to.

Edmund Guerrier, the half-French, half-Cheyenne who often acted as go-between for the Indians and military, said that these Cheyennes were well disposed toward the government. He had heard nothing that led him to think they meant mischief. Guerrier advised the post commander at Larned not to believe the lies that had been brought in from other sources, but said he knew nothing concerning the Indians south of the Arkansas.[16]

The tone of the Indians' talk during the early spring was defiant, but there was no sound evidence that they were planning an outbreak. Even where there was talk of war, it was simply that—talk. Although several of the post commanders, especially commanders stationed on the Smoky Hill route, thought the raiding season was about to begin, there was no definite evidence to support that view.

[16] *Ibid.*

8. HANCOCK'S EXPEDITION

General Hancock planned to march into the Indian country with an expedition strong enough to overawe the Indians or to fight them, depending on their own attitude and actions. His intentions do not seem to have been unduly warlike, for, in his letter to Wynkoop and Leavenworth, Hancock stated: "We desire to avoid if possible any trouble with the Indians and to treat them with justice; and I wish especially to act through the agents of the Indian Department . . . ."[1]

Although his force has been described as the largest ever seen on the plains, no doubt this former corps commander did not consider it large. Actually it was only a small reinforced brigade. The fighting components consisted of parts of two regiments—eleven companies of the Seventh Cavalry, seven of the Thirty-seventh Infantry, and a battery of the Fourth Artillery. There was also a wagon train, a small pontoon train, and a detachment of Delaware Indian scouts. The whole force contained 1,400 officers and men.[2]

The cavalry and infantry were not ready for combat. The men were recruits, and the units had only been organized for a few weeks. The cavalrymen scarcely knew how to ride and the infantry had not been hardened for marching. Although they knew the manual of arms and had had loading exercises, neither had actually been trained in the use of their weapons. The infantry were still armed with single-shot, muzzle-loading muskets. In experience and ability, the soldiers were far inferior to the Indians, but they made up for it by the use of tactical methods in which they acted in concert, under the orders of their officers. The Indians, on the other hand, fought as individuals and seldom made serious attacks unless they had great numerical superiority.[3]

General Hancock was forty-three and, excepting a wound he had received at Gettysburg which had never healed properly, in the prime of life.

---

[1] Hancock to Wynkoop, March 11, 1867, Report of the Commissioner of Indian Affairs, 1867, 40 Cong., 1 sess., *Sen. Exec. Doc. 1308*, 78.

[2] *Army and Navy Journal*, Vol. IV (April, 1867), 510.

[3] Major General John Gibbon, "Arms to Fight the Indians," *United Service*, Vol. I (April, 1879), 239–42 ff.

He was intelligent and brave, and he had been in service on the plains before the war. However, for dealing with the Indians, he was not a good choice. He was genial socially but when speaking officially, he was inclined to be stern, blunt, and undiplomatic. And although he had led fifty thousand men in battle, he knew nothing of the guerrilla type of warfare that characterized Indian fighting.[4]

His second in command was Colonel Andrew Jackson Smith, Seventh Cavalry, who as a major general of Volunteers had commanded a corps at Vicksburg. He was four years older than Hancock and had been a dragoon before the war. He was a fine officer, who liked to share all the hardships of his men.[5]

The cavalry was commanded by Lieutenant Colonel George Armstrong Custer, one of the "boy generals" who had commanded a division under Sheridan. He had never served on the plains and knew nothing of Indian fighting, but he made a big show.[6] The infantry commander was Brevet Major John Rziha, and the artillery was under Lieutenant Colonel C. C. Parsons. Two other former generals were with the expedition—Lieutenant Colonel John Davidson, inspector general on Hancock's staff, and Major A. M. Gibbs, who joined the column at Fort Harker.

The force arrived at Fort Larned on April 7, where the post commander, Captain Henry Asbury, greeted Hancock with the eleven-gun salute prescribed for a major general.[7] The troops settled in a tent camp outside the post. Two days later an eight-inch snow fell. The snow delayed the Cheyenne chiefs whom Mayor Wynkoop was bringing from the camp on Pawnee Fork but Hancock held a council with them on the night of the twelfth, after they had been fed.[8] In order to impress his uncivilized brothers and because it was a formal occasion such as Hancock relished, he and his staff were in full dress. Colonel Parsons was particularly impressive, wearing a tall black hat with a scarlet horsehair plume. The Indians thought him an important medicine man.

The chiefs were also dressed for the occasion. Their women had washed them carefully and brushed and combed their hair, braided it, and wrapped strips of otter fur or bright yarn around the braids. Two or three chiefs wore large, silver "Washington" medals suspended by ribbons from their

---

[4] Stanley, *My Early Travels and Adventures,* I, 2, 24.

[5] *Ibid.,* 24–25.

[6] Heitman, *Historical Register,* 348.

[7] Hancock's visit to Fort Larned is described in detail in Stanley, *My Early Travels and Adventures,* 28–36.

[8] *Ibid.,* 29–35.

necks—the medals had been presented by President Lincoln or Andrew Johnson on the occasion of a junket to Washington. Others were decorated with large thin discs of German silver beaten from metal they had bought from Charles W. Whitacre, a trader known to them for a decade or more, when he had visited their camps in the summer of 1866.[9] A few chiefs wore shirts of soft, white doeskin decorated with beadwork and fringes. Several had knotted bits of human epidermis, still carrying strands of hair, attached to the fringes of their leggings—each knot represented a vanquished enemy. Some of the Indians had army overcoats; others wore red blankets they had bought from traders. All were armed but not as an evidence of fear or hostile intention. A weapon was the honorable badge of a fighting man.

Hancock, in the opening address, offered the Indians a choice of peace or war. He said that during the recently concluded war (the Civil War), he and his officers had fought in many great battles, while the Indians had fought only in small skirmishes. There was, therefore, no renown to be gained in fighting Indians, and they did not desire to do so. Two Cheyenne children captured at Sand Creek would be returned to their people, and he wished the Cheyennes to surrender any white captives in their possession. He reminded the chiefs that the whites were building roads and railroads through the country and said the Indians must leave these routes alone. Any Indian guilty of wrongs against the whites would be punished, and any white man who wronged an Indian would likewise be punished. The last statement astonished the Indians.

Hancock said that he noticed that only a few of the chiefs had come to the meeting; consequently, in the morning he was going to the Indian camp, where he would have more to say.

Tall Bull replied for the Indians. He said the Indians had made a treaty with the agent, Wynkoop, they had not harmed the white man, and they did not intend harm. "Whenever you want to go on the Smoky Hill Road you can do so. You can go on any road. We are willing to be friends of the white man."

The chief said that they did not recognize the Indian boy Hancock had brought. They thought he must belong to some other band. He spoke of the fact that game was disappearing, and that, when the Indians approached a military post to get something to eat, they were fired upon by Hancock's

---

[9] Mooney, "Calendar History," 319; Nye, *Bad Medicine and Good: Tales of the Kiowas*, 77–81 (hereinafter referred to as Nye, *Bad Medicine and Good*). A Kiowa family named Botone is probably descended from Whitacre.

young men. He suggested that Hancock also talk to the tribes south of the Arkansas. Tall Bull added that when Hancock came to his village he, Tall Bull, would have nothing to add to what he had said here.

Actually Tall Bull and the other chiefs were alarmed at the announcement that the expedition would visit the Indian camp. They knew that the women and children, mindful of what happened at Sand Creek, would panic and flee.

On the following day the expedition headed up Pawnee Fork. After Hancock had marched for a day and a half he was met by three hundred warriors from the Cheyenne and Brûlé Sioux village. They were in all their war trappings and carried weapons ready for instant use. They did not intend to attack, but were ready to defend their women and children or cover their flight if Hancock's advance was for the purpose of war. The chiefs rode out in front for a parley.[10]

Hancock, not knowing the Indians' intentions, deployed his infantry, which was in the lead, into a battle line facing the Indians. The artillery cannoneers positioned themselves to the right of the infantry and swung their guns around to face the front. The cavalry galloped into line on the right of the battery and drew sabers. Anything could happen.

But Wynkoop quickly arranged for a council between the lines. The senior officers met the chiefs and shook hands. Hancock told the Indians he had come in peace, not to fight. Roman Nose, a prominent war leader of the Dog Soldiers, whom Hancock had been told was principal chief of the tribe, was in front. The two leaders sat on their horses for a few minutes staring at each other. The Indian was as imposing as the General, and dressed much the same. He had on an officer's uniform with epaulettes. He was over six feet tall, well muscled, and full of pride and dignity. In his belt were several revolvers. At his side a cavalry carbine hung muzzle down in its scabbard in the manner of the old dragoons. In his left hand was a bow and several arrows. He was ready for a fight. Hancock asked him if that was what he wanted.

"If I did, I wouldn't come so close to your big guns," Roman Nose replied sarcastically. Then he explained that he and several other Cheyennes had failed to attend the council at Fort Larned because their horses were too weak to travel that far, especially in the snow.

---

[10] This parley is described in detail in Stanley, *My Early Travels and Adventures*, 37–38, and George A. Custer, *My Life on the Plains; Or, Personal Experiences with Indians*, 26–27 (hereinafter referred to as Custer, *My Life on the Plains*).

With Roman Nose were the Cheyenne chiefs—Bull Bear, Tall Bull, White Horse, Gray Beard, and Medicine Wolf—and the Sioux chiefs—Pawnee Killer, Bad Wound, Little Bear, and Little Bull.

During the conversation Hancock noticed that many of the Indians in the background were beginning to fade away and ride back toward their village. He told the chiefs he was going to move forward and camp near the Indians, but would keep his soldiers from visiting the village. He invited the chiefs to come to his tent that evening for another talk. They agreed, and promised to hold the village in place.

That night Hancock learned that the whole village had fled, leaving their lodges standing. He awoke Custer and sent him to investigate. Custer found the village deserted except for two aged Sioux, a man and woman whom the Indians had abandoned, and an eight-year-old girl who was almost dead from having been raped repeatedly. There was a difference of opinion as to whether she was white, Indian, or half-blood. She was sent to the hospital at Fort Dodge, but she and the old man died.[11]

Hancock was greatly disturbed over this turn of events, and by the duplicity of the Indians. He was determined to burn the village, but waited a few days to hear from Custer, whom he sent with the bulk of the cavalry to follow the Indians. Custer failed to find them, but sent word a few days later that the Indians had started attacks along the Smoky Hill. Hancock put the village to the torch, which started a controversy on the part of Wynkoop and others about the timing—whether Hancock burned the village before or after he heard from Custer. But this point seems inconsequential, for the attack on the Smoky Hill was made before Hancock destroyed the village.[12]

Historians still debate the justification of Hancock's act—the consensus being that he probably was not in the right. It is usually charged that he precipitated the war of 1867; the Indians and their agents made much of this point. However, previous experience indicates that the Cheyenne Dog Soldiers would probably have commenced raiding even if Hancock had not had his bonfire. But even if the act was justified, it was unwise and accomplished no good.

Custer marched north to the Smoky Hill without overtaking the Indians or even picking up a large trail. At Downer's station he learned that small parties had been crossing the Smoky Hill Road, headed north. Therefore, he turned east, hoping to intercept some of them. On the eighteenth he reached

[11] Stanley, *My Early Travels and Adventures*, 139–40.
[12] Custer, *My Life on the Plains*, 33–37; Stanley, *My Early Travels and Adventures*, 39–47.

Lookout Station, which was still smoking, and found the bodies of the three attendants in the ashes. Custer, after sending a message to Hancock, continued east to Fort Hays, later stating that he went there for rations and forage. Neither were available at the post, but Custer's wife was there.

Hancock sent word to the posts along the Arkansas to be on the watch for Indians who might cross the river to the south. Major Douglass at Fort Dodge received this dispatch on April 17. He at once directed Major Wickliffe Cooper, who had been left there with two companies of the Seventh Cavalry, to go to Cimarron Crossing, a likely place for Indians to cross. On the nineteenth a detachment from Cooper's squadron encountered several Cheyennes near their camp. The Indians took position in the bushes on a sandy island and exchanged shots with the soldiers for a time, then tried to get away. Two were killed. Grinnell claims that these warriors were "friendly" Cheyennes from Black Kettle's village who were trying to steal horses at the stage station. One of the dead had a white woman's scalp tied to his belt.[13]

Hancock has been the object of considerable derision from writers who point out that he killed only two Indians, both friendly. They overlook the fact that Hancock had an unrivaled opportunity to kill a large number of Indians had he wanted to do so. When his force lined up facing the Indians short of the village and the two sides sat staring at each other at a range of less then three hundred yards, Hancock could have loosed a blast of rifle and artillery fire that would have wiped out Tall Bull's entire force. A volley even from untrained men would have been devastating.

On April 30, Hancock started across country toward Fort Dodge. It was a three-day march for the infantry, and there was no road, though ground was firm and there was ample water and firewood along the way. At Fort Dodge, the General was gratified to receive the honors of the garrison—an eleven-gun salute from the Parrotts and a guard of honor.[14] Major Douglass had the post in a neat and orderly condition. The garrison had been undisturbed by gunfire for months, except for the occasional differences of opinion between frontiersmen in the refreshment parlors of the sutler's store. In these affairs, the loser was interred in the growing post cemetery and the survivor lodged in the guard house until the sheriff came to get him. Major Douglass had no jurisdiction in such cases.

Henry Douglass, USMA, 1852, had stayed in the Regular Army during

---

[13] Stanley, *My Early Travels and Adventures*, 50; Post Adjutant Fort Dodge to Wickliffe Cooper, April 17, 1867, "Letter Book, Fort Dodge"; *Army and Navy Journal*, Vol. IV (May 11, 1867), 605.

[14] Stanley, *My Early Travels and Adventures*, 47–48.

the war while many of his contemporaries accepted Volunteer commissions and rose to high rank. Now he was at a disadvantage among all the high brevets who visited his post. He was a conscientious and hard-working officer, but he managed to offend both the Indian agents and several other civilians, who made a great deal of trouble for him. He took the part of Hancock when Wynkoop and Leavenworth were writing reports to their own department charging Hancock with having brought on an Indian war and costing the government millions of dollars. In talking to Hancock directly, however, the agents presented another face. Wynkoop told Hancock confidentially that it was Leavenworth's Kiowas and Comanches who had been causing all the past trouble. Leavenworth took the General aside and informed him that it was Wynkoop's Cheyennes and Arapahoes who were guilty and deserved severe treatment.[15]

While at Fort Dodge, Hancock camped outside the post and ate the salt pork, boiled beans, and hardtack that the Quartermaster General furnished field expeditions from war surplus. He declined the more palatable fare offered him by Douglass, explaining that it was only right that he share the food his men had to eat.[16] It is to be doubted that this had the desired effect, because his men were deserting by the dozens, especially from the cavalry. The desertion rate in that regiment climbed to an incredible 52 per cent for the year.[17] There were numerous causes—the cruel and arbitrary punishments often imposed by Custer among them.

Until recently the Kiowas, Comanches, and Little Raven's Arapahoes—and possibly some of Black Kettle's Cheyennes—had been camped a short distance south of the Arkansas. Hancock wanted to visit them but thought this unwise while his cavalry was absent. He was pleased, therefore, when Kicking Bird, Stumbling Bear, and several other Kiowas came to Fort Dodge to pay their respects. During a talk with them on April 25, Hancock cautioned these Indians not to wander north of the Arkansas, because troops then in the field could not distinguish between friendly and hostile Indians and might attack them. He offered the opportunity to the Kiowas, Comanches, and Arapahoes to enlist in the army as scouts. They would receive the same pay and allowances as soldiers, be rationed, and wear the uniform.[18]

The chiefs replied that they appreciated the offer but thought that when

---

[15] Letter from General W. S. Hancock in *Army and Navy Journal*, Vol. V (Sept. 7, 1867), 43.
[16] Stanley, *My Early Travels and Adventures*, 48.
[17] Report of the Adjutant General, 40 Cong., 2 sess., *House Exec. Doc. 1324*, 475; 40 Cong., 3 sess., *House Exec. Doc. 1367*, 768–69.
[18] Stanley, *My Early Travels and Adventures*, 51–53.

the promised annuities were delivered it would be time enough to talk about furnishing young men as scouts.[19]

On Hancock's invitation, several other chiefs, including Little Raven, Cut Nose, and Big Belly came in for a friendly interview on April 28, and, later that same day, Satanta came in. Little Raven agreed to surrender twenty-five mules that some of his braves had captured east of Fort Lyon.[20]

After these talks were concluded, General Hancock and his troops started back for Fort Harker by way of Forts Larned and Hays. He intended to disband the force and distribute the troops among the various posts when he reached Fort Harker.

[19] *Ibid.,* 53.
[20] *WDAGO, Letters Received,* April 28, 1867.

9. SATANTA GETS TWO STARS

General Hancock had now conferred with most of the Indians whose declarations for peace or war he had come to hear. There still remained Satanta, the spectacular Kiowa, who had achieved increased notoriety in 1866 for his latest raid in Texas. Summoned by Colonel Leavenworth, he came to Fort Larned on April 29 for a talk with Hancock.[1] In addition to Satanta and several of his fellow Kiowas, Wynkoop and Leavenworth, Hancock and his officers, three interpreters, and William Bent and David Butterfield, who were invited to be present presumably as disinterested witnesses, were present at the meeting.

Prior to the oratory, the three interpreters, F. F. Smith, John A. Atkin, and a man named Kinkaid, testified that, on previous occasions when they were used as interpreters, Leavenworth had paid them in annuity goods he had withheld from the Kiowas. They also claimed that the agent had sold to a merchant in Leavenworth City goods which the government furnished him for issue to the Indians. They further stated that Leavenworth had hidden several bales of goods in the ground, goods which were supposed to have been issued to the Indians. Smith said Leavenworth had told Satanta to keep quiet about his dealings and say little at the council. In return, he had promised Satanta that, if he would come to the agency at Fort Zarah, Leavenworth would "make it right" with him.[2]

Leavenworth, invited by Hancock to reply to these charges, categorically denied every one of them. He could have explained that he was compelled to store Indian goods at Leavenworth because of the inadequate facilities at Forts Larned or Zarah. But, having already reported this in writing, he made no comment at this time. Major Douglass had reported his own lack of confidence in the veracity of Smith, and he therefore kept quiet.[3]

Satanta was then invited to speak. He rose to his feet, took position in front of his tribesmen, and cast his sharp, glittering eyes about the assembly before launching into his oration. A Kiowa making a formal address speaks

[1] *Army and Navy Journal*, Vol. IV (May 18, 1867), 621; Stanley, *My Early Travels and Adventures*, I, 61.
[2] Stanley, *My Early Travels and Adventures*, I, 63.
[3] *Ibid.*, 64.

slowly and with emphasis. His gestures are in the grand tradition. His voice is deep and sonorous. Many of the sounds are guttural and some are explosive, making a powerful yet not unpleasing effect. Satanta, who was proud of his title, "Orator of the Plains," always made an impression, though his words lacked the sincerity and logic of those spoken by Kicking Bird, Satank, and the Comanche Ten Bears. Nevertheless, his expressions were rich with imagery and symbolism. The following is an excerpt from his speech at Fort Larned:

> I look upon you and General Smith as my fathers. I want friends, and I say by the sun and earth I live on, I want to talk straight and tell the truth. All other tribes are my brothers, and I want friends, and am doing all I can for peace. If I die first, it is all right . . . . I want the Great Father in Washington and all the troops and soldiers to go slowly. I don't want the prairies and country to be bloody. Just hold on for awhile. I don't want war at all. I want peace.[4]

Satanta then made several complaints, stating that the country belonged to the Indians but the soldiers were ruining it by cutting down the trees. He chided Hancock for burning the Cheyenne and Sioux village on Pawnee Fork. He referred to those tribes as his "brothers," although he knew full well they had been, until recently, traditional enemies of the Kiowas and had driven his fathers out of their former homeland in the north. But Satanta's strongest complaint was that Leavenworth had been withholding presents due his people under the terms of the 1865 treaty.

Leavenworth interrupted to explain that Satanta and his band were the chief culprits in the murder of James Box and members of his family in Texas, and even now were holding two or three girls in captivity. He said his instructions from his superiors were to withhold the goods until Satanta released the captives without ransom and promised to abstain from further raiding.[5]

Satanta did not deny that he had participated in the Box massacre. He was proud of exploits of this kind. He simply grumbled that Stumbling Bear and Mow-way, a Comanche chief, had been on the same raid but had been given their annuities.[6]

Hancock did not propose to get into a wrangle over this, especially as he knew little about it. He said he would report the matter fully to Washington,

[4] *Ibid.*, 63–66.
[5] *Ibid.*
[6] *Ibid.*, 81–82.

and he did. (Leavenworth also reported it, sharply criticizing Hancock and Douglass.)[7]

Satanta asked for a letter that he could show to sentries and others in authority that would enable him to visit various posts. Hancock knew that the Indian wanted a pass that would admit him to a military post at any time, but he pretended not to understand. He told Satanta he would give him a copy of the transcript of the council.[8]

The meeting closed on a cordial note. Hancock presented Satanta with a major general's coat, complete with shoulder straps and insignia.[9] The Indians were familiar with army insignia. For example, in sign language the motion of flapping wings followed by the sign for a soldier chief, and pointing to the shoulder, meant eagle chief, i.e., colonel. The sign for a star was made by gathering the fingers of the hand like an artichoke bud, then opening the fingers suddenly. A man branded on the shoulder with two stars was a major general, quite rare on the plains. Satanta now felt that he had been elevated to this rank and thus was a great chief indeed. During his speech he had sneered at Kicking Bird, Stumbling Bear, and several of his fellows, saying they did not amount to much, that their bands consisted of only two or three lodges apiece. Now he had conclusive evidence that he was the big chief.

After the council, Hancock's column marched northeast and reached Fort Hays in two days. This post, named for Brigadier General Alexander Hays, who was killed in the Battle of the Wilderness, had the usual two-company arrangement. It was built in the form of a square, with small log barracks for the soldiers. It was on level ground bordered on three sides by a deep ravine in which flowed a small stream, forming a moat. Hancock did not like the location and directed that the fort be moved, for he thought it would be inundated in a flash flood.[10]

Custer and his five companies of the Seventh Cavalry were waiting at Hays when Hancock arrived. Their horses were in sorry condition from malnutrition, several of them dying each day. Forage ordered from the quartermaster had not arrived.[11]

The men were also suffering from an inadequate diet. There were a dozen cases of scurvy, difficult to excuse in view of the variety of game and the

[7] *Ibid.*, 82.
[8] *Ibid.*
[9] *Ibid.*
[10] *Ibid.*, 83–84.
[11] *Ibid.*, 84.

wild plums, wild onions, and certain edible roots existing in the surround-ing prairie.[12]

Hancock now distributed his troops as planned. Two companies each went to Forts Dodge, Larned, Lyon, and Hays and one went to Fossil Creek Station. Orders were issued to reoccupy and rebuild Fort Zarah, and a fort was to be built at Monument Station. The artillery and wagon train were sent to Fort Riley—the former to be stationed there, the latter to pick up supplies. Custer and his command were to make a circuit of the country between the Arkansas and the Platte in an endeavor to round up the Indians who had not yet been contacted and those who had fled from the village burned by Hancock.[13]

These arrangements having been made, Hancock and his staff departed for Fort Leavenworth. The *Army and Navy Journal* reported,

> General Hancock's campaign has now ended. His object was to make peace with the tribes that would accept it and to make war with those who would not. In the hostile part of the expedition little has been accomplished; but the pacific conferences with the Comanches, Arapahoes, and Kiowas promise good results . . . .[14]

Disillusionment followed quickly. Shortly after Hancock's brigade was broken up, the Indians, chiefly Cheyenne Dog Soldiers, resumed their attacks along both the Smoky Hill and the Arkansas routes. Whether these attacks were caused by Hancock's burning of the village at Pawnee Fork or because the Indians thought it now safe to steal horses will never be known. It could have been either or both.

The Kiowas held their sun dance early this year, in the latter part of May or early June. The various tribal bands started to assemble for the big festival and to travel to the place the *Tai-me* keeper had selected for the ceremony. This year it was on the north bank of the Washita near the Oklahoma-Texas border. Nearly all the Arapahoes, Cheyennes, and Comanches who were south of the Arkansas gathered to watch the dance.[15]

As soon as the dance was over and war parties were permitted to leave, Satanta returned to the Arkansas to make a raid on Fort Dodge. This occurred at eight o'clock on the morning of June 12. A patrol had been sent out from the post at dawn to scout through the hills surrounding the area, but

[12] *Ibid.*
[13] *Ibid.*, 86.
[14] *Army and Navy Journal*, Vol. IV (May 18, 1867), 621.
[15] Mooney, "Calendar History," 319–20.

had seen nothing amiss. Then seventy-five horses of Company B, Seventh Cavalry, were taken to graze one mile east of the post, attended by Sergeant Totten and Private James Spillman. The quartermaster's mule herd, watched by a young Mexican, was similarly grazed west of the post. A fourth herdsman was posted on a hill to the north to watch for interlopers.[16]

Suddenly Satanta and his band rode out of a gully and dashed toward the cavalry herd, yipping like coyotes. Satanta was arrayed in his new uniform and wore an officer's dress hat with plume.

Spillman was shot several times with a pistol and arrows. Totten raced back to the post while the Indians drove the horses toward the river. The shooting attracted the attention of the garrison. Ten cavalrymen, mostly non-commissioned officers, mounted and galloped after the Indians, who, instead of crossing the river, were moving downstream. Fifteen or twenty soldiers, well strung out, followed within moments. Some were mounted, while others toiled on foot well to the rear.

Meanwhile, west of the post a smaller group of Indians shot the Mexican boy, wounding him mortally, and attempted to steal the mules. They were driven away by armed civilian teamsters and employees of the stage line, but they did capture a few animals.

Lieutenant Stanley Brown, Third Infantry, mounted his horse and went alone after the Indians. Three miles down the river he saw Indians "signalling"—probably making obscene gestures of defiance as was their habit. They were on the other side of the river, which was not fordable in the vicinity of the post. He expended a few rounds without noticeable effect. However, the sound of his firing brought several soldiers and civilians mounted on mules, and together they resumed the chase. The Indians with the stolen herd continued along the near side of the stream, followed by Brown and his reinforcements.

Little by little the mules fell behind, but after a hard run of eighteen miles, Brown came upon the Indians, who were now swimming the captured herd across the Arkansas. Brown thought the water was too swift and too deep, and his mules agreed. The Indians protected their crossing by posting a rear guard in the bushes, thus forcing the soldiers to witness the operation from a safe distance. When the crossing was completed, Satanta galloped up to the bank on the far side, tipped his hat courteously to the troops, wheeled, and disappeared.

[16] Satanta's raid on Fort Dodge is described in the following letters: Thompson to Hesselberger, June 12, 1867; Brown to Hesselberger, June 13, 1867; De Graw to Hesselberger, June 13, 1867 and June 15, 1867; Douglass to McKeever, June 14, 1867—all from the "Letter Book, Fort Dodge"; Smith to Douglass, June 21, 1867, "Letter Book, Fort Harker."

Spillman died of his wounds the next day, and the Mexican died on the following day. Douglass reported the episode to higher headquarters, drawing wrath upon himself from the exasperated district commander, Colonel A. J. Smith.

The post itself was not again disturbed by the Indians during the summer, but within a few days, a series of attacks on wagon trains commenced and continued intermittently until fall. Most of these affairs took place near Cimarron Crossing or on the Dry Route farther to the southwest. The victims were mostly citizens from New Mexico who used this unprotected route through habit and because it was shorter. The trains were accompanied by numerous armed guards, but apparently they were deficient in spirit and fighting ability. The Indians soon observed this apathy and acted with great boldness, thus adding to their success.[17]

After one such attack, the owner of the train told newsmen in Leavenworth that Major Douglass had refused to give aid. This report was untrue, but the subsequent publicity reacted against Douglass.

The hapless Douglass had other problems at this time which were much more tragic. On July 9, a detachment of the Thirty-eighth Infantry, a Negro troop en route to New Mexico, camped at Fort Dodge. Within a few days they developed cholera, which had been incubating since the men had been exposed to the disease in New Orleans, where it had been brought in from Asia. The dread disease, for which no cure was known, spread through the troops while they were on the plains, and over five hundred were dead within two weeks. Thirty cases developed at Fort Dodge, a light attack when compared with others, but the post was gripped in terror.[18] Major Douglass' wife, who volunteered to nurse the sick Negroes, became ill and passed the infection to her husband. The post commander and his wife lay in their mud hovel for a few hours until she died. He was then carried to a slab shanty that had been erected for some purpose other than as a dwelling, and there he managed to stay alive. Sherman's inspector general, who came through while Douglass was convalescing, criticized the unfortunate major for living in a "palace" while the other officers remained in sod huts.[19]

Neither the epidemic nor the Indian attacks on nearby wagon trains were permitted to interrupt construction work at Dodge. By the winter of 1867, Douglass and his civilian employees and soldiers completed one company

[17] Brown to Douglass, July 21, 1867, "Letter Book, Fort Dodge."

[18] The terror, tragedy, and mortality caused by cholera in the frontier posts in the summer of 1867 is portrayed in the medical histories, letter books, post returns, and letters to service journals such as the *Army and Navy Journal* for June and July.

[19] Douglass to AAG, Dept. of the Mo., November 19, 1867, "Letter Book, Fort Dodge."

barracks and part of another. The hospital, commissary, and bakery were completed and the storehouse half finished. Officers' quarters were not built until 1868.[20]

From time to time there were pistol duels between civilians, and the post cemetery had to be enlarged. These affairs set a trend that led to the growth of the notorious boothill cemetery at Dodge City which was built later.

[20] "Medical History, Fort Dodge," 11, 12.

The summer raids of 1867 were more frequent and vicious along the Smoky Hill Road than along the Arkansas route. The first attack occurred on April 24 at Russell's Springs, twenty miles west of Fort Wallace.[1] This happened after the conclusion of Hancock's expedition, and from the time of that attack forward, there was, on the average, one raid every other day somewhere along the road.

The Indians seemed to establish a pattern. They would ride up to a station about two o'clock in the morning, set fire to the haystack—and also the station if it was made of combustible material. Then while some of the Indians rode whooping in a circle around the station, firing into it, a few others would steal the stock, or try to do so. As soon as the station attendants and soldier guards had crawled through the tunnels to the redoubt and could return the fire, the Indians would ride away. They were usually in groups of ten to twenty, and seldom took chances of getting hurt. If one of the raiders was shot from his horse, two Indians would ride up at full speed and lift him from the ground without dismounting, and often without stopping. This was a difficult and spectacular stunt which they had practised since childhood, and it made the tallying of Indian casualties practically impossible.

Most of the stage stations were now fortified and able to resist ordinary attacks if the defenders did not lose their nerve or fail to stay alert. When this happened, someone lost his scalp. Favor and Thompson, who after the episode at the Goose Creek Station in the fall had returned to their ranches, were killed because they became careless of danger. On the morning of June 3, they rode to the vicinity of the station, looking for strayed mules. From there they went up along the Smoky Hill. At midafternoon, when they had not returned, the station master notified Fort Wallace. Lieutenant Joseph C. Hale with several soldiers came to search for the missing men. They found them fifty yards from the road and about one mile from the river. Both had been shot many times and looked like pin-cushions because of the arrow shafts protruding from their naked, white bodies. They had been

[1] Keogh to Weir, April 26, 1867, "Letter Book, Fort Wallace."

scalped, and the top of Thompson's head down to his eyes hacked off with a hatchet. Marks on the ground told the story. The two men had been jumped near the river and had made a running fight back toward the station. When they saw there was no chance to escape, they had dismounted, taken cover, and fired at the Indians until both were seriously wounded or killed. It was known that Favor had a Henry rifle and Thompson a Starr, both repeaters. They must have hit some of their assailants, for there was a great quantity of blood on the grass. This attack happened within eight miles of Fort Wallace.[2]

Three days later, two civilians stopped at Goose Creek Station and said they were on their way east. The sergeant in charge of the guard detachment urged them to wait until the detachment went to the post to be relieved by another. They declined, saying they were old hunters from the mountains, and could take care of themselves. The detachment later found them part way to the post, full of bullets and arrows and scalped. There was nothing to identify them. It was heard later that they had told people at one of the stations that they were returning to Missouri with $5,000 they had made in mining.[3] Their roadside graves were marked: "Unknown. Killed by Indians."

These episodes are cited not because they were unusual, but because they were typical. The records of Fort Wallace for the period April 26–June 14 show that twenty-seven Indian attacks were reported, undoubtedly with others unreported, along that portion of the Smoky Hill route protected by Fort Wallace. The loss of life was not great; six civilians and three soldiers were killed and two soldiers wounded, but the Indians were getting bolder, attacking ever nearer the post and in larger numbers. On June 15, three hundred Indians attacked a convoy of three stages escorted by twenty-three soldiers. In a running fight thirty miles west of Fort Wallace, the convoy was able to shake off the pursuit and continue the journey, but Privates McNally and Waldruff of the Third Infantry were killed and Private Morehouse was wounded. Two passengers were killed and one wounded. Because of the heavy fire, the soldiers were unable to pick up their fallen comrades. On the return trip two days later, the detachment found the bodies, but they were so cut up that they could not be recovered decently. The pieces were buried by the roadside.

A woman passenger had been in one of the stages during the fight. When the stage was opened at its destination, and the blood-spattered interior

---

[2] *Ibid.*, June 4.
[3] *Ibid.*, June 7.

seen, the woman was asked if she had been frightened. "Not especially," she said. "It wasn't too bad."[4]

At Fort Wallace, Captain Keogh could see that the post itself would soon be attacked, for the Indians obviously realized that they could make such an attack without fear of reprisal. Keogh noted that the Indians habitually approached from the east or southeast and departed in the same direction. He thought they had a camp on some stream about fifty miles in that direction, and there were reports of another village some fifty miles north of Big Timbers. He was convinced that the way to combat the Indians was to shift to the offensive—to follow one of their raiding parties to its village, where the Indians could be surprised and destroyed. He had already written district headquarters:

> It is ridiculous to expect me to protect the different stations unless I close up the post and divide the garrison between Willow Creek and Monument station. If the Indians are not followed up to their village and killed, then it is useless to expect peace or rest on this route.[5]

Keogh was sharply reprimanded for this remark. The attacking of Indian villages, or even the burning of empty ones was not an approved policy. The truth of this statement can be seen from the mounting criticism of Hancock. He would by fall be relieved from command and replaced by Sheridan. In the meantime, Keogh and his men had to maintain their posture of passive defense.

Actually, Keogh did not have the forces necessary to undertake an expedition, and his guide, Billy Comstock, was with Custer. There was not a soldier in the command who could follow an Indian trail except by riding at a slow walk with his eyes continuously on the ground. Even then he would lose the tracks on a rocky surface or at night.[6]

Fort Wallace was short-handed. The paper strength of the garrison at this time was 175. Of these, twenty or more men were usually off duty because they were in the infirmary, on furlough, or en route to join or be discharged from the army. Twenty were in the guard house charged with desertion, and an equal or greater number had not been apprehended. Fifteen or twenty men were operating the warehouses, the commissary, the

[4] Hale to Weir, June 18, 1867, "Letter Book, Fort Wallace"; W. A. Bell, *New Tracks in North America, A Journal of Travel and Adventure Whilst Engaged in a Survey for a Southern Railroad to the Pacific Ocean During 1867–68*, 36 (hereinafter referred to as Bell, *New Tracks*).

[5] Keogh to Weir, June 18, 1867; Keogh to Weir, May 31, June 4, "Letter Book, Fort Wallace"; Post Returns for May and June, 1867, Fort Wallace.

[6] *Ibid.*, June 4.

hospital, and the post headquarters; herding animals; or hauling wood and water. From twenty to fifty men were on escort duty or guarding stage stations. Twenty were guarding wood trains.[7] There was also the post to guard. The old army saying certainly applied here: "I am on guard so often that when I march off guard I meet myself marching on." Some of the men were not getting enough sleep, and, all in all, it is a wonder the desertion rate was not even higher.

By June 16 the strength of the garrison seemed stretched to the breaking point. On that day General Hancock arrived while on an inspection of the route to Denver. He took with him Captain Keogh and forty men of the post as a personal escort.[8]

Lieutenant Hale, the post adjutant, was left in command. Keogh had issued arms to fifty civilian employees—stonemasons, carpenters, teamsters—and, otherwise, Hale's situation would have been desperate. He was forced to recall the guard detachment at Goose Creek and close down that station. A welcome reinforcement came when Greenwood's survey party with an escort of twenty-five men from the Thirty-seventh Infantry came to Fort Wallace for supplies and more men. They were held at the post in hopes that the Indian threat would diminish.[9]

Towards noon on June 21, several hundred Indians rode from the northeast over the low range of hills that partly encircled the post three miles away.[10] Some of the Indians headed for the quarry at the foot of the hills southeast of the fort, while the main body continued straight toward Fort Wallace. Two wagons hauling stone had just left the quarry. The drivers whipped up their teams when they saw the Indians. The leading wagon made it to the post, but the other, driven by Patrick McCarty, was overtaken. While the men at the edge of the quarry and at the post watched in helpless horror, the Indians pulled McCarty from the wagon seat and shot and speared him. The Indians then unhitched the mules and drove them off. Because of the fire directed at them from the post, they overturned the wagon but did not burn it. The raiders did not pause to scalp McCarty, who was still alive.

When the Indians first appeared, Lieutenant Hale assembled twenty-seven cavalrymen who had been on various post duties and sent them under

[7] Keogh to McKeever, June 11, 1867; Keogh to Weir, May 31, June 4, "Letter Book, Fort Wallace"; Post Returns for May and June, 1867, Fort Wallace.

[8] Hale to Weir, June 18, 1867, "Letter Book, Fort Wallace."

[9] Hale to Weir, July 2, 1867; Post Return for July; Bell, *New Tracks*, 52.

[10] The description of the battle on July 21 is based on: Hale to Weir, June 22, "Letter Book, Fort Wallace"; Post Return, June; and Bell, *New Tracks*, 53–56.

Lieutenant James Bell to the relief of the workmen at the quarry. They rescued the stonecutters, who were about to attempt a dash back to the post. After they left, the Indians looted and burned the sheds and tents at the quarry.

While the buildings at the quarry were being destroyed by one band, a larger crowd of Indians advanced from the north toward Fort Wallace. They were opposed by soldiers and civilians on foot, who took up an ir-regular line on the forward edge of a low slope north of the post. Presently Bell's mounted platoon came up and passed to the front to delay the enemy advance. Halting just out of effective musketry range the Indians dismounted and formed a line standing ready to mount. Then, instead of circling the soldiers in their customary tactic, they attempted a maneuver similar to that used by cavalry, with skirmishes out in front followed by a battle line. Twenty or thirty Indians rode out as skirmishes, but, when the bullets began to crack around them, they wheeled and galloped back to the main line.

The infantry composing Greenwood's escort came up from the rear and formed a reserve line behind the dismounted troopers and civilians. Then Sergeant Dummell, Company G, Seventh Cavalry, with ten men he had managed to assemble and mount, rode forward over the knoll to extend the battle line to the left. As they arrived, they were met head-on by fifty or more mounted redskins. Shouting to his men to follow him, Sergeant Dummell dashed into the very midst of the enemy, firing his Spencer carbine. Only three men followed him, and all four were knocked down by the In-dians, who clustered around the prone soldiers, firing pistols and thrusting at them with lances to count coup. Before any of the Indians could jump to the ground to collect scalps, they were driven away by other cavalrymen.

One of Sergeant Dummell's men was dead and the Sergeant and one other were badly wounded. A fourth man, also wounded, was missed at first because he had crawled into some bushes in a hollow. An ambulance was brought forward, and, just as the dead and wounded were being loaded into it, a rescuer spotted and went after the fourth victim.

The Indians withdrew under heavy fire, taking with them their dead and wounded and the horses and equipment of Dummell's men.

Hale reorganized the dismounted men and posted them to present a continuous line in case the Indians made another mounted attack. But they did not. Instead, ten or twenty warriors cantered out to the front, brand-ishing their spears and shouting defiance. No doubt they called, as was their custom, "Watch me! See how brave I am!" This was standard practice for young Indians in their first fight, when they were trying for battle honors and the right to be known as warriors. Some of them were probably trying to work up their nerve to make a "run."

The hills to the north were black with Indians; they were milling around and possibly trying to decide if they should advance. In a determined fight, a noted leader such as Roman Nose, or perhaps a medicine man, would circle close to the enemy, and, if he returned unscathed, others would try it. But this time the heavy fire of the cavalry's repeating carbines, with the fire of the infantry and civilians, discouraged any such attempt.

One individual duel seemed about to take place. Lieutenant Bell rode forward in an attempt to see more clearly through the dust and smoke how many Indians were actively opposing the troops and whether they were forming for another charge. One of the Indians, mounted on a white or gray horse, apparently interpreted this as a challenge. He also rode out to the front and then stopped. Bell continued toward him. The Indian fired one shot then turned and galloped away. Bell later said that the man may have been Charles Bent, the half-blood son of William Bent.

After some two more hours of desultory firing at long range, the Indians vanished over the hills in the direction from which they had come. They had captured fewer than ten mules and had suffered an undetermined number of casualties. It was thought at the post that the Indians had been encouraged by their earlier raid to believe that they would have an easy victory over the few soldiers left at Fort Wallace, and that their main motive, as usual, was to steal horses.

The troops were exhilarated by the fight, as is often the case when danger is over and men feel they have done well. Sergeant Dummell died of his wounds, but, before he died, he told Lieutenant Hale that he thought he had recognized Charles Bent among the attacking Indians. He also said that the Indian who seemed to be in command was a chief whom he had seen drawing annuities at Fort Zarah the previous fall. The defenders thought the arrows they picked up were mostly Cheyenne, but a few had Sioux and Arapaho markings.

The people at Fort Wallace spent a sleepless night, for they expected a renewal of the attack. The next morning they buried their dead.[11]

Two days later a column of dust was seen six or seven miles to the northeast. As this was the direction in which the Indians had disappeared on the twenty-second, it was supposed that they were returning for another fight. Once more the bugler sounded "Boots and Saddles." The entire garrison

[11] Bell, *New Tracks*, 56.

promptly assembled under arms on the parade ground where they were assigned places at the breastworks.

The dust cloud drew steadily nearer. Presently a long column came over the hill on the stage road, three or four miles away, and the sun shone on the white canvas tops of escort wagons and glinted from the scabbards and gun barrels of cavalry escorts riding on either side of the wagons. Lieutenant Hale, watching through field glasses from the roof of the sutler's store, announced that it was probably "General" W. W. Wright's railroad survey party which, because an advance number had already arrived with Hancock, had been expected for several days.

An hour later the wagons pulled up at the entrance of the post. The newcomers were greeted with hearty handshakes and a barrage of questions. They said they had seen no Indians. They were eager to hear about the recent fight at Fort Wallace. The mules were unhitched, unharnessed, and turned loose to roll and graze. Tents were pitched outside the post in a grassy plot used for transient parties, and all hands came to get their mail, which had just been delivered by two stagecoaches. In the evening, the engineers and scientists of Wright's party were invited to a social gathering in the quarters on the "line," and the threats of an Indian attack were temporarily put out of mind.[12]

At this time, Custer, with 350 men of the Seventh Cavalry was scouting the country around the forks of the Republican River and accomplishing nothing in his mission to round up hostile Indians or to bring in additional chiefs for a conference with Hancock. He was supposed to locate the Cheyennes and persuade them to move to the vicinity of an army post where they would be safe from attack and where the military could keep an eye on them to insure that no raiding parties went out. Custer, however, was merely skirmishing with the Indians (who made several attempts to steal his horses) and affording them a bit of amusement.[13]

General Sherman had directed Custer to march to Fort Sedgwick for supplies and to receive fresh orders. Instead, Custer planned to march to Fort Wallace; he had sent a message to his wife to meet him there. Thus, instead of going to Sedgwick for supplies, he sent his wagons in the opposite direction—to Fort Wallace—where, on June 24, Custer's men filled their wagons from Lieutenant Hale's diminishing stores. During their return to Custer's camp, they came under Indian attack but suffered no loss.

[12] *Ibid.*, 57–58.
[13] Custer's expedition is set forth in Custer, *My Life on the Plains*, 124–44; and Berthrong, *The Southern Cheyennes*, 285–87.

Meanwhile, Sherman had sent Lieutenant Lyman S. Kidder with nine men and an Indian scout with changed orders for Custer. This party was intercepted by Indians and destroyed. Custer later found their skeletons while on his way to Fort Wallace.[14]

At daybreak on June 26, a large war party attacked Pond Creek Station two miles west of Fort Wallace. A stage had just driven up, and the men were unhitching the teams before replacing them with four fresh animals from the corral. The attendants and passengers took refuge in the station building. The horses, frightened by the Indians, dashed away toward Fort Wallace. The men at the garrison, who heard the gunfire and saw the Indians, again began to assemble for defense.[15]

Within ten minutes, Lieutenant Hale's men had saddled their horses and were ready for action. Hale sent an orderly to Wright's camp with a request for assistance from Brevet Colonel (Captain, Seventh Cavalry) Albert G. Barnitz who, with his Company G, constituted Wright's escort. Barnitz and Company G moved out within a few minutes. They were joined by ten men under a sergeant from the post garrison, making a total of fifty cavalrymen.

By this time the leading Indians had approached to within one mile of the post in pursuit of the coach horses, which were still hitched in pairs. Two animals were bleeding from wounds. When Barnitz and his men appeared, the Indians slowed down and began riding in small individual circles. This was a signal employed by scouts of all Plains tribes, which meant, "Enemy sighted." These few advance Indians then turned and dashed back toward their main body, trying to decoy Barnitz away from the protection of the post. But he kept his company together and did not let them string out in a wild pursuit.

As the cavalry drew near, the Indians began to collect on the brow of a low hill two miles west of the post, where they awaited Barnitz' expected charge. A big warrior on a white horse seemed to be their leader, and Barnitz, who had previously shaken hands with Roman Nose, thought it was he.[16]

The cavalry deliberately approached the Indians on the hill, exchanging shots as they advanced. Suddenly other groups of Indians, who had been concealed in swales on either flank, appeared and moved toward the troops.

---

[14] Report of General W. T. Sherman, 40 Cong., 2 sess., *House Exec. Doc. 1324*, 35.

[15] The description of the fight on June 26 is based on: Hale to Weir, June 27, 1867, "Letter Book, Fort Wallace"; Post Return; Bell, *New Tracks*, 58–62.

[16] Bell, *New Tracks*, 61–62.

Both sides halted. The Indian leader, a powerful fellow wearing a long war bonnet decorated in front with swatches of downy white feathers from the breast of an eagle, galloped along the front of the Indian groups, shaking his lance and shouting orders. Barnitz bent back his line on the flanks forming a half moon.

At this moment all three groups of Indians sped forward and began to converge on Barnitz' command. The cavalry leader should have dismounted his company and formed a base of fire, for the men were no match for the Indians in mounted combat, and they were sorely outnumbered. But it was too late. Bowstrings twanged, and there was a crackling of pistol fire. Several saddles were emptied, and the cavalry were forced back.

Bugler Charles Clark fell, pierced by five arrows. At once a brawny Indian leaned far over the side of his horse and picked up the boy, much like an eagle would snatch a rabbit. He stripped the bugler, smashed his head with a hatchet, and flung him back to the ground under the pounding hoofs.

The attack on the left pierced the blue line, isolating Sergeant Frederick Wyllyams and four men. One by one they fell, and none could be rescued. The soldiers continued to retreat.

The Indians were getting the best of it, for the troopers could scarcely control their mounts, much less fire their carbines with one hand from the backs of their rearing, plunging horses. Barnitz disengaged and had his men dismount. Now their repeating carbines poured out such a volume of fire that the Indians recoiled. Barnitz withdrew still farther to reorganize his company and redistribute ammunition. Once more he formed in a half moon, three men of each set of fours kneeling in the firing line while the fourth man in each set held the horses a little in the rear.

Again the Indians advanced in front and on both flanks. A well-directed volley stopped them. They began to leave the field. Barnitz waited two hours, expecting another attack, but the Indians merely sat on their horses, well out of range, and argued among themselves. Finally they withdrew entirely and disappeared over the hills.

Dr. William A. Bell, an English physician and scientist who was with Wright's party as a photographer, came with his camera and took a picture of Sergeant Wyllyams. The sergeant was a fellow Briton, a graduate of Eton, and in line for a commission. The night before the engagement, he had helped Bell prepare his photographic plates, little dreaming that on the following day he would become the subject of what may be the first photograph of a white man killed and mutilated by wild Indians. Dr. Bell recorded his sensations:

I have seen in days gone by sights horrible and gory . . . but never did I feel the sickening sensation, the giddy, fainting feeling that came over me when I saw our dead, dying, and wounded after this Indian fight. A handful of men, to be sure, but with enough wounds upon them to have slain a company. The bugler was stripped naked, and five arrows driven through him, while his skull was literally smashed to atoms. Another soldier was shot with four bullets and three arrows, his scalp torn off, and his brains knocked out.

A third was riddled with balls and arrows; but they did not succeed in getting his scalp, although, like the two, he was stripped naked. James Douglas, a Scotchman, was shot through the body with arrows, and his left arm hacked to pieces. He was a brave fellow, and breathed out his life in the arms of his comrades. Another man named Welsh was killed, but all subsequent search failed to discover his remains. Sergeant Wyllyams lay dead beside his horse; and as the fearful picture met my gaze, I was horror stricken. Horse and rider were stripped bare of trappings and clothes, while around them the trampled, bloodstained ground showed the desperation of the struggle.

A portion of the sergeant's scalp lay near him but the greater part was gone; through his head a rifle ball had passed . . . . In all there were seven killed and five wounded.[17]

The Indians were hovering not far away when Bell made his memorable photograph and rushed the plate back to a darkroom for development. Later he sent a print to Washington, as he said, "to show the authorities how their soldiers were treated on the plains."

Post Surgeon T. H. Turner took excellent care of the wounded. Two men who had been shot through the body with arrows recovered without complications. Bell wrote:

One soldier, I watched from the extraction of the arrow until he was able to walk about. The arrow had entered the back two inches from the spine; and the point had reappeared just below, and about two inches from the navel. Probably it had passed quite through the liver without touching any other organ; still, four layers of peritoneum must have been pierced, and his recovery says much for the skill of the surgeon and the healthiness of the climate.[18]

Wright kept his expedition at Fort Wallace for two weeks, partly to provide the post with additional protection and also to obtain a larger escort for himself when Hancock returned. The men were so heavily armed, however, that they would have preferred to move on.

When Hancock did arrive, he had left so many of his soldiers at stations

[17] *Ibid.*, 63.
[18] *Ibid.*, 65.

along the way that he could not spare any for Wright. Wright was about to abandon his project and return to the East when Greenwood offered to escort both parties, although the remainder of the wilderness was considered unsafe. The combined parties had more than seventy soldiers, and they suffered no further annoyance from hostile Indians.

For a week following Captain Barnitz' fight with the Cheyennes nothing occurred to upset the routine at Fort Wallace. Then, on July 2, two coaches traveling together under escort approached Goose Creek Station from the west; they were the first stages to arrive in ten days. As they neared the station they were fired upon from the buildings, and realized that the station had been taken by Indians. The vehicles went by in a hurry.

Two miles east of the station they came upon a corralled wagon train. The teamsters were fighting Indians at long range. The escort with the stages joined in the skirmish, which continued for two hours. At length the Indians tired of the fighting and went away. Two soldiers had been wounded, one seriously.[19]

This was virtually the last of the Indian troubles in that area during 1867. One can only speculate about why the Indians stopped raiding so early. It was not through fear of Custer's expedition, though he came to Fort Wallace on July 13.[20] He left his broken-down and useless horses at the post, and, taking seventy-five of his best men as an escort, he abandoned his command and rode to Fort Riley to see his wife.[21] She had not received his message to come by stage to meet him at Fort Wallace, or, despite the great risk involved, she would have done it.

General Hancock preferred charges against Custer for abandoning his command without leave and for having a number of deserters shot without a court-martial. He was tried by a general court-martial, convicted of some of the specifications, and sentenced to be suspended from command for one year.[22]

Captain Keogh, who had returned to Fort Wallace on July 8 with General Hancock, still had problems, although the Indians were quiet. Someone stole the horse belonging to Hancock's orderly, and there was considerable unhappiness over this.

Construction work was resumed; the hospital was completed, and other stone buildings were rising. The stage company was getting replacements

19 Hale to Weir, July 2, 1867, "Letter Book, Fort Wallace."
20 Post Return for July, 1867, Fort Wallace.
21 W. A. Graham, *The Custer Myth*, 202.
22 *Ibid.*, General Courts-Martial Orders, 1867, No. 93, WDAGO Washington, November 20, 1867.

for the stock taken by the Indians and was promising that the stages would soon be running again.[23]

On August 9, General Sherman sent instructions to all commanders that a new peace commission was preparing to negotiate with the Indians. Officers were enjoined to refrain from annoying the Indians while this was going on. The meeting of the commissioners and the Indians would occur south of the Arkansas during the full moon in September.[24]

[23] Keogh to Weir, July 29, 1867, "Letter Book, Fort Wallace."
[24] Sherman to Hancock, Records of U.S. Army Commands, Records of Fort Wallace, Box 1.

11. VAIN HOPES AND EMPTY BOASTS

General Sherman met Hancock at Fort Harker on July 12, and they considered ways of securing more troops to combat the Indian attacks along the Smoky Hill route. Although Fort Wallace and its subposts were now enjoying a period of relief from raids, the Indians seemed to be transferring their attention to the Fort Hays–Fort Harker area, where the railroad was being built. Because six companies of the Seventh Cavalry had been shifted to the north of the Platte River to meet Indian threats in Nebraska, a shortage of cavalry existed. The Tenth Cavalry (a Negro unit) had been formed but was not yet ready for service on the frontier.[1] Sherman's solution to the problem was to ask Governor Samuel J. Crawford of Kansas to furnish militia.

Accordingly, four companies of the Eighteenth Kansas Volunteer Cavalry were raised for a four-months tour and were mustered at Fort Harker where they were placed in tents.[2] The Seventh Cavalry was brought back and distributed, with the Thirty-seventh Infantry, to the several posts. A battalion of the Fifth Infantry was brought from New Mexico. The two Negro regiments—the Tenth Cavalry and the Thirty-eighth Infantry— were shipped west without waiting for them to be trained and were also distributed to the posts on the Smoky Hill and Arkansas routes. When all these shifts had been made, Fort Hays had six companies, Harker seven, Larned eight, Dodge four, and Wallace six. One company each was stationed at the stage stations at Monuments, Downer's, and Cedar Point.[3] This more than doubled the number of troops in these stations and posts. But the troops did not become available immediately, and nearly all the companies were composed mostly of recruits.

At Fort Harker the first cavalry reinforcement was Company F, Tenth Cavalry. This unit was shipped to the post on June 29, having been assembled at Fort Leavenworth. The fact that the men of this company had not yet been mustered into the service of the United States, although they

[1] Report of General W. T. Sherman, 40 Cong., 2 sess., *House Exec. Doc. 1324*, 34–35.
[2] *Roll of Officers and Enlisted Men of the 3d, 4th, 18th, and 19th Kansas Volunteers* (Topeka, 1902), reprint of Appendix 4, *Report of Adjutant General (Kansas), 13th Biennial Report*, 99.
[3] 40 Cong., 2 sess., *House Exec. Doc. 1324*; 39.

had enlisted in the Regular Army, is indicative of the belief at division and department headquarters that an emergency existed.[4] The commander was George A. Armes, the same beardless youth who had reported at Fort Wallace as a second lieutenant less than a year before. He was now a captain, there having been vacancies in nearly all ranks in the new regiment. In those days promotion was by regiment and was much faster in some units than in others.

Captain Armes placed his men in a tent camp near Fort Harker, which he called Camp Grierson in honor of Colonel (Brevet Major General) Benjamin F. Grierson, the commander of the regiment. Grierson, a professional musician who had been commissioned in the cavalry early in the Civil War, although he hated horses and wished to serve in the infantry, had become prominent as a cavalry raider in Mississippi. Now part of his regiment was being sent to Kansas and part to Fort Arbuckle in southeastern Indian Territory.

Armes, by direction of General A. J. Smith, who was still commanding the District of the Upper Arkansas, mustered his men at the tent camp, the special mustering officer not having appeared. Lacking the required muster form, he used a plain piece of paper for this purpose. One can imagine the curled lip of the minor bureaucrat in the Office of the Adjutant General in Washington who received this heretical document.

Armes was not allowed to settle down to a comfortable regime of army paperwork and morning drill. Two days after the tents had been erected at Camp Grierson, he was ordered out to scout Indians observed in the vicinity of Fort Harker. The company saw no Indians, only a few tracks of unshod ponies.[5] Scouting, instead of drill, was to be the chief occupation of this unit during July. Perhaps it was better training than drill; at least the men were learning to ride. A little marksmanship training would also have been beneficial, but two more decades were to elapse before this kind of instruction received much attention in the army.

William Edward Armes, the captain's younger brother, was a guest at Camp Grierson, he being on a short vacation prior to reporting to West Point as a new cadet. Before daylight on July 3, Captain Armes was ordered out with his company to rescue a railroad construction crew who were being attacked by Indians in a camp several miles west of Fort Harker. The unit assembled quickly, their horses were saddled, and they were ready to depart. Armes told his young brother that he had to leave him in charge of

[4] George A. Armes, *Ups and Downs of an Army Officer*, 231.
[5] *Ibid.*

the small detachment remaining to guard the camp. Eddie said he was not afraid; he would build a fort out of sacks of grain.

When Captain Armes returned next day he was told that his brother had been stricken with cholera shortly after the column left camp, and was dead by midafternoon. Captain Armes was prostrated with grief. The two young men had been very close. It did no good to tell Armes that the surgeon and the ladies at Fort Harker had done all they could to save the boy. Mrs. Sternberg, the wife of the surgeon, had nursed young Armes. She caught the disease within ten days and also died a few hours later.[6]

This was the beginning of the cholera epidemic that struck all the posts that summer. Causing far more terror and greater losses than all the Indian attacks, the cholera manifested itself with appalling symptoms, and at that time there was no knowledge about its cause or cure.

The cholera appeared at Fort Wallace late in July; the first cases developed in the camp of the Seventh Cavalry. It did not then spread to the post, but early in August a battalion of the Fifth Infantry, marching from Fort Union, New Mexico, brought it in. By the middle of the month the disease was raging in all companies at Fort Wallace, in common with other posts. Deaths were occurring daily, and something like panic was building up.[7]

Mrs. Bankhead, the twenty-nine-year-old wife of the new post commander, Brevet Colonel (Captain, Fifth Infantry) H. C. Bankhead, volunteered to help nurse the soldiers. On August 16 she started vomiting blood and within a few hours was dead. She was described as being a person "of rare loveliness and the daughter of the late Bishop Wainwright of New York." In addition to Mrs. Bankhead and Mrs. Douglass, the wife of another post commander, Captain Rife at Fort Arbuckle, died of cholera at this time.[8]

The post medical histories have little to say about the cholera epidemic, though it is clear from the surgeon's annual report that special reports were made on the epidemic. The routine post records reflect a preoccupation with injuries, including those caused by Indian attacks, and with milder ailments. Surgeon Turner at Fort Wallace recorded: "The percentage of sick (other than from cholera and scurvy) continues to be light. Most cases of the class zymotic were traceable to individual indiscretions, while nothing

[6] *Ibid.*, 232–34.
[7] Keogh to Mitchell, July 29, "Letter Book, Fort Wallace"; Keogh to Weir, August 16; Report of the Surgeon General, U.S. Army, 40 Cong., 2 sess., *House Exec. Doc. 1324*, 592.
[8] Keogh to Weir, August 16, 1867, "Letter Book, Fort Wallace"; *Army and Navy Journal*, Vol. V (August 13, 1867).

beyond the usual contusions from cavalry were received."[9] What he meant was that the ailments were mostly scurvy, "intermittent fever," venereal disease (post surgeons reported the Indian camps to be ripe with gonorrhea and syphilis), and injuries incurred in drunken fights or falling from horses. Many of the recruits suffered from gout; the surgeon said they should never have been enlisted.

The continued affliction of so many men with scurvy is inexplicable in view of the general knowledge accumulated at that time concerning its cause and prevention. Vitamins had not yet been invented, but antiscorbutics were used. The early experimenters in the medical profession had given undue prominence to the use of vinegar to prevent scurvy, not realizing that a man would have to drink a gallon a day to get much benefit.[10] Most surgeons knew that fresh potatoes were desirable in controlling scurvy, and it is evident in the correspondence that there was a bit of borrowing and lending between posts when one unit ran short.

The post adjutants were responsible for the post vegetable gardens, and they were eager to grow fresh vegetables during the summer to supplement the monotonous diet of salt meat, beans, and hardtack that the Commissary General was cannily issuing to get rid of his mountains of war surplus. But the gardens did poorly at some posts, among them Forts Dodge and Wallace. There was ample organic fertilizer at the cavalry posts to grow anything, but insufficient water. Water pipes and hydrants were unobtainable, and rubber garden hose did not appear until the late eighties. Lieutenant Fred Beecher at Fort Wallace built a dam across Pond Creek to get more water (and ice) for the post, but at this period of history, irrigation ditches were not thought of in the Midwest—or in the East. Furthermore, as Dr. Turner noted in his medical history, "The grasshoppers consume what nature had allowed to grow."[11] During the Kansas summers, the grasshoppers moved in clouds, eating every leaf and every blade of grass.

Most of the small prairie posts were built to accommodate from one to three companies, but, owing to the influx of additional troops in the summer of 1867, they were crowded. Fort Wallace's garrison jumped from 120 men to 456. Units had to be doubled up in barracks or placed in tents. By winter of that year, they were again living under miserable conditions.

On July 21, Captain Armes and his company were transferred to Fort Hays, seventy-six miles west of Fort Harker, where they went into a tent

[9] "Medical History, Fort Wallace," 3.

[10] Byron Stinson, M.D., "Scurvy in the Civil War," *Civil War Times Illustrated*, Vol. V, No. 5 (August, 1966).

[11] "Medical History, Fort Wallace," 4.

camp once more. The railroad had progressed so far westward that this area was now the scene of Indian raids.

The cholera epidemic struck this camp and the nearby post about the end of the month, and two or three deaths occurred in each company every day. Armes moved his camp to higher ground, trying to get away from the source of the disease. It was realized vaguely that contaminated ground somehow contributed to the spread of cholera, although it was not known that some intestinal ailments were contracted by ingesting food or drink that had been contaminated by flies from open garbage pits or unprotected latrines. Army posts and camps in the plains were kept neat and orderly even under difficult conditions, but it was not appreciated that the mere appearance of cleanliness was insufficient to prevent infection and contagion. In Armes's camp, as at several posts, the epidemic would continue for two or three weeks and then end as suddenly and mysteriously as it had appeared.

The Indians may have been aware of the cholera epidemic, for they had an intermittent contact with the whites through traders and the few squaw men who lived in the Indian camps but who occasionally visited army posts. It is noticeable that during the period of the epidemic the Indians did not raid any post or come in for a visit. They did, however, attack the railroad construction camps. These raids were probably made by the Dog Soldiers, together with a number of Sioux and a few Arapahoes who were consistently hostile.

Captain Armes and his men were called out on frequent scouts despite the sickness in the command. Until August 1, these short expeditions were unsuccessful. At 2:00 P.M. on that day, Armes received word from Fort Hays that Campbell's railroad construction camp thirteen miles to the west was under attack. An hour later he was headed for the scene with forty-four men. When they arrived, the Indians had gone, but they had left seven men lying dead in the grass amidst great clots of blood. They had been scalped and the stock stolen. The few survivors had hidden in the brush.[12]

Armes followed the tracks of the Indians' horses for eighteen miles up the north branch of Big Creek but lost the trail after nightfull. He led his men back to Campbell's camp and sent six troopers to Fort Hays for reinforcements. He asked for thirty men and a howitzer; the railroaders had told him there were more Indians than he could handle with his small company.

[12] The expedition of August 1–2, 1867, is described in Armes, *Ups and Downs of an Army Officer*, 236–41. Included are his diary entries and the official reports.

As morning approached, Armes's impatience grew. The reinforcements did not arrive. At daylight he started off with thirty-four men, four others having come down with cholera. After riding north for fifteen miles, he reached the Saline River, which he followed upstream for an additional fifteen miles.

Suddenly seventy or eighty Indians rode at the column from a side canyon. At once Armes formed a line and had his men dismount. He realized that the soldiers were too inexperienced as horsemen to do any shooting from the backs of their mounts. But he kept them moving forward, leading their horses; he was unwilling to turn back without having made a determined effort to recover the stolen stock.

Within a few minutes the Indians were on all sides of the company, but remaining at a respectful distance. The country favored the Indians, for it was cut up by gullies and small canyons that offered concealed approaches. On the bluffs flanking the soldiers, the enemy began building small fires and sending up smoke signals. This brought other Indians.

About mid-morning Armes saw several hundred other warriors approaching. At once he turned his men around and started back in the direction of Fort Hays. The Indians followed, pressing closer. Now and then a pair of braves, or a larger group, would dash forward and ride at top speed entirely around the cavalry. Both sides fired rapidly during such displays, but there were few casualties. Once Captain Armes saw two men he was certain were either white or half-blood, but he did not recognize them. He also claimed that Satanta was the Indian leader, but this is not likely, for the Kiowas were well south of the Arkansas at this time. The whites usually accused Satanta or Roman Nose of being the leader of Indian attacks, but it is doubtful that they were able to recognize the tribe of the attackers. I have asked Kiowas how it was possible to recognize the tribe of strange Plains Indians, and they admitted that only the decorations, such as beadwork, supplied such identification. Many Kiowas, however, wore their hair in a unique manner—cut off level with the ear lobe on the right side.

Armes was surprised at the poor shooting displayed by the Indians, which he thought resulted from unfamiliarity with their weapons. The government (Interior Department) had recently issued them new models of the Spencer carbines with which to shoot at the warriors of the War Department. The soldiers did not distinguish themselves as sharpshooters, either, though Armes claims his men shot six of the enemy, who were carried off by their comrades. Armes lost one sergeant killed and was himself wounded in the hip. Even worse, six more men were overcome with cholera and had to be strapped to their horses, doubled over with pain and in agony from constant vomiting and diarrhea.

Armes was soon unable to walk, and had to mount, although it was very painful to sit in the saddle. Some of the men, seeing the blood oozing through his trousers, lost their nerve and rushed to the center of the line for better protection. Armes made them return to their places lest the Indians should think them out of ammunition. Under good leadership the men gradually calmed down and began firing steadily.

By taking the most direct route to Fort Hays, Armes and his men had only thirty-seven miles to march. That would have been almost too much for such green soldiers, for, being cavalry, their legs and feet had not been toughened to walking. Fortunately, the Indians vanished after the first fifteen miles, and the soldiers were able to mount once more. For the sick and wounded, the ride back to Fort Hays was torture, and there must have been great anxiety among the other men. But they made it.

Armes learned at Fort Hays that the reinforcements he had requested were sent to him, but did not arrive at the railroad camp until after he left. This detachment consisted of twenty-five Negro infantrymen from the Thirty-eighth Regiment, whom the post commander at Fort Hays had mounted on horses. They had brought the howitzer Armes had asked for. Shortly after leaving the post, the lieutenant in charge had come down with cholera and returned to Hays. Then a Sergeant Pittman had taken charge. Although Pittman had failed to overtake Armes, he did encounter fifty Indians. Three shells from the howitzer caused the Indians to scatter and disappear, whereupon Pittman led his men back to Hays.

Armes went to the infirmary at Fort Hays, where the surgeon dug the bullet out of his hip. Then the doctor put him to bed.

Second Lieutenant John A. Bodamer, Tenth Cavalry, took command of the company for a few days, but Armes was out of bed every day to lead the men after the Indians, for they were probing the line of the railroad and terrorizing the construction crews. The first day, he rode in an ambulance, but thereafter he was on his horse, moving along the railroad to show the workmen they had protection.

On August 12, several battalions were ordered out by district headquarters to run down the numerous small parties of Indians who had been seen here and there on the plains about Fort Hays. One battalion, consisting of Captain (now Brevet Major) Armes's company, with two companies of the Eighteenth Kansas attached, marched to the Saline River and thence westward until, about 4:00 P.M. on August 14, they met the other two companies of the Eighteenth Kansas under Major Horace L. Moore coming down the river. They decided to comb the country to the north—Moore to march northwest and Major Armes northeast—after which they would come together again on the Solomon River.[13]

The meeting on the Solomon failed to occur, although Armes searched along the stream for forty miles. He then moved southwest toward Monument Station until, on the seventeenth, he found a large Indian trail running northwest. He followed this until he came to a construction camp on the railroad forty miles west of Fort Hays. Since he now needed rations and forage, Armes placed Captain Edgar A. Baker, Eighteenth Kansas, in command, while he rode to Fort Hays with three men for supplies and additional men. He was furnished with five wagonloads of food and forage and, with twenty-five men as escort, started back to his battalion. During this trip Armes met Major Joel H. Elliott with a battalion of the Seventh Cavalry, also looking for Indians. Elliott gave Armes the impression that this battalion would start for the Republican River on the Nineteenth and would cooperate with him. But he did not see Elliott again.

Thus the situation on August 18–19 was that, in an area infested with large numbers of hostile Indians, three small battalions of inexperienced cavalry led by young officers having only slightly more service than the men were riding in different directions without any over-all direction or planning and without making positive arrangements for mutual support. This was asking for trouble, and Armes got it.

Armes was blithely unconcerned, however, when he returned to his command on the morning of the eighteenth. He now had 164 men, a fairly respectable force if he kept them together. Instead, he divided them into three detachments. All marched north, but they were well separated and not in contact with each other. Captain George B. Jenness, Eighteenth Kansas, with 29 men searched the country out to one flank and Armes with 70 men were on the other side. They were eight or ten miles apart. Lieutenant John W. Price with 65 men came along with the wagons, at least a march of one-half-day behind. The Indians, who were well out of sight, must have been keeping the soldiers under constant surveillance, and doubtless they were pleased at the opportunity this dispersion of forces offered them.

Armes's detachment marched northward in this formation until, on the morning of August 21, his portion of the command ran into a large war

[13] The expedition of August 12–23 is covered in Armes, *Ups and Downs of an Army Officer,* 242–49.

party near Beaver Creek. The soldiers were immediately surrounded. Armes dismounted his men and had them take cover in folds in the ground. This was the beginning of a day that stretched out interminably. The Indians maintained a constant fusillade of long range firing and made continual attacking feints and runs. Again Armes thought he recognized Satanta, mounted on a fine gray or white horse and dressed in full uniform, as the leader of the Indians. Again this was unlikely. Satanta's battle colors were bright red. He carried a red shield, and, if he followed the usual custom of the Kiowas, his horse would have been painted to match. The "full uniform" sounds like Roman Nose of the Cheyenne Dog Soldiers. Furthermore, the Kiowas went on a notable raid against the Navahos in New Mexico that summer. Most of their chiefs were members of the party, and it is unlikely that Satanta would have stayed behind to operate with the Cheyennes. The two tribes were no longer enemies, but they were not close allies. The Arapahoes usually joined the Cheyennes, while the Comanches and Kiowas rode together.

The fighting continued until dark; eleven soldiers were seriously wounded, including the first sergeant in Armes's own company. Under cover of darkness, Armes tried to locate the other portions of his battalion but failed. At four o'clock in the morning, he halted in a ravine to rest his men and horses until sunrise.

The previous afternoon Captain Jenness had seen the Indians circling in the distance and realized that Armes was surrounded. He tried to effect a junction with Armes but was surrounded by Indians and forced to take up a defensive position in a ravine. He remained in a precarious position until the next day, when Armes joined him. Armes had also located Price and the wagons, who similarly had been surrounded and were fighting Indians all day. The fighting continued all of this second day until about 4:00 P.M., when a charge by Armes drove the Indians out of range. But they still remained within sight, and the troops could hear their calls during the night.

The next day several Indians approached carrying a white flag and attempted to parley with Armes's two guide-interpreters. This broke down in an exchange of insults and mutual defiance. The guides claimed that they recognized Roman Nose, Charley Bent, and several other prominent Cheyennes.

Later that day, Major Armes continued his retreat to Fort Hays. He had lost three men dead and thirty-five wounded. His men had fought well, but there is no escaping the conclusion that the Indians had achieved a substantial victory. This confirmed for the Indians what the Sioux had told them—that their victories in the north had forced the soldiers to give up the Powder River Road and that by warlike action the Cheyennes could secure similar results on the Smoky Hill route.[14] The young men in the Dog Soldier band commenced to boast of their victory over Armes. Their cocky attitude was well stated by the Sioux chief Spotted Tail in an interview with an army officer: "We don't fear your cavalry because we can ride down within a hundred paces of them, and then if we give our whoop and shake our buffalo robes, one half of your men will fall off their horses and the other half will run away."[15]

Nevertheless, the declared objectives of the Cheyennes had been only vain hopes and empty boasts. They had not permanently stopped traffic on the Smoky Hill Road. Far from evacuating the country, the white men had established additional military stations and were building towns along the lengthening railroad. The Indians had captured much stock, and their young men had collected a few scalps and counted coups. But when they met the government officials they could not brag about this because at the Little Arkansas peace council they had promised to abstain from such acts. They had to fall back on the old excuse that their raiding was done in revenge for General Hancock's burning of the village.

And so, as summer turned to fall, even the attacks on the railroad camps ceased, and the time drew near for the great peace council on Medicine Lodge Creek.

[14] Report of General W. T. Sherman, 40 Cong., 3 sess., *House Exec. Doc. 1367*, 3.
[15] *Army and Navy Journal*, Vol. V (October 12, 1867), 117.

Well before the cessation of hostilities in 1867, the government had decided to secure peace by negotiation with the Indians instead of permitting the army to undertake another military expedition like that led by General Hancock. In Washington, Hancock had become the object of a storm of criticism, caused mainly by the strong denunciations contained in the reports of both Wynkoop and Leavenworth. They said flatly that he was responsible for the Indian war of 1867. The army, whose lifeblood depended on Congressional appropriation, reacted by relieving Hancock and ordering him transferred to New Orleans.[1] General A. J. Smith temporarily replaced him in command at Fort Leavenworth. In the spring, Major General Philip H. Sheridan would take over command of the department. Wynkoop and Leavenworth had twisted a mighty corkscrew, but the wine was bitter to their taste—Sheridan was no man of peace.

The Congress, by an act approved on July 20, 1867, provided for a board of commissioners who were to proceed to the Indian country and negotiate a peace with the southern Plains tribes. General Sherman was detailed as a member of that board, the other members being Commissioner of Indian Affairs Nathaniel G. Taylor; Senator John B. Henderson of Missouri; Samuel F. Tappan, a former lieutenant colonel of the Second Colorado Cavalry; John B. Sanborn, late major general of Volunteers; and Generals William S. Harney and Alfred H. Terry, commanding the Departments of the Platte and the Dakota, respectively. The board assembled in St. Louis and began making plans for meeting with the Indians.[2]

Since Sherman had ordered the military commanders in the Indian country to keep quiet while the agents were trying to round up the Indians, the several posts utilized this respite to accelerate construction projects and

---

[1] Naturally, no such reason was given for Hancock's transfer. It has long been customary for the War Department to transfer to another assignment an officer who has been "under fire" by the press or some other agency—to protect both the officer and the department itself from further criticism.

[2] Report of General W. T. Sherman, 40 Cong., 2 sess., *House Exec. Doc. 1324*, 37; 40 Cong., 3 sess., *House Exec. Doc. 1367*, 2.

improve living conditions. They were following the spirit of the old peace-time army: "Let's get this damned war over so we can go back to work"—"work" meaning the nomal routine of paperwork, post guard and police, whitewashing of fences and rock borders, repair or building of offices and quarters, and two hours of daily drill.

Because General Sherman was busy with other duties, he was relieved as a member of the peace commission and replaced by General C. C. Augur. Following a visit to the northern tribes, the commissioners went to Fort Larned, where they waited until the tribes assembled for the treaty council. This took several weeks, but General Sherman had allowed for the delay by postponing the date from September to October.

In August, nearly all the Indians were south of the Arkansas—the Cheyennes and Arapahoes (except for the warring bands) were on the Cimarron and Beaver Creek, and the Kiowas were sixty miles south of Fort Larned. The Comanches were either near the Kiowas or along Red River on the northern border of Texas. The Indians were brought to the vicinity of Fort Larned for a preliminary assembly. There, they could be fed and watched while all waited for the main assembly to occur. (Many years ago, old Indians told me they attended these councils because they were promised food, and for no other reason.) In August and September of 1867, they camped south of the Arkansas River, within a few miles of Larned, and rations were distributed by Wynkoop and Leavenworth.[3]

The Arapahoes, who had remained quiet and had not wandered about on the plains during the summer—preferring to stay out of trouble—had not found many buffalo. They were destitute and querulous. The Cheyennes were better off, but the older chiefs admitted that they had lost most of their control over the young warriors. The Dog Soldiers were aloof in demeanor when visited by messengers from the commissioners. Since they were even then engaged in making attacks along the Smoky Hill route or farther north, they were uncertain what kind of a reception might await them at the peace meeting. Nevertheless, some of the older chiefs seemed amenable, and Wynkoop was optimistic that they would bring in their bands. According to Thomas Murphy, head of the Central Superintendency, even Roman Nose promised to come to the preliminary assembly as soon as the raiding parties had returned from their current activities along the railroad.[4]

---

[3] *Report of Commissioners of Indian Affairs for 1867*, 18; Mooney, "Calendar History," 321; Report of General W. T. Sherman, 40 Cong., 3 sess., *House Exec. Doc. 1367*, 3.
[4] Berthrong, *The Southern Cheyennes*, 292.

There was no difficulty in reaching the Kiowas. They had celebrated the sun dance on "Timber-hill River," named for a low timber-covered hill on the east bank of the river. They had built their medicine lodge just across the river from the hill, and the lodge was still standing when the treaty council was held in the vicinity. Because of this circumstance, the white people called the stream Medicine Lodge Creek. The council was held on its east side, three miles above its junction with Elm Creek. The town of Medicine Lodge, Kansas, now stands on the site. Towards the end of June, when the sun dance was over, nearly all the Comanches and half of the Kiowas and Kiowa-Apaches went on a big raid against the Navahos on the Pecos River. They were successful and returned to Kansas in time for the treaty gathering.[5]

A substantial number of Comanches attended. These included the Penetekas, or Southern Comanches; the Nokoni and Kotchateka, or Middle Comanches; and the Yapparikas, or Northern Comanches. The Quohada, who roamed the Staked Plains, either were not reached by the messengers or refused to come.[6] Several groups of Cheyenne Dog Soldiers, including those led by Roman Nose and Medicine Arrow, also stayed away. Some 850 tipis were counted at the final assembly—about 5,000 Indians.

The assembled Indians and government officials left Fort Larned on October 13 and headed for Medicine Lodge Creek. There were about one hundred white men, including the commissioners, interpreters, clerks, a dozen or so newsmen, observers, and servants. They were escorted by a battalion of the Seventh Cavalry under Major Joel H. Elliott.[7] This assembly was the largest and most colorful gathering of Indians and officials ever witnessed on the plains, and it received full coverage in the press. Free food and plenty of coffee were provided to ensure that the Indians did not wander away.

When the council opened, the commissioners told the Indians that they had been violating the provisions of previous treaties and that the killing of white people and taking their property must stop. They were then invited to state their side of the case.[8]

[5] Mooney, "Calendar History," 319–21.

[6] These are the simplified names of the major subdivisions of the Comanche tribe, popularly in use for many years. The more exact nomenclature used by ethnologists is given in Wallace and Hoebel, *The Comanches*, 25–32.

[7] Berthrong, *The Southern Cheyennes*, 295–96.

[8] The Medicine Lodge Peace Council is described in detail in a number of works, including: Mooney, "Calendar History," 184–86; Berthrong, *The Southern Cheyennes*, 295–98; Stanley, *My Early Travels and Adventures*, 223–37; and Douglas L. Jones, *The Treaty of Medicine Lodge*.

A number of chiefs spoke, Satanta, as usual, leading off. The old Kiowa, Satank, also made a short but clear and pointed address. However, Ten Bears, the venerable chief of the Yapparika Comanches, was the most impressive. He had visited Washington and thus realized that the powerful and numerous white race could not be stopped. Nevertheless, he set forth the fading hopes and desires of the Indian in phrases that deserve repetition:

My heart is filled with joy when I see you here, as the brook fills with water when the snow melts in the spring, and I feel glad as the ponies do when the fresh grass starts in the beginning of the year. I heard of your coming when I was many sleeps away, and I made but few camps before I met you. I knew you had come to do good to me and my people. I looked for benefits which would last forever, and so my face shines with joy as I look upon you. My people have never first drawn a bow or fired a gun against the whites. There has been trouble on the line between us and my young men have danced the war dance. But it was not begun by us. It was you who sent out the first soldier and we who sent out the second. Two years ago I came upon this road, following the buffalo, that my wives and children might have their cheeks plump and their bodies warm. But the soldiers fired upon us, and since that time there has been a noise like that of a thunderstorm, and we have not known which way to go. So it was upon the Canadian. Nor have we been made to cry once alone. The blue-dressed soldiers and the Utes came from out of the night when it was dark and still, and for campfires they lit our lodges. Instead of hunting game they killed my braves, and the warriors of the tribe cut short their hair for the dead.

So it was in Texas. They made sorrow come in our camps, and we went out like buffalo bulls when their cows are attacked. When we found them we killed them, and their scalps hang in our lodges. The Comanches are not weak and blind, like the pups of a dog when seven weeks old. They are strong and farsighted like grown horses. We took their road and we went on it. The white women cried and our women laughed.

But there are things I do not like. They are not sweet like sugar, but bitter like gourds. You said that you wanted to put us on a reservation, to build us houses and make us medicine lodges. I do not want them. I was born upon the prairie, where the wind blew free and there was nothing to break the light of the sun. I was born where there were no enclosures and everything drew a free breath. I want to die there and not within walls. I know every stream and every wood between the Rio Grande and the Arkansas. I have hunted and lived over that country. I live like my fathers before me and like them I live happily.

When I was in Washington the Great White Father told me that all the

Comanche land was ours, and that no one should hinder us in living upon it. So why do you ask us to leave the rivers and the sun, and the wind, and live in houses? Do not ask us to give up the buffalo for the sheep. The young men have heard talk of this, and it has made them sad and angry. Do not speak of it more. I love to carry out the talk I got from the Great Father. When I get goods and presents, I and my people feel glad, since it shows he holds us in his eye.

If the Texans had kept out of my country, there might have been peace. But that which you now say we must live in, is too small. The Texans have taken away the places where the grass grew thickest and the timber was the best. Had we kept that, we might have done the things you ask. But it is too late. The whites have the country we loved, and we only wish to wander on the prairies until we die. Any good thing you say to me shall not be forgotten. I shall carry it as near my heart as my children, and it shall be as often on my tongue as the name of the Great Spirit. I want it all clear and pure, and I wish it so that all who go through my people may find peace when they come in and leave it when they go out.[9]

The negotiations resulted in the Treaty of Medicine Lodge, which was signed by the Kiowa and Comanche chiefs on October 21, the Kiowa-Apache chiefs on the twenty-second, and the Cheyenne and Arapahoe chiefs on the twenty-eighth. By its terms, the Indians agreed to move to areas set aside for them in Indian Territory, to stop killing white people and interfering with traffic on the roads across the plains, and to permit military posts and railroads to be built. They were to accept agencies; compulsory schools for their children; farming tools, seeds, and instructors; doctors; and artisans.[10] They wanted none of these things. But they signed.

In return, the Indians were promised reservations and supplementary hunting grounds that presumably would allow them to support themselves by hunting so long as the buffalo were plentiful, and such Indians as elected to become farmers would each be given 320 acres of land—the title to the land, however, would remain with the government. This would have been ample for farming but not for stock raising. Had the commissioners been more sensitive to the lessons of history, and applied them to the future, they would have realized that the Indians, like many other races, were not adapted by inclination or background to agricultural life. They might have made good stockmen.

The Indians were to be issued, at their agencies, some rations, but not

[9] Ten Bears' address is from a photographic copy furnished me by the Department of the Interior in 1935. It can also be found in the "Sheridan Papers."
[10] Mooney, "Calendar History," 184.

enough for their entire support, and certain annuities or "presents." Congress was to appropriate $25,000 annually for the purchase of the annuities.[11] An army officer was to witness each issue to ensure that the Indians were not cheated.

Since the treaty gave the Indians much they did not want, while taking away their hunting grounds and the life they loved, it is surprising that they signed. According to Wallace and Hoebel, the chiefs were probably convinced that if they refused to sign the treaty they would receive no rations and presents, and the troops would be sent to attack them. The following chiefs, many of whom have been immortalized on photographic plates by William Soule, signed the treaty:

Kiowas: Satank, Satanta, Black Eagle, Kicking Bird, Fishemore, Woman's Heart, Stumbling Bear, Lone Bear, Crow Bonnet, Bear Lying Down.

Kiowa-Apaches: Wolf's Sleeve, Poor Bear, Bad Back, Brave Man, Iron Shirt, White Horn.

Comanches: Ten Bears, Painted Lips, Tosawi (Silver Brooch), Cear-Chi-neka (Standing Head Feather), Howeah (Gap in the Woods), Horse Back, Esa-naninca (Wolf's Name), Little Horn, Iron Mountain, Saddy-yoh.

Cheyennes: Black Kettle, Little Robe, Bull Bear, Tall Bull, White Horse, Whirlwind, Spotted Elk, Buffalo Calf, Slim Face, Gray Head, Little Rock, Curly Hair, Heap of Bears.

Arapahoes: Little Raven, Yellow Bear, Storm, White Rabbit, Spotted Wolf, Big Mouth, Young Colt, Tall Bear.

The Medicine Lodge Treaty was the last treaty made between the government and the five tribes, except for some agreements wheedled out of them several decades later when the white man coveted the Indians' land. The government then paid them less than two dollars an acre to open their reservations to homesteading. At the time of the Medicine Lodge Treaty, General Sherman remarked that the peace commission "has assigned them a reservation which if held for fifty years will make their descendants rich."[12] Unfortunately for the Indians, this land was taken away from them in less than fifty years, and they are poor today.

That the Medicine Lodge Treaty was a failure will be seen presently. But it is not quite fair to say that when they signed the treaty the Indians had

---

[11] *Ibid.*, 185.
[12] 40 Cong., 3 sess., *House Exec. Doc. 1367*, 6.

no intention of abiding by its provisions. Many of them did, especially the chiefs; but they could not keep their followers in line.

The major portions of the Cheyenne and Arapaho tribes, those who had participated in the treaty, went into winter camps on the Cimarron River sixty miles south of Fort Dodge. Their agent, Wynkoop, did not establish an agency with them, but continued to live at Fort Dodge and issue rations there, outside their reservations. George Bent and John Smith, who remained with the Cheyennes, kept Wynkoop partly informed about the attitude and activities of the Indians.[13] The agent had little exact knowledge about the location of the Dog Soldiers who under Roman Nose and Medicine Arrow, had not participated in the treaty. Early in April, 1868, evidences of their camps were seen eighty miles northwest of Fort Wallace by Lieutenant Beecher, who said there were seventy-six lodges.[14] This would mean more than 450 persons. They were definitely outside their reservation, and the troops were entitled to attack them, but no such campaign was launched, and some of these Indians actually came to Fort Larned to draw rations.[15]

The Cheyennes and Arapahoes left the overland routes and army posts undisturbed for ten months following the Medicine Lodge Treaty, but a large war party recruited from all the bands rode east to attack the Kaws and Osages. The reason for this attack was more the fulfillment of the Indian custom of exacting revenge for wrongs suffered, than because fighting was a primary occupation of the Plains Indians. The Kaws had stolen ponies from Little Raven, and possibly from other bands, while the Cheyennes and Arapahoes were camped at Medicine Lodge. The Kaws had to be "paid back." In November, the war party had a fight with the Kaws twenty-five miles east of Fort Zarah and were defeated. This only increased their determination to settle with the Kaws on a later occasion, and another battle was planned for the spring of 1868.[16] The Indian Bureau officials were upset over this intertribal warfare, for they feared it might be the spark that would start another Indian war.

The Kiowas, Kiowa-Apaches, and Comanches also moved on to their assigned reservation. They camped in the vicinity of Fort Cobb, where they

---

[13] Berthrong, *The Southern Cheyennes*, 299.

[14] Butler to AAG, Hq District of Upper Arkansas, April 11, 1868, "Letter Book, Fort Wallace." Lieutenant Beecher said these camps were on Thickwood Creek. In Butler's opinion the Indians were seeking a retired area as a camp site for their families, preparatory to making war on the Utes, some of whom were near Lake Station hunting buffalo.

[15] Douglass to AAG, Dept. of the Mo., March 1, 21, 1868, "Letter Book, Fort Dodge."

[16] Boone to Taylor, June 4, 1868, 40 Cong., 3 sess., *House Exec Doc. 1366*, 524–25.

expected Jesse Leavenworth, still their agent, to resume the issue of rations. Leavenworth followed the Indians to this area, which was three hundred miles south of Fort Dodge, and set up a new agency with temporary accommodations in Eureka Valley, near the site of Fort Cobb.[17] The Kiowas were still displeased with Leavenworth because they continued to believe he had cheated them out of the presents they were supposed to be issued after the treaty of the Little Arkansas. Satanta and others had asked that John Tappan, the sutler at Fort Dodge, be appointed as their agent in place of Leavenworth,[18] but this was not done. Leavenworth had been commended by the peace commissioners for his efforts in assembling the Indians for the council, and was currently in favor with the Commissioner of Indian Affairs.

During the winter of 1867–68, the Indians clustered about the agency, begging for food and annuities, and becoming surly when these were not forthcoming. Leavenworth and his superiors had not made definite and timely arrangements to stock the agency with supplies or to make issues from that point. Fort Cobb and Eureka Valley were remote from any railhead or route over which supplies could be hauled by wagon. No military protection had been requested, possibly because the Agent felt that it was not needed. At any rate, in his differences with the military in Kansas, and his reports to his superiors, he had proclaimed that his Indians were peaceable.

On the contrary, the Kiowas and Comanches, with the exception of two or three chiefs, were as warlike as ever. For several months they abstained from attacking routes and military posts in Kansas, but, like the Cheyennes and Arapahoes, they found an outlet for their bloodthirsty propensities by attacking other Indians. Lean Bull, known to the whites as Poor Buffalo, led a party of warriors against the Navahos, partly to steal horses and partly to avenge the killing of Kaun-pah-te in an earlier fight with the Navahos. On reaching the salt beds near the head of the South Canadian River, on the border between Texas and New Mexico, Poor Buffalo's raiders met a group of Navahos who were on their way east to give them a similar treatment. In the ensuing fight one Navaho was killed and one Kiowa, the stepson of Poor Buffalo.[19] The score was even numerically, but the Kiowas were not satisfied. Another raid would have to be made into New Mexico to assuage the sorrow in Poor Buffalo's family over the death of their young

[17] Nye, *Carbine and Lance*, 46–47.
[18] Foreman, "Col. Jesse Henry Leavenworth," *Chronicles of Oklahoma*, XIII (March, 1935), 28.
[19] Mooney, "Calendar History," 322.

kinsman. This revenge was to be gained the following summer, or so the Kiowas planned.

White Horse, another minor Kiowa war chief, also led a party against the Navahos. In a fight on the South Canadian, he killed one of the enemy, who, when examined, was found to have no external ears. One of the Kiowa calendars commemorates this summer as "the winter Spoiled Ear was killed."[20] Other parties went out against the Navahos on the Pecos River during the winter. As usual, these groups included Comanches and Kiowa-Apaches as well as Kiowas.

Since Leavenworth failed to issue rations to the Kiowas and Comanches, they obtained food by robbing two small, inoffensive tribes—the Caddoes and Wichitas—who lived in Cottonwood Grove, a few miles downstream from Fort Cobb.[21] During the same month, January, 1868, they commenced raiding the farms and settlements of the civilized Chickasaws, who lived still farther east. On January 27, Cyrus Harris, governor of the Chickasaw Nation, wrote to department headquarters for authority to raise a troop of militia, explaining:

> Times are getting too hot to lay still. Government has taken no steps to put down this thing; and in order to save life and property, we have got to shoulder our arms and march . . . . No less than four thousand head of horses have been taken out of the country by these very naked fellows . . . . The wolf will respect a treaty as much as Mr. Wild Indian.[22]

During the first week in February, the wild Indians again raided the Chickasaw settlements and killed some of these Indians, including the family of Overton Love, a Chickasaw living on Red River twenty miles from Fort Arbuckle.[23]

The Kiowas and Comanches could, and probably did, allay their hunger by eating some of the horses they obtained by raiding the civilized Indians. In addition, Satanta and his band went back to Fort Dodge for rations, especially the sugar and coffee to which the Indians were now addicted.

Satanta also had a big thirst which could not be satisfied by coffee. After Major Douglass had fed him and issued ten days rations to his entire band, the chief asked Douglass for liquor. This was refused. Satanta then went from the post headquarters to the Major's quarters, and no one being there

[20] *Ibid.*, 320–21.
[21] Old Files, Fort Arbuckle (in Fort Sill Library).
[22] Foreman, "Col. Jesse Henry Leavenworth," Vol. XIII, XXVIII, *Chronicles of Oklahoma*.
[23] *Ibid.*, 27.

to stop him, drank a bottle of wine he found there. Next, he visited the home of a lieutenant, likewise absent, and swallowed a full bottle of sarsaparilla extract. By this time he was feeling good, but not entirely satisfied. He rode from the post to the nearby house of the stage station proprietor. There he seized and drank a bottle of strong physic the agent had prepared to purge a sick horse.[24] Later he complained to the Indian bureau, through John Smith, that he had been poorly treated at Fort Dodge. Satanta also demanded that Leavenworth be required to establish his agency on the Arkansas River.

Satanta returned to Dodge later in April and repeated his request that Leavenworth, whom he called "that foolish old man," be moved to the Arkansas, where he could issue rations.[25]

In May, the Comanches in Eureka Valley raided the Wichita agency and robbed the agent and the trader's store. They burned the buildings and told the agent that he was not to cut down any more timber or erect any more buildings. They instructed all white men in the vicinity to move out, and the white men did so. Meanwhile, the Kiowas took Leavenworth out on the prairie, tied a rope around his neck, and told him he would be hanged if he remained much longer. Leavenworth left, not stopping to turn over his property to his assistant, S. T. Walkley, who acted as interim agent until the government should appoint another.[26] Albert Gallatin Boone, a grandson of Daniel Boone, was appointed in September, 1868, but owing to illness did not arrive until about February, 1869, when the agency was at Fort Sill.

A short time after Leavenworth's departure, Mr. Walkley noticed that the Kiowas and Comanches had a good deal of liquor, which, he learned, was being sold to them by two white men who had been living in the vicinity since before the Civil War. They were having it hauled in by Caddo George Washington, an eccentric, old Caddo chief who also bootlegged weapons to the wild Indians, and would continue doing so for ten more years.[27]

In May, most of the Indians started north, following the spring migration of the buffalo and planning to reach Fort Larned in time for the first issue of annuities due under the terms of the treaty. This was scheduled for July, but the Kiowas wished first to hold their sun dance, again on Medicine Lodge Creek near the site of the 1867 ceremony. As before, many of the other Indians planned to attend as spectators. The Nokoni and Kotchateka

---

[24] Douglass to McKeever, March 1, 1868, "Letter Book, Fort Dodge.
[25] Douglass to Barr, May 2, 1868, "Letter Book, Fort Dodge."
[26] Nye, *Carbine and Lance*, 48–49; General P. H. Sheridan, *Annual Report*, October 15, 1868, 16.
[27] Walkley to Hazen, October 10, 1868, "Sheridan Papers."

Comanches, however, remained behind to conduct two extensive raids into Texas, where they secured much booty and a number of captives.[28]

The Kiowas and Comanches were not the only Indians who were obtaining large quantities of whisky. The Cheyennes and Arapahoes were trading buffalo robes for liquor at Fort Dodge and Fort Harker, and possibly at Fort Larned. The post commanders admitted in their reports that they were unable to stop this traffic because the traders concealed their merchandise on the prairie and sold it at night.[29] Hunting had been good during the fall and early spring and the Indians had collected many bundles of buffalo robes, which they could trade for whisky. Uncle John Smith reported that the Cheyennes and Arapahoes were returning to their camps carrying liquor in kegs, and that the occupants of entire villages were roaring drunk most of the time. One man alone—Big Mouth—had enough liquor for his whole band. Smith wrote to Superintendent Murphy that the situation was serious and could lead to an outbreak. An aged Apache once told me that liquor was usually the cause of Indian misdeeds. He said that the Indian character had two basic weaknesses—addiction to whisky and to revenge. Both caused brutal, animal-like fights among the Indians and aroused all their warlike instincts, sooner or later leading to attacks on white settlements.[30]

At Fort Dodge, Major Douglass finally obtained evidence that led to the trial and conviction, for selling liquor to soldiers and Indians, of two illicit traders, E. P. Wheeler and William "Dutch Bill" Seamans. They retaliated by swearing out a warrant for the arrest of Douglass and two of his staff for selling liquor to Indians. The officers had to be absent from the post for some time to appear before a court and absolve themselves of the charges.[31]

Kiowas began to arrive on Medicine Lodge Creek late in April, and the assembly for the sun dance started soon afterwards. Satanta and the two hundred people comprising his band continued on to Fort Dodge for his customary talk with the post commander; his talk again included complaints concerning Leavenworth. The Cheyennes and Arapahoes notified their agent that they were going to move to the Middle Branch of Pawnee Fork. This was outside their reservation, but Wynkoop did not object. The treaty permitted them to hunt outside the reservation under certain conditions, for instance, when the buffalo had congregated north of the Arkansas.

[28] Foreman, "Col. Jesse Henry Leavenworth," *Chronicles of Oklahoma,*" XIII (March, 1935), 29; Nye, *Carbine and Lance,* 51–52; Walkley to Hazen, October 10, 1868, "Sheridan Papers."
[29] Douglass to AAG, Dist. of Upper Arkansas, March 24, 1868, "Letter Book, Fort Dodge."
[30] Jason Betzinez, cousin of Geronimo, told me this in 1960.
[31] Douglass to Townsend, May 5, 1868, "Letter Book, Fort Dodge."

Big Mouth's and Little Raven's Arapahoes camped near Fort Dodge during May, and Satanta came in again on June 8 for a brief visit.[32] Meanwhile, the young braves, led by experienced war chiefs, were on the warpath against their traditional enemies.

On June 3, three hundred Cheyennes under Tall Bull, Whirlwind, and Little Robe attacked a Kaw camp near Council Grove. The fight seesawed for four hours, and at dusk the Cheyennes withdrew, their vengeance still unsatisfied.[33]

The Kiowas held their sun dance in June, the celebration again being watched by large crowds of Comanches and other tribes. Following the dance, the base camps were moved to the vicinity of Fort Larned to wait for the issue of annuities. Meanwhile, Satanta went raiding in Texas, and Poor Buffalo carried the pipe to other Kiowa bands and to Comanche villages to enlist a war party for the revenge raid he had been planning against the Navahos. Over two hundred Kiowas and Comanches joined the expedition. A Kiowa named Heap of Bears asked his father, the Tai-me keeper, if he might take with him two of the tribal idols constituting the Tai-me. The permission was given, and Heap of Bears strapped to his back a kidney-shaped pouch containing one of the medicines and gave the other to a friend to carry. It was supposed that these sacred objects would ensure success on the raid.[34]

The expedition headed for a place called Red River Spring, in the salt flats north of the Canadian, where the young Kiowa had been killed by the Navahos. En route the Comanches killed, cooked, and ate a bear. The Kiowas were appalled. Nothing but bad luck could result from this, for the bear was one of their legendary ancestors. The Comanches were unimpressed, and even the leader of the raid, Poor Buffalo, was determined to go ahead. Quite a few of the Kiowas turned back, however, and the others were apprehensive. Their fighting spirit was disappearing rapidly.[35]

About July 10, forty Utes met the war party near Red River Spring. The Utes had come five hundred miles on foot to raid the Kiowas. In the fight that followed, the Kiowas and Comanches were routed with the loss of seven killed. Among the slain was Heap of Bears and his friend, who was carrying one of the Tai-me gods. The Utes captured both Tai-me, a disaster of the first order.[36]

[32] Douglass to Belger, June 13, 1868, "Letter Book, Fort Dodge."
[33] Boone to Taylor, June 4, 1868, 40 Cong., 3 sess., *House Exec. Doc. 1366*, 524–25.
[34] Mooney, "Calendar History," 322–23.
[35] *Ibid.*, 323.
[36] *Ibid.*, 323–24.

On their return to Fort Larned, the Kiowas went into mourning. The chiefs implored Superintendent Murphy to recover the Tai-me for them at any cost. They would even make peace with the Utes, who had been their enemies for as long as they could remember. But the medicine was not returned, and its whereabouts still remains a mystery.[37]

Toward the middle of July, Satanta and his Kiowas, and the Nokoni, Kotchateka, and Penateka Comanches returned from their raids into various parts of Texas. They had committed a series of ghastly atrocities and brought back scalps, horses, and a number of captives. Kicking Bird's band came to Fort Dodge on July 13 after having been fighting with the Utes. One Bear's Kiowas and a small party of Kiowa-Apaches under Spotted Wolf had also been out against the Utes.[38]

All five tribes were assembling near Fort Larned for the annuity payments scheduled for mid-July. There is evidence that the Cheyennes and Arapahoes, and perhaps some of the Kiowas and Comanches, expected to be "cheated" by the white man in this, the first payment promised under the provisions of the Medicine Lodge Treaty.[39] Colonel Leavenworth, before abandoning his post, had sent in a report recommending that payments to the Kiowas and Comanches be held up until they gave up the captives they had taken in Texas. He also recommended that if the tribes did not surrender the Indians guilty of outrages, they should all be turned over to the military, "supported by the Navajos and the civilized tribes, to make short work of them until they can see, hear, and feel the strong arm of the government."[40] This was an about-face for Leavenworth, and some hint of his strong words may have leaked out to the Indians.

Similarly, the Cheyennes and Arapahoes may have heard that Superintendent Murphy, angered by their raid against the Kaws, had ordered the withholding of arms and ammunition at the annuity issue.

Shortly after July 1, Brevet Brigadier General Alfred Sully arrived at Fort Harker to take command of the District of the Upper Arkansas. A contemporary correspondent of the *Army and Navy Journal* describes him as a "fine military-looking gentleman, about 45 years of age, of agreeable manners, and greatly beloved by the soldiers of his command." He had the reputation of having been a successful commander in campaigns against the Sioux in the Dakotas. Soon after his arrival at Fort Harker, General Sully

---

[37] *Ibid.*, 325.

[38] Douglass to Barr, July 18, 1868, Douglass to Belger, August 22, 1868, "Letter Book, Fort Dodge."

[39] Beecher to Sheridan, June 13, 1868, "Sheridan Papers."

[40] *Army and Navy Journal*, Vol. V (June 27, 1868), 718.

117

inspected the posts along the Arkansas route and found them and their garrisons in good shape.[41]

Sully was present when Wynkoop issued the annuities at Fort Larned. The Cheyennes refused to accept theirs when they were told that arms and ammunition were not included. Sully reported that the tribesmen were cross and sullen. The Kiowas and Comanches were also impudent, but all the Indians remained quiet, for Sully had concentrated the troops from Fort Harker and Fort Larned at the latter post.[42]

Newspaper accounts in Kansas stated that the Cheyennes would first place their women and children in remote camps; then they would return and take the arms and ammunition from Wynkoop by force. The entries in the Fort Dodge letter book during the last half of July and the first week of August suggest that there was some truth in the news accounts. The entries reflect a curious situation, for there were over a dozen movements by Indian bands past the post—first small groups with women and children going to Larned for rations, then north or south, and finally successive large groups of warriors heading for the Middle Branch of Pawnee Fork. By the end of the first week in August, two thousand or more Cheyennes had collected on Pawnee Fork. This did look like a concentration in preparation for hostilities, and Sully predicted war by September.[43]

On August 9, Murphy and Wynkoop, reversing themselves, issued arms and ammunition to the entire tribe. The reason they gave was that the Indians needed these articles for their fall hunt.[44] It would have looked better if they had not given such a specious excuse; the Indians used bows and arrows during controlled hunts in order not to frighten and scatter the buffalo.

41 *Ibid.*, 763.
42 Berthrong, *The Southern Cheyennes*, 304–305.
43 *Ibid.*, 305; Douglass to Belger, August 22, 1868, "Letter Book, Fort Dodge."
44 *Ibid.*

13. "I'LL TAKE THE STARCH OUT OF THEM"

Wynkoop issued arms and ammunition to the Cheyennes on August 9. At that very time a large raiding party was on its way to kill civilians living on farms and ranches in the valleys of the Saline and Solomon rivers, thirty miles north of Fort Harker. Edmund Guerrier, the half-blood who often furnished information to government officials, made the following sworn statement concerning the make-up of the raiding party:

> I was with the Cheyenne Indians at the time of the massacre on the Solomon and Saline Rivers in Kansas early in August, and I was living at this time with Little Rock's band.
>
> The war party who started for the Solomon and Saline was from Little Rock's, Black Kettle's, Medicine Arrow's, and Bull Bear's bands; and, as near as I can remember, nearly all the different bands of the Cheyennes had some of their young men in the war party.
>
> Red Nose and The-Man-who-breaks-the-marrow-bones were the leaders in this massacre; the former belonging to the Dog Soldiers, and the latter to Black Kettle's band . . . .[1]

Black Kettle and the other chiefs were, without doubt, in their villages when the criers were calling among the tipis for warriors to assemble for the preliminary war dance and smoker at which plans for the raid would be discussed. Indian raids were always carefully planned, and the medicine man was called upon to determine whether the omens were favorable. The chief of each village must have been aware that a foray was in the making.

Perhaps the so-called friendly chiefs tried to prevent the raid. More likely they did not. In any event, they continued to profess friendship to the whites and to receive government bounty, even after the war party had started on their way. And they did nothing to warn their white "friends" that some of their people were about to be murdered by Indians who had recently promised to give up such practices.

The blow fell on August 10. Major General Philip H. Sheridan, who

[1] Report of General P. H. Sheridan, 41 Cong., 2 sess., *House Exec. Doc. 1412*, 47.

119

personally investigated the atrocities, described what happened in the opening raid:

> A party of about 200 Cheyennes, 4 Arapahoes, and 20 Sioux, then visiting the Cheyennes, organized and left their camp on the Pawnee Creek and proceeded first to the Saline Valley, north of Fort Harker. They were kindly received by two farmers living in the advanced settlements, and given coffee, etc. After throwing the coffee in the faces of the women serving them, because it was given them in a tin cup, they commenced the robbery of the houses, violated the women until they were insensible from brutal treatment. Then they crossed to the settlements on the Solomon, where they were again kindly treated and served with coffee; after which they commenced robbing the house, taking the stock, ravishing the women, and murdering 13 men. Two of the women outraged were also shot and badly wounded. A small party crossed the Republican and killed two persons there; but the main party returned to the Saline, carrying two children . . . .[2]

In all fairness to the Indians, their version, which was told to General Hazen at a later date, should be given. Hazen reported the Indians' story to Sherman:

> Being about Fort Larned, where abundant whisky was to be had, a war party went to attack the Pawnees—their old foe—and were beaten. When returning, and on the Saline in the settlements, one of them rode to a house for something to eat, without any intention of doing harm. A man came to the door and ordered him away. The Indian, not knowing what was said to him, continued to ride toward the house, when the citizen came out with a shot gun and fired on him. At that, the fracas began and the war started.[3]

The Cheyennes followed these initial outrages with attacks in many other areas. They struck in forty localities during the sixty-day period ending October 24, killing seventy-nine civilians and wounding nine. They also killed six soldiers and wounded ten. The total number of captives was never published, but there is mention in the reports of fourteen captive children being found frozen to death in one winter camp.[4] The impact of the raids on the widely scattered farms and small settlements was so great that the governors of Kansas and Colorado made urgent, even frantic appeals for help.[5] The post commanders and officers in higher headquarters did what they could, but, because of the slowness of communication and the dis-

[2] Sheridan to Sherman, September 26, 1868, 40 Cong., 3 sess., *House Exec. Doc. 1367*, 11.
[3] Hazen to Sherman, November 10, 1868, "Sheridan Papers," Container 72, 381–82.
[4] Report of General P. H. Sheridan, 41 Cong., 2 sess., *House Exec. Doc. 1412*, 49.
[5] Report of General W. T. Sherman, 40 Cong., 2 sess., *House Exec. Doc. 1367*, 4–5.

tances involved, in nearly every case the troops arrived after the Indians had vanished from the scene.

It was impossible to predict where the next attack would occur; if the military commander attempted to concentrate on an area supposed to be threatened, the Indians, with their superb scouting, would immediately be aware of the commander's intentions and strike elsewhere.

During the Civil War, General Sheridan had attempted to thwart John Mosby and his Rangers in the Shenandoah Valley by organizing a special scout detachment under Harry Young. Sheridan decided to try the same scheme here. There were only a few men with the necessary qualifications and on whom he could rely, but, before the outbreak occurred, he had hired three civilian scouts to serve under Lieutenant Beecher. They would have been most useful at this time, but unfortunately, they were put out of action shortly after the first raid. Beecher sent two of the three scouts— William Comstock and Abner S. Grover—to obtain information from the Indians in Turkey Leg's camp on the Solomon River, for he was supposed to be an old friend. The Indians pretended to be friendly only to shoot and kill Comstock and seriously wound Grover, who managed to escape in the darkness.[6]

General Sherman was visiting General Sheridan at Fort Leavenworth when the first reports of the Saline and Solomon outrages were received. Sheridan at once went to the front to investigate conditions and initiate emergency measures. In his reports, he described the outbreak to be an explosion of attacks occurring simultaneously along the line of the Smoky Hill and Arkansas. Such was not the case. For two days after the first attack nothing happened. Then on August 12 there were two raids in the Fort Dodge area, with stock stolen, but no casualties. During the succeeding ten days no attacks were reported. Then, beginning on August 22, there were robberies or killings, or both, nearly every day until October 21.[7]

The official list of "murders, outrages, and depredations" shows that they occurred in succession, not simultaneously. They were, however, in different areas, and could not have been perpetrated by one band or war party. General Sheridan claimed that the raids along the Smoky Hill were the exclusive work of the Cheyennes, Arapahoes, and part of the Sioux, while the raiding on the Arkansas and Cimarron was done principally by the Kiowas "under their chief, Satanta, aided by some of the Comanches."[8]

[6] P. H. Sheridan, *Personal Memoirs*, II, 292–94.

[7] "List of murders, outrages, and depredations committed by Indians from the 3rd of August to 24th of October, 1868, officially reported to Hdqs. Dept. of the Missouri, in the field," 40 Cong., 3 sess.; *House Exec. Doc. 1367*, 12–16.

[8] Sheridan, *Personal Memoirs*, II, 294.

121

There is no evidence implicating the Kiowas and Comanches whatever, except a report by Brevet Brigadier General William Penrose stating that an attack on a train near Sand Creek on October 14, in which Mrs. Clara Blinn and her child were captured, was made by Satanta's Kiowas.[9] But Satanta was raiding near Fort Griffin, Texas, at this time. Furthermore, in November Mrs. Blinn and her child were found dead in what was probably a Cheyenne village, not a Kiowa, during the Battle of the Washita.[10]

It is possible, even probable, that a few individual Kiowas were members of the war parties in 1868; and it is still more likely that Arapahoes participated in the raids, for they were closely associated with the Cheyennes. But it appears that, with a few exceptions, the attacks were mostly made by Cheyennes. This idea is borne out by the affidavit of Edmund Guerrier and by statements made by the Cheyenne women captured by Custer at the Battle of the Washita. They stated that even the depredations along the line of the Arkansas were committed by the Cheyennes and Arapahoes.[11]

Wynkoop, though disturbed by the murders in the Solomon and Saline valleys, was still inclined to make excuses for his Indians. He thought that the majority of the Cheyennes were not in favor of the raids, but that the chiefs were unable to restrain their young men. He even told Sheridan that Little Rock and his band were innocent and should be protected. In this idea he was mistaken, for ample evidence was found later that Little Rock's band did furnish members to the raiding party. Superintendent Murphy disagreed with Wynkoop about the innocence of the Indians. He believed that they deserved punishment. The difference of opinion between Wynkoop and his superior was probably the reason for Wynkoop's terminal leave of absence late in August.[12]

Sheridan agreed that Little Rock, if innocent, should be protected. But instead of bringing his band to Fort Larned, where he would be safe from attack, Little Rock fled southward, and so did many others of the Cheyenne and Arapaho tribes. Brevet Brigadier General (Lieutenant Colonel, Third Infantry) Alfred Sully, who was now the commander of the District of the Upper Arkansas, invited Little Raven and other Arapaho chiefs to come to

[9] "List of murders, outrages, etc.," 40 Cong., 3 sess., *House Exec. Doc , 1367*, 15.

[10] Older Kiowas, including Satanta's daughter, told me in 1934, that their camps during and after the Battle of the Washita were at the mouth of Rainy Mountain Creek, over fifty miles downstream from the battle. However, there may have been a few Kiowas camped near Black Kettle's village.

[11] *Army and Navy Journal*, Vol. VI (January 2, 1869), 306.

[12] Edward W. Wynkoop, "Story of Edward Wanshear Wynkoop," *Kansas Historical Collections*, Vol. XIII (1913–14), 73–78, shows that Wynkoop never held any job for more than a few years.

Fort Dodge under a flag of truce. They were interviewed there on August 20 by General Sheridan, who offered to feed them during the winter if they would surrender. The Indians agreed to this proposal, but did not come in. Sheridan claims that they were the first to attack Sully's expedition, which marched south from Fort Dodge on September 7.[13]

The purpose of Sully's expedition was to locate and attack the villages of the runaway Indians, which were reported to be on the Cimarron, some forty or fifty miles south of Fort Dodge. Sully had nine companies of the Seventh Cavalry, a twelve-pounder howitzer, and a supply train of thirty wagons escorted by Company F, Third Infantry—a total of nearly six hundred men.[14] The guides were John Smith, a squawman who spent a good deal of his time with the Cheyennes, Ben Clark, another frontiersman who had married a Cheyenne woman, and Amos Chapman. All three were experienced plainsmen, and the Indians' skill in concealing their tracks is indicated by the failure of these men to locate the villages or even the main trails leading away from the vacated sites.

On the afternoon of August 10, the head of the column encountered an Indian rear guard of some twenty braves below the Cimarron. The Indians withdrew, skillfully delaying Sully's advance, which was geared to the rate of the wagon train and its infantry escort.[15]

The next morning the Indians attacked the rear of Sully's column as it was pulling out of camp, and killed one man and wounded another. Soon afterwards a heavier attack was made on the left rear of the column. The Indians kept up this harassment throughout the day, until, in the evening, Sully reached camp on the North Canadian (also called Beaver Creek), upstream from the confluence with Wolf Creek. During the day, the cavalry had made several fruitless attempts to run the Indians to earth. This convinced Sully that he could not overtake the savages, so he closed his column on the wagon train and plodded steadily southward, hoping finally to come upon the villages.

On the following day, the twelfth, the column was again attacked when it reached Wolf Creek. The march was similar to that of the previous day, with the Indians executing delaying tactics to cover the flight of their villages. One of the soldiers later said they marched down the North Canadian, on which they camped that night. This statement indicates that they

---

13 Sheridan to Sherman, Sept. 26, 1868, 40 Cong., 3 sess., *House Exec. Doc. 1367*, 12.

14 Report of Major General P. H. Sheridan, October 15, 1868, 40 Cong., 3 sess., *House Exec. Doc. 1367*, 18.

15 "General Sully's Expedition," *Army and Navy Journal*, Vol. VI (October 3, 1868), 102.

struck Wolf Creek near its confluence with the North Canadian and marched southeast along the latter stream.

> The following day we progressed easily until we reached the middle fork of the Canadian. On the south bank of this stream is a range of steep and heavy sand hills, covered with a thick growth of scrub dogwood. In these hills the Indians had ensconced themselves, and when we came up essayed to stop our progress.
>
> They delayed us only so long as was necessary to halt and deploy, when, after a few desultory shots, they gave up a position that 100 men could have held against us for at least a day. Here we encountered a difficulty which no amount of bravery could overcome. The sandhills were absolutely impassible for the wagons. The trail scattered. We were in a country no white man had ever traversed and our guides were perfectly at sea. The season is unusually dry. To venture into these hills without a guide would have been perfectly useless, because we were convinced that the lodge-pole trail which led into the hills was not the true trail of the village but merely a decoy. The other trail we have not been able to find . . . . We keep them from hunting, and when we get some guides we have sent for, we will have their [the Indians'] families, which to them will be a disheartening blow. Mutual confidence exists between the troops and General Sully, who has convinced us all that his experiences and wisdom will eventually carry us to success.[16]

The optimistic note on which this dispatch ended was not justified by the results of the expedition. The soldiers ran out of food before the Indians did, and had to turn back to Fort Dodge.

It should not be surprising that such reliable scouts as Ben Clark and Amos Chapman failed to follow the Indian trail and were unacquainted with the country south of the Cimarron. They were now in Kiowa and Comanche country, while they had spent their lives with the Cheyennes in villages north of the Arkansas.

Sheridan now had a scout detachment of the type that had proved so useful to him during the Civil War organized by his aide, Major (Brevet Colonel) George A. Forsyth. It contained fifty civilian frontiersmen; Lieutenant Fred Beecher, who had been so active in scouting while stationed at Fort Wallace; and Doctor John M. Mooers.

The chief scout was Abner "Sharp" Grover, whose back wound, suffered when Comstock was killed, had not entirely healed. Two other scouts, whose names later became familiar around Fort Reno and Fort Sill, were Pierre Trudeau and Simpson E. Stilwell, better known as Jack Stilwell.

[16] *Ibid.*

Forsyth had enlisted his men at Forts Harker and Hays, where, according to Sheridan, there were numerous bushy "Petes," "Jacks," and "Jims" hanging around. Though most of these self-designated "Indian scouts" were false alarms, Forsyth had rounded up several good shots who were to prove themselves in battle. While Sully was chasing the Arapaho and Cheyenne bands south of the Arkansas, Forsyth took his detachment to Fort Wallace, and from there rode northwest, where William F. "Buffalo Bill" Cody said they would probably find the villages of the Cheyenne Dog Soldiers.

On September 17, Forsyth was attacked by several hundred Indians on the Arikaree Fork of the Republican River. The fight was a classic, full of excitement and heroism on both sides and with all the color and drama of a battle with Plains Indians. It has been recounted too many times to be told in detail here, and it has been made into at least one film story.[17] The site of the battle is a few miles inside Colorado and near the boundaries of that state, Nebraska, and Kansas. The engagement is known as the Battle of the Arikaree or Beecher's Island. The latter name is in memory of Fred Beecher, who was one of the first killed. Forsyth also lost Dr. Mooers, six enlisted scouts, and was himself seriously wounded. The Indians made numerous close charges, but did not succeed in overwhelming the detachment. The most prominent Indian killed was the famous Cheyenne war chief, Roman Nose.

After a three-day siege, Jack Stilwell and Trudeau volunteered to go for help. They succeeded in evading the Indians and made their way toward Fort Wallace. En route they met a company of the Tenth Cavalry, which rode to Forsyth's relief, as did Colonel Bankhead from Fort Wallace with a large detachment. Stilwell, only nineteen at this time, was an experienced scout. Trudeau, a small, uneducated man, was called "Avalanche" because he had applied that name to an ambulance. He had been the butt of a number of jokes played by his rough companions, but they regarded him with great respect after his brave exploit.[18]

While Sully was in the field, Captain George W. Graham with a company of the Tenth Cavalry was also sent out from Fort Wallace to afford protection to the stage road leading west toward Denver. On September 15, he was attacked on Big Sandy Creek, some twenty miles west of Cheyenne Wells,

[17] This engagement is covered thoroughly in George A. Forsyth, *Thrilling Days of Army Life*, 1–75; Sheridan, *Personal Memoirs*, 302–306; and George Bird Grinnell, *The Fighting Cheyennes*.

[18] Colonel Homer Wheeler, *The Frontier Trail*, 34, 37.

by a hundred Indians, and another typically indecisive battle occurred.[19] Graham was an enthusiastic fighter but of a character not often found among army officers. He had been paroled from a penitentiary in New York State to enlist in the army during the Civil War and had actually attained the rank of captain. Some time subsequent to 1868, he was dismissed for selling government horses. Then he shot two men while trying to rob a paymaster. He was arrested, but escaped, was recaptured and sentenced to the penitentiary in Colorado. He again escaped, was recaptured in St. Louis, and served out his term. He was finally shot and killed while serving as a mine guard in Colorado.[20] The West seemed to attract men of this type in those stormy days.

On September 29, seven companies of the Fifth Cavalry arrived at Fort Harker from the East, and after being re-equipped were sent out under Brevet Colonel W. B. Royall, Major, Fifth Cavalry, to hunt Indians in the country north of Harker. Royall was a veteran cavalryman with a fine reputation, but he did not find any Indians.[21] Shortly after this expedition, Major Eugene A. Carr, Fifth Cavalry, arrived and superseded Royall, for Carr was a brevet major general. The Fifth Cavalry was reinforced at Fort Wallace by Graham's and Carpenter's companies of the Tenth Cavalry and moved north from Fort Wallace on the basis of better information of the enemy. Carr was attacked by the Indians on Beaver Creek. In a fight that lasted six hours, he reported having killed nine Indians while suffering only three men wounded.[22] In this engagement the Indians were, as usual, on the offensive and certainly were not defeated.

On October 12, General Sully ordered Custer's portion of the Seventh Cavalry, who were camped south of Fort Dodge, to make another scout to the south as far as Medicine Lodge Creek, then turn north to the Big Bend of the Arkansas. Custer saw a few Indians and had several small skirmishes, but what Indians he did encounter were probably scouts. Customarily, the Indians scouted in pairs, for the purpose of keeping the military forces under observation. Custer saw no villages or traces of villages.[23]

During the army's summer and fall operations, the Indians were not struck in their most vulnerable points, for their food supplies and extra

[19] Report of Major General P. H. Sheridan, October 15, 1868, 40 Cong., 3 sess., *House Exec. Doc. 1367*, 18ff.
[20] Wheeler, *The Frontier Trail*, 75.
[21] Report of Major General P. H. Sheridan, 40 Cong., 3 sess., *House Exec. Doc. 1367*, 19.
[22] *Ibid.*, 19–20.
[23] *Ibid.*

horses and ammunition were kept in their villages, which had not been touched. Thus, they had not yet suffered defeat. In most fights, they either had the initiative or were carrying out skillful covering and delaying operations. The Indians were having the best of it.

While the Cheyennes, with some of their allies—the Arapahoes—were carrying out their successful raids in Kansas and Colorado, the Kiowas and some of the Comanches remained near Fort Larned. Their chiefs, who were in favor of maintaining the peace, notably Kicking Bird and his cousin Stumbling Bear, thus far had generally been successful in keeping their warriors in hand. Satanta went on a raid to the Brazos River in Texas and did not return to the villages until after they had departed for Fort Cobb.[24] The Kiowas do not recall any parties out during the summer and fall of 1868, at least north of the Canadian, except possibly a small one led by Stumbling Bear. He took a few men back to the scene of the disastrous fight with the Utes to recover the bodies of Heap of Bears and his companions who were slain there. They found the spot and bundled up the remains of their tribesmen, by this time skeletons.[25]

Sheridan, however, thought that the Kiowas were dealing falsely with him, that the warriors were out aiding the Cheyennes or attacking Sully. He wished to get them away from the Arkansas River and preferably back to Fort Cobb. The Kiowas were willing to go, and so were the Comanches. In fact, when the Kiowas left the Arkansas River in the fall of 1868 they never again, as a people, returned to that river.[26] But Sheridan wished them to move under the charge of their new agent, General Hazen. William B. Hazen (Colonel, Sixth Infantry, and Brevet Major General), had been loaned by the War Department to the Commissioner of Indian Affairs to act as an agent or local superintendent for the five tribes in place of Wynkoop and Leavenworth, both of whom had departed, until regular agents could be appointed and brought to the field.

Hazen's instructions from Sherman were to go to Fort Cobb and set up an agency for all Indians who wished to stay out of the war:

> The object is for the War Department and the Interior Department, to afford the peaceful Indians every possible protection, support, and encouragement . . . . It may be that General Sheridan will be forced to invade the reser-

[24] Nye, *Carbine and Lance*, 51, 58; Mooney, "Calendar History," 324.
[25] Statement to author by Andrew Stumbling Bear, son of Chief Stumbling Bear, 1935; Mooney, "Calendar History," 324, 326.
[26] Mooney, "Calendar History," 324.

vation in pursuit of hostile Indians; if so I will instruct him to do all he can to spare the well-disposed; but their only safety now is in rendezvousing at Fort Cobb.[27]

The Indians were allowed to go on a buffalo hunt while Hazen was making arrangements for their subsistence after they arrived at Fort Cobb. They were supposed to return to Larned after the hunt, and then go to Cobb with Hazen. Instead, they followed the herds so far south that they decided to report to Cobb and not to return to Fort Larned. This caused Sheridan some anxiety, for he thought the Indians had employed a trick to get their families to a safe place while the braves again went on the warpath. But when Hazen came to Fort Cobb, the Kiowas had already arrived and had left on a hunting expedition to the Washita. The Comanches were on the Canadian, but were expected to arrive shortly.[28]

Captain Henry Alvord and one company each of the Tenth Cavalry and the Sixth Infantry had been sent to Fort Cobb from Fort Arbuckle to act as military protection to the new agency. Since the post was in ruins, the troops started to rebuild it. Colonel Hazen arrived on November 7, and the Indians began coming in soon afterwards. He received a friendly reception from the Penateka chiefs Tosawi and Asa-Havey, who had been on good terms with the whites since before the Civil War. The Yapparikas and the Kiowas began their bullying tactics with Hazen, just as they had with Leavenworth, showing that they respected only force. Hazen asked for a back-up force and was supplied to a limited extent—Major Kidd and his squadron of the Tenth Cavalry were sent from Arbuckle. En route they were met at Cottonwood grove by a large band of Kiowas and Comanches, who ordered Kidd to return to Arbuckle. Kidd kept on to Fort Cobb. When he reported this episode to Sheridan, the General said, "I'll take the starch out of them before I get through with them."[29]

[27] William B. Hazen, "Some Corrections of 'Life on the Plains,' " *Chronicles of Oklahoma*, Vol. III (December, 1925), 303. A full account of Hazen's activities is in his report, "Hazen to Sherman," "Sheridan Papers," Container 72, 377–78.

[28] Nye, *Carbine and Lance*, 55–56.

[29] *Ibid.*, 56.

14. SHERIDAN'S WINTER CAMPAIGN

Before the end of August, 1868, General Sheridan realized that he was facing a widespread outbreak rather than isolated raids. He also knew that his two cavalry regiments, the Seventh and the Tenth, could not round up and punish the elusive savages while the Indian ponies were in good flesh. A winter campaign would be necessary, one that would comb the prairie from several directions and strike the Indian winter camps and destroy their food supplies.

He applied for more cavalry, and seven companies of the Fifth Cavalry were shipped from Virginia and the Carolinas.[1] The postwar army was so small and its commitments so numerous that General Grant could do no better. Governor Samuel J. Crawford of Kansas raised and turned over to General Sheridan the Nineteenth Kansas Volunteer Cavalry. General Sherman could not leave the Platte country unprotected, but he sent six companies of the Twenty-seventh Infantry under its lieutenant colonel, Brevet Brigadier General L. P. Bradley, across the Republican to help drive the Cheyennes south from the Smoky Hill and the Arkansas. These troops did not reach the Republican until September 25, however, and the Fifth Cavalry did not arrive at Fort Harker until the twenty-ninth.[2]

While these reinforcements were being brought into the district, Sherman and Sheridan, who had demonstrated during the Civil War that they were master logisticians, carefully prepared for the campaign by bringing in over five hundred tons of rations and distributing them in advance depots and by securing other supplies. Some of these rations had to be hauled five hundred miles by wagon, and this, together with the huge trains that would accompany the main column, used all the wagons and animals in that part of the state. As a result, the Interior Department was unable immediately to send rations to Fort Cobb, where the new agency for the Kiowas and Comanches was to be built.[3]

[1] Report of General W. T. Sherman, November 1, 1868, 40 Cong., 3 sess., *House Exec. Doc. 1367*, 5.

[2] Report of General P. H. Sheridan, October 15, 1868, 40 Cong., 3 sess., *House Exec. Doc. 1367*, 19.

[3] Report of General P. H. Sheridan, November 1, 1869, 41 Cong., 2 sess., *House Exec. Doc. 1412*, 45.

Sheridan's plan was to send his main column, under Sully and consisting of the Seventh Cavalry with a battalion of infantry as support, south from the vicinity of Fort Dodge to the confluence of Beaver Creek (in Indian Territory) and Wolf Creek, where they would be joined by the Nineteenth Kansas Cavalry. Here Sully would establish an advance base from which the cavalry would search for the Indian villages. A smaller force from Fort Bascom, New Mexico, under Major Andrew W. Evans, would move east and operate along the Canadian River. A third auxiliary column under General Eugene A. Carr would march southeast from Fort Lyon. Sheridan regarded the last two forces as "beaters-in," and he did not expect them to strike much.[4]

It was a task of considerable magnitude to haul the vast quantities of rations, forage, ammunition, and other supplies for a campaign estimated to last at least three months. Furthermore, some refitting of units was required. The troops were already a bit bedraggled from spending two months of hot weather fruitlessly chasing the depredating Indians. New equipment was needed in some instances and repairs in other cases. Some remounts were needed by the cavalry.

With all this, the harassed post commanders still tried to keep up the normal post routine and, above all, not to neglect their paperwork. They were always under the threat that an inspector general would descend upon them from district or department headquarters. Below are samples of the problems they faced.[5]

At Fort Wallace the post commander took time out to requisition letter-size paper, foolscap paper, pens, and pencils. When these were not forthcoming through normal supply channels he told his post quartermaster to buy them on the open market. The AAG, Headquarters District of the Upper Arkansas tore his hide off for this action, and for a time the poor fellow feared he would have to pay for the articles out of his own pocket.

The post adjutant subscribed to the Cincinnati *Commercial* so that the people on the post might read about the murders and robberies that were being committed back in civilization. District headquarters noted, with deep suspicion, that he was taking ten copies. The adjutant was in a quandary about whether to give some plausible but imaginative excuse or tell the truth, which was that the post was taking ten copies to fill the mail sack. Otherwise the postmaster at the rail terminal would hold up delivery of the mail until a full sack had accumulated.

---

[4] *Ibid.*
[5] The examples are from the "Letter Book, Fort Wallace."

Post headquarters at Fort Wallace was in a stew all summer over the shortage of forms; administration nearly broke down.

Captain Lauffer, the post quartermaster, had an office adjacent to that of the adjutant. Nevertheless, communications such as the following were delivered to him in writing rather than orally, a standard procedure:

> Sir: What necessity exists that seven enlisted men be kept on duty in the QMD as carpenters, when you report no lumber on hand to repair the guard house?[6]

The post commander noted that he was signed for three cannon, a mountain howitzer, and two 3-inch Parrotts. Unfortunately, he could not fire them, not even for ceremonies, because his troops consisted only of cavalrymen and infantry. He requisitioned an artillery manual. This request was referred to Headquarters Department of the Missouri, who indorsed it to the Adjutant General who indorsed it to the Chief of Ordnance. This hearty fellow indorsed it all the way back down through channels, disapproving the request. He said that, since there were no artillery units at Fort Wallace, there was no basis for issue.

Captain Edmund Butler, who was temporarily post commander while Colonel Bankhead was out chasing Indians or rescuing Forsyth's scouts, had this to say to the Chief Commissary of Subsistence at district headquarters: "The A. C. of S. at this post has not been able to purchase beef, and the contractors still fail to deliver beef. We are forced to take buffalo meat, for which I have paid four cents a pound."[7]

Since Lieutenant Bates's deep well remained dry, the post used water from the creek, which occasioned the following letter:

Mr. Nichols
Agent U.S. Express Co. Pond Creek Station.

Sir:

The Commanding Officer direct me to say to you that the stream which supplies the post with water is enclosed in the corral of your station, and in consequence the drainage from the manure and offal finds its way into it. As this is very unpleasant he requests that you remove the corral from the course of the stream.

Very respectfully
your obedient servant
1st Lt. Granville Lewis
5th Inf. Post Adjutant[8]

[6] *Ibid.*, April 16, 1869.   [7] *Ibid.*, May 14, 1868.   [8] *Ibid.*, March 30, 1868.

By far the most difficult problem faced by Captain Butler, however, and one that caused him to seek advice from higher headquarters, is set forth in his letter to the AAAG, District of Upper Arkansas:

> Private George Paul and Private Patrick Kean of Company C, 7th Cavalry were tried for desertion and larceny and sentenced to be confined at hard labor for six months, and at the expiration of that time to have their heads shaved and be drummed out of the service. Subsequently they were again tried for assault on a citizen while they were undergoing sentence, and were sentenced to be confined for one month.
>
> In order to carry out the second sentence it is impossible to fully execute the first at the present time. The second period of confinement commencing at the expiration of the first, the prisoners cannot be drummed out of the service at that time. Is that portion of their first sentence to be executed at the end of the additional month, or can it be executed at that time without an order from the Department Commander authorizing its postponement until then?
>
> Respectfully ask instructions in the matter, as I have to act upon it, as early as the District Commander's convenience will permit.[9]

This was indeed a puzzler, but the action of the district commander is not in the record.

The campaign began in November. On the twelfth, General Sully started, with the Seventh Cavalry (under Custer, whom Sheridan had had restored to duty) and its supporting troops, from the Seventh Cavalry's camp twelve miles below Fort Dodge. Sully's destination was the point at which his previous expedition had turned back—at the confluence of Beaver and Wolf Creek. It was a cool day, though the sun was shining on the prairie, when the column lined up for departure. The cavalry was organized into a column of platoons, each platoon in line. The cavalry had often marched in this formation during the Civil War when contact with the enemy was imminent, for it permitted quick deployment. Custer had arranged the horses so that each platoon had horses of one color. There were the chestnuts, the bays, the sorrels, the blacks, and so on. The mounted band, who had white or gray, were near the head of the column, just to the rear of the commander and his staff. The band made a colorful display; for the drummer, with his drums fastened to either side of the pommel, twirled his batons and crossed them in striking the drums, and the trumpeters flourished their brass horns between the phrases of the music. It was like a circus parade, even including the "wildmen" in the procession—a dozen or more Osage warriors riding

[9] *Ibid.*, May 13, 1868

132

near Sully, all decked out in feathers and scarlet blankets. The wild animals were present, too, not in cages but sprinting away from the column as it approached—buffalo, antelope, deer, and smaller game such as jack rabbits. The Indian scouts and some of the military were permitted to stage an occasional chase.[10]

Mingled with the music of the band was the clank and rattle of trace chains and wagon bodies from Major Henry Inman's three hundred wagons, moving in columns abreast. The vehicles were loaded with rations, forage, and tools and materials to construct shelters for the supplies at the supply base.

Reveille sounded in darkness the next morning, breakfast followed quickly, and the force was under way as the eastern sky turned to rose. Camp was made early in the afternoon to permit several hours for grazing the horses before dark, when they were brought close to the tent lines and tethered to picket ropes pinned to the ground.

On the following day, the column crossed the trace of an Indian war party that had recently passed on its way north. Sully refused Custer permission to follow the track south to the village from which it had come. Later, after the Battle of the Washita, it was found that this war trail came from Black Kettle's village. After being supplied with food and ammunition by William "Dutch Bill" Griffenstein, the Indians left to raid the settlements along the Arkansas.[11] They killed Sheridan's couriers between Fort Dodge and Fort Larned and ran off the mules belonging to a wagon train. Then they rode to the vicinity of Fort Dodge where they killed and scalped two civilians. One of these was a hunter named Ralph Morrison, whose body was photographed shortly afterwards by William Soule, the only photograph Soule made of an atrocity, although he had many opportunities.[12]

On the fourth day, a sudden snowstorm whirled down from the north. The snow was mushy and mixed with rain, but on the following day the temperature dropped and the flakes turned dry. It was still snowing when the column reached its destination on November 20. Captain Hale, commanding the infantry, at once started his men cutting timber along the two creeks, to be used in building palisade storehouses for the supplies. The men, when not so engaged, quickly dug little burrows for themselves which they roofed over with their shelter halves.[13] In their year of service on the plains, they had learned how to take care of themselves in the field.

[10] *Army and Navy Journal*, Vol. II (January 2, 1869), 310.
[11] Nye, *Carbine and Lance*, 59.
[12] *Harper's Weekly*, January 16, 1869, p. 42.
[13] "Medical History, Camp Supply," 1.

The name "Camp Supply" first appeared in the post letter book on December 9, 1868; consequently, this may be taken as the first official mention of the name of the post. However, General Sully apparently used the term somewhat earlier, perhaps on the day the troops arrived at the spot.

As is often the case, the official correspondence files of the post fail to describe the truly historic events that were occurring in the area. The Battle of the Washita, the arrival of the Indian captives, and other matters of more than passing interest are not even mentioned. Instead, the post commander and his adjutant seem to have been concerned chiefly with such routine administrative matters as forwarding the proceedings of a Board of Survey (an army device for relieving supply officers of accountability for government property lost, stolen, or damaged).[14] Fortunately, the surgeon, Dr. George M. Sternberg, who many years later became surgeon general, faithfully recorded the more important events in his medical history of the post. In numerous instances medical histories of frontier posts give more and better information than do other sources.

The Nineteenth Kansas Volunteer Cavalry departed from Topeka on November 5, with orders to march straight through to the rendezvous at Camp Supply. But they had not arrived on November 23. Since their commander, Governor Crawford, was a full colonel, Sully—only a lieutenant colonel—would be outranked by the militia officer. Sully therefore issued an order assuming command of the expedition by virtue of his brevet rank of brigadier general. Custer, not to be outdone, issued an order taking command as a brevet major general. Sheridan, who arrived on the twenty-third sent Sully back to Fort Harker to resume his duties as district commander, thus confirming Custer as commander of the field expedition.[15]

Sheridan had seen the same trail of the Indian war party that Custer had wanted to track back to its source. On his arrival at Camp Supply, he told Custer to move out with the Seventh Cavalry, not waiting for the Nineteenth Kansas, and march north until he again found the Indian trail. He was to follow it back to the village from whence it came, and attack that village.[16]

Custer set forth on November 23. The Indian trail, if indeed such had been seen, must have been invisible by this time, for the snow was again falling heavily. Perhaps the pointed mention made of this trail by Sheridan and Custer in their reports was for the effect it would have on the public.

14 "Letter Book, Camp Supply," entry for December 9, 1868.
15 Nye, *Carbine and Lance*, 60.
16 Sheridan, *Personal Memoirs*, II, 312.

Sheridan and Custer must have learned the location of the Indian villages from their white scouts, several of whom had Indian wives and children in the tribes. If the place was familiar to Griffenstein, it must have been known to other plainsmen of the area. Sheridan must also have received word of the village from Henry Alvord, who had been visited by Indians from these villages early in the fall—in time for a copy of his report to have reached Sheridan's headquarters. Hazen also knew the location of Black Kettle's village but Hazen and Sheridan do not appear to have been in direct contact by courier at this time.

Black Kettle and several other Cheyenne and Arapaho chiefs and warriors had visited Hazen at Fort Cobb on the same day Sully arrived at Camp Supply. The chiefs gave Hazen the usual excuses for the summer raids—"I tried to keep my young men quiet but they wouldn't listen"—but protested that they all wanted peace. They said they were willing to move their villages to Fort Cobb and asked Hazen to stop the soldiers from coming down to fight them.

General Hazen gave the chiefs no comfort, explaining that he could not control General Sheridan, who was a war chief. He advised them to return to their country and make their peace with General Sheridan.[17]

In reporting this powwow to General Sherman, Hazen explained:

> Big Mouth was accompanied by Spotted Wolf and Black Kettle by Little Robe. To have made peace with them would have brought to my camp most of those now on the warpath south of the Arkansas, and as General Sheridan is to punish those at war, and might follow them in afterwards, a second Chivington affair might occur, which I could not prevent . . . . The Kiowas and Comanches are all of the opinion that the suit for peace by the Cheyennes and Arapahoes is not sincere beyond the chiefs who spoke.
>
> The young men who accompanied these chiefs expressed pleasure that no peace was made, as they would get more mules, and that next spring the Sioux and northern bands were coming down and would clean out this entire country.[18]

The snow was dazzling in the bright sunshine when Custer set forth on the morning of the twenty-third. He did not go north in accordance with his alleged instructions because, as he knew full well, the Indian villages were on the headwaters of the Washita, due south of Camp Supply. He rode fifteen miles south, following Wolf Creek to what is now known as Custer's Crossing, where he crossed and went into camp. When the Osage scouts confessed that they could not find the Indian trail, Custer set the course

[17] Hazen to Sherman, November 20, 1868, "Sheridan Papers."   [18] *Ibid.*

135

south with his pocket compass, proof enough, if any was needed, that he knew where his quarry lay.[19]

After a march of some forty-five miles, they reached the Canadian north of Antelope Hills. They crossed the hills and on the morning of the twenty-sixth found a fresh Indian trail in the snow, perhaps made by a returning raiding party. Custer sent a squadron ahead under Major Elliott to follow the trail. The wagon train was corralled and left under the guard of the infantry escort. Toward evening the advance party sighted the Indian villages, partly concealed by trees, along the Washita. The regiment closed up and waited within one-half mile of the most westerly village to make an early morning attack.

The Seventh Cavalry charged into Black Kettle's village at dawn on the twenty-seventh while the soldiers cheered and the band played "Garry Owen," the regiment's marching song.

At first most of the Indians tried to flee, resulting in a massacre, although without much of the exaggerated brutality that had stained the Chivington affair. A number of women and children were killed, for it was not easy to distinguish them from warriors in the confusion and twilight. However, fifty-three women were captured. Custer admitted that, except for women and children under eight, they did not try to take captives.[20]

Black Kettle and Little Rock were killed. No doubt this was a result of soldiers firing at all fleeing Indians without knowing who they were. But, since many of the officers had on previous occasions shaken hands with Black Kettle, and might be said to have been acquainted with him, the affair must be regarded with a certain distaste.

Custer reported having killed 103 Indians and capturing 875 horses, besides large quantities of supplies. The Indians claim far fewer were killed. This illustrates a feature of casualty reporting by Indians. In talking to old Indians about fights of this kind, it is noticeable that the informants mention very few deaths on their side. This is not due to an effort to deceive or to play down their own losses. Indians tend to state only what they saw themselves or were told by a close relative. Further, the Indians are superstitious about mentioning the names of dead tribesmen, and this custom has, over the years, made accurate tallying of Indian casualties impossible. In the case of the Battle of the Washita, Custer had ample opportunity to count the dead on the field, and this tally was verified by Sheridan when he visited the site a few days later.

19 Custer's Report, "Sheridan Papers," Container 73.
20 *Army and Navy Journal*, Vol. VI (January 2, 1869), 306.

Custer lost two officers killed, Captain Louis M. Hamilton, the grandson of Alexander Hamilton, and Major Joel H. Elliott who, with nineteen men, had become separated from the command while pursuing Indians. They were surrounded and killed. Three officers and eleven enlisted men were wounded. One of these was Captain Albert Barnitz, who had led his company in the fight against the Indians at Fort Wallace in June, 1867. Barnitz' wounds caused his retirement and death in 1870.

All the Indian ponies were rounded up and shot. This was a distasteful task for the cavalrymen, but it was the most effective method of eventually bringing about the subjugation of the Plains tribes. Once their means of transportation was gone, they could neither fight nor feed themselves. They were subdued finally by starvation, not bullets.

After the ponies were killed, Custer withdrew. Many Indians were coming up from camps farther down the Washita, and the situation was dangerous. Before pulling out he burned the village, but he made no effort to find Elliott and his detachment. For this reason, Custer lost some of his former admirers among the Seventh Cavalry.

Sheridan, at Camp Supply, received the first word of Custer's fight from California Joe, a woolly, unkempt scout who came to the post on November 29 with the news. The following day Custer arrived with his regiment and the Indian prisoners. Colonel Crawford returned the same day with a few men, and the remainder of his Kansans followed shortly. They had been lost in the snow-filled canyons of the Cimarron and had been subsisting for over a week on buffalo meat. Many of their horses were dying from starvation and exposure, and the regiment had to be partially dismounted [21]

Sheridan had wished to follow Custer's strike with an immediate pursuit to the south, but it was December 7 before the two regiments were sufficiently rehabilitated to make another march. On that day they set forth for Fort Cobb, going first to the Washita to visit the scene of Custer's fight and then following the Washita southeast. Near the Washita battlefield they found the bodies of Elliott and his men and obtained identification of Mrs. Clara Blinn's remains—one of the Kansas Volunteers recognized her even though her features were disfigured from powder burns when she had been killed by an Indian. Other evidence implicating Black Kettle's band in recent atrocities was collected.[22]

The march to Fort Cobb was hampered by deep snow and rough terrain. The temperature was sixteen degrees below zero. Instead of following the

[21] Sheridan, *Personal Memoirs*, II, 321–22.
[22] Nye, *Carbine and Lance*, 71.

divide between the Canadian and the Washita, Sheridan stayed close to the Washita to avoid making dry camps at night. Consequently, there were many tributaries that his supply wagons could cross only after much pioneer work.[23] To their surprise, the guides noticed an old wagon road. They had believed that the area had never before been traversed by wheeled vehicles, not knowing that Captain Randolph B. Marcy had passed that way in 1849 with a party of wayfarers bound for California.[24]

The bulk of the Kiowa tribe and many of the Comanches had been camped at the mouth of Rainy Mountain Creek at the time of the Custer attack on Black Kettle's village. When they heard of this disaster, they fled to the west end of the Wichita Mountains and camped at the confluence of Sweetwater Creek and the North Fork of the Red River. A few days later, a few of them recovered from their fright sufficiently to return to Rainy Mountain, a locality much frequented by Kiowas even today. Eagle Heart and Satanta talked to Captain Alvord who reassured them sufficiently that by December 10 three-fourths of the Kiowas were again camped at the mouth of Rainy Mountain Creek and many of the Comanches were back at Fort Cobb.[25] A band of Nokonis was at Soldier Spring, and the Kiowa band led by Woman's Heart was nearby at Sheep Mountain.[26]

General Hazen, acting under previous instructions from Sherman, gave the Kiowas a letter stating that the Kiowas camped twenty miles upstream from Fort Cobb were friendly.

On the night of December 16, the Indians saw the lights of Sheridan's campfires. The next day several of their chiefs, including Satanta and Lone Wolf, rode out on the high ground west of the present town of Mountain View and met Custer and Sheridan. They showed Hazen's letter and proposed that their bands accompany the soldiers to Fort Cobb. Custer and Sheridan's adjutant, Colonel J. Schuyler Crosby, who still thought Satanta guilty of the capture and slaying of Mrs. Blinn and her child, refused to shake hands with him. When Sheridan joined the parley he and his staff drew their pistols and made prisoners of the two chiefs. He told them to send Satanta's handsome son, Tsa'l-aute (Cry of the Wild Goose), to the rest of the band with an order that they come in at once and move under troop escort to Fort Cobb.[27]

The other Indians, who had remained at a little distance, saw this action,

23 Sheridan, *Personal Memoirs*, II, 332.
24 Nye, *Carbine and Lance*, 71.
25 *Ibid.*, 72.
26 *Ibid.*
27 *Ibid.*, 73.

138

and the whole village immediately took flight, not stopping until they reached Elk Creek, twenty miles away.[28]

The expedition went on to Fort Cobb, where Sheridan found the Indians so frightened they did not sleep at night and kept their ponies saddled for instant flight. Satanta and Lone Wolf, held shackled in a guard tent, kept promising that their people were on the way in. Finally Sheridan informed them that if the Indians did not arrive by sundown he would hang the chiefs to the nearest tree. Tsa'l-aute scooted off to carry the ultimatum to the tribe. The Indians came in as ordered, and were issued rations. Sheridan was convinced that his stern threat had produced the desired results.[29]

The Kiowas assured me, however, that Tsa'l-aute had said nothing to them about the threatened hanging of Satanta and Lone Wolf. Tsa'l-aute had told them that if they arrived at Fort Cobb that evening they would receive food in plenty.[30]

[28] *Ibid.*

[29] Sheridan, *Personal Memoirs*, II, 335–36.

[30] Nye, *Carbine and Lance*, 75. Several Kiowas told me in 1934 that if they had known of the threat to hang Satanta and Lone Wolf they would not have come in at all. Satanta's son was clever enough to know this; hence he used the never failing bait of free food.

15. NO MORE TREATIES

$\mathbf{M}$ost of the southern Comanches and the Kiowa-Apaches were clustered about Fort Cobb when Sheridan arrived, and most of the Kiowas came in as a result of the message delivered to them by Tsa'l-aute. Those still out included the Cheyennes, Arapahoes, Woman's Heart's Kiowas, the entire band of Quohada, and Mow-way's Kotchatekas. A Nokoni village under Arrow Point was at Soldier Spring, or arrived there from farther north after being flushed out by Evans.[1]

Evans' force departed from Fort Bascom on November 17 and marched down the North Canadian to Monument Creek. Here he barricaded his wagons and left them and all heavy impedimenta, guarded by his infantry company, while with his six cavalry companies and an artillery battery he continued toward Antelope Hills. He reached this region after the Battle of the Washita, which he did not know had occurred, but he struck the trail of some of the fleeing Indians, which led him southward toward the North Fork of the Red River.[2]

By December 23, Evans was near the west end of the Wichita Mountains. Instead of following the Indian trail into a gorge between the peaks, he circled around the west end of the range until he came to the southern end of the gap, where he hoped to intercept the Indians as they emerged. On Christmas Day, he located a village at Soldier Spring and made a surprise attack on it. At this time of year the sand hills bordering the North Fork are generally shrouded in a cold fog, at least until noon, and the fog probably enabled Evans to get close to the camp before the Indian sentries saw him.

The warriors rode forth, led by Arrow Point, and began firing on Evans' advance troops to cover the withdrawal of the women and children. The artillery came up at a trot, their guns were put in position, and two rounds were fired into the village. This scattered those Indians who had not yet fled, and stampeded their horses. Those Comanches who could catch their mounts rode away in haste. Others scrambled up the granite sides of the

[1] Nye, *Carbine and Lance*, 72.
[2] *Ibid.*, 78–79.

mountain and hid among the boulders. For the next hour or so both sides indulged in long-range shooting, but few casualties resulted.[3]

The Indians in the flats made a number of mounted charges, but Evans maneuvered his troops skillfully and drove the Comanches away. The Kiowas, having heard the artillery fire, came up to aid the Comanches, but they too were driven away. At length all the Indians disappeared, probably because their villages were now at a safe distance. A great many leaden balls had been flattened against the rocks, but few had found their marks. Evans reported twenty-five Indians killed, but in 1934 Comanche participants could remember only one—Arrow Point, who was hit in the mouth early in the fight. Evans had one man killed and two wounded.[4]

Horseback, Howea, and Habby-wake, all well known at Fort Sill in later years, were members of Arrow Point's band, but at the time of this fight they seem to have been at Fort Cobb.[5]

Colonel Evans destroyed the Indian lodges and their contents, including the winter supply of dried buffalo meat. He then returned to his supply train on the upper Washita and from there marched downstream to the mouth of Rainy Mountain Creek. He sent a detachment and wagons, under an officer, to Fort Cobb to pick up supplies and report the results of his campaign to General Sheridan. When his wagons returned, Evans went back to Fort Bascom.[6]

Major (Brevet Major General) Carr's column, which had gone southeast from Fort Lyon and scouted along the Canadian west of Antelope Hills, also carried out its assigned role in the general campaign. They fought no battles, and indeed saw no Indians other than a few strays, but the men suffered severely from frostbite and exposure, and lost many horses owing to the lack of good water and adequate forage. The hostile Indians saw this force from time to time, but kept out of its way. Thus the villages were forced to keep moving, and could not pause to hunt buffalo or rest their ponies. Soon they were exhausted, nearly starved, and ready to surrender.[7] Nevertheless, when peace emissaries visited them from Fort Cobb, most of the Cheyennes and Arapahoes still had enough spark to resist going to the reservation. Few of them returned until after Custer visited them in March.

Mow-way's Kotchatekas had been on the Staked Plains with the Quo-

[3] *Ibid.*, 79–80.
[4] *Ibid.*, 80–81.
[5] *Ibid.*, 79.
[6] *Ibid.*, 82.
[7] Report of Major E. A. Carr, "Sheridan Papers," Container 73, 655ff.

hada Comanches. The appearance of the forces of Evans and Carr, where it had been thought the white man would never go, frightened and discouraged these Indians. They went to Fort Bascom, where their chiefs surrendered. Major General George W. Getty, commanding the Department of New Mexico, seized Mow-way and six other Comanches and confined them in the guardhouse. Later they were transferred to Fort Leavenworth. On June 23 they were sent under guard to Fort Sill to be turned over to the post commander. The officer in charge of the guard and his men got drunk and were in a stupor during the latter part of the trip. Mow-way and his companions carried their guards on to Fort Sill and turned themselves in to General Grierson, much to his astonishment.[8]

Part of this long trip had been by rail. The Indians saw things that were beyond belief—scores of towns, thousands of white people, and above all the railroad train and the engine. Mow-way was so impressed that he never again thought seriously of fighting the white man, though he did take part in the stampede of 1874.

General Sheridan did not remain long at Fort Cobb. The cold weather abated and was succeeded by heavy rains that turned the area into a sea of mud. The troops were forced to abandon their little dugouts and move to higher ground. The officers sat on their bunks with their feet up to keep dry, and swapped stories about the Civil War. In retrospect it seemed more pleasant than the present campaign.[9]

At length Sheridan decided to move south to a better place described to him by Grierson, who had reconnoitered it the previous summer. On December 27, Grierson led a small party to the east end of the Wichita Mountains to check on the site, especially to see if the grass was still abundant.[10] Forage supposed to be forwarded from Fort Arbuckle was not coming through, and the horses were dying.

Grierson returned to Fort Cobb on the twenty-ninth and made a favorable report. Sheridan thereupon decided to move everything—troops, supplies, Indians, and agency—to the new location. On January 6, the rains stopped for a few days, permitting removal. Sheridan liked the new site so much that he decided to build a permanent post there. On January 8, he staked out the outline for the new post on a plateau where lay the remains of a long abandoned Wichita village.[11] It was near the junction of Cache

[8] Alvord to Grierson, May 5, 1869, "Sheridan Papers," Container 73, 706, 784; Nye, *Carbine and Lance*, 104.

[9] Nye, *Carbine and Lance*, 75.

[10] *Ibid.*, 75–77.

[11] *Ibid.*, 84–85.

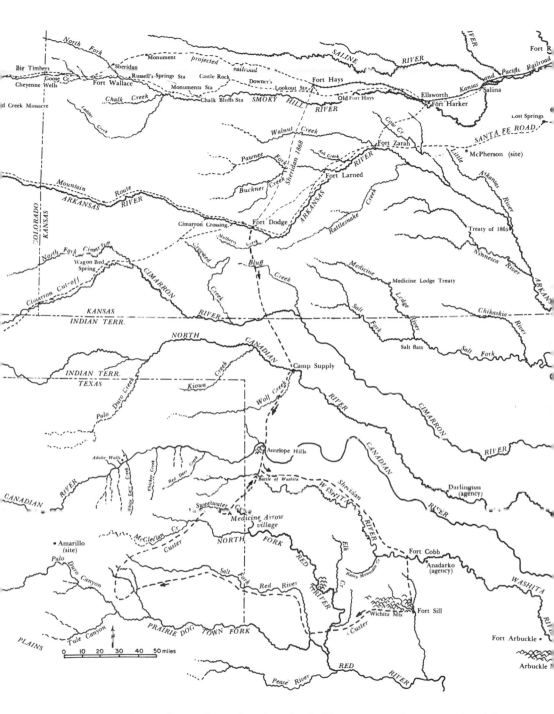

Sheridan's Winter Campaign, *showing the Indian country in 1868–69, with the initial routes of Sheridan and Custer from Fort Hays to Fort Sill and Custer's route to Medicine Arrow's Cheyenne village on Sweetwater Creek in March, 1869.*

Creek and Medicine Bluff Creek, and along the stream there was a good stand of hardwood trees. Also nearby was a plentiful supply of sweet water and a limestone outcrop from which building stone could be quarried. The stone buildings erected by the Tenth Cavalry during 1869 and 1870 are still in use by the United States Army Artillery and Missile Center.

At first the installation was called Camp Wichita, but Sheridan later named it Fort Sill in memory of his classmate Brigadier General Joshua W. Sill, who had been killed at the Battle of Stone's River in Tennessee.[12] The agency for the Kiowas, Kiowa-Apaches, and Comanches was built about a mile southeast of the post, but a few years later was moved to the present site of Anadarko. Sheridan expected the agency of the Cheyennes and Arapahoes to be at Camp Supply.

Sheridan went to Fort Arbuckle to speed up the hauling of supplies from there to Fort Sill. When he found that the trouble lay in the almost impassible roads from Arbuckle to Fort Gibson, he purchased fields of corn from Chickasaw farms and had the corn sent by wagon to Fort Sill.[13] This helped feed the cavalry horses, though it was too late to save many of them. But when the agent tried to issue corn to the Indians he met a storm of protest. The Indians complained that it hurt their teeth and made them sick. They did not know how to prepare it as food. Satanta and Taw-Haw with their bands rode north to Camp Supply to obtain rations but were rebuffed.

Sheridan held several conferences with the Indians, in which he spoke some plain words. He told them that there would not be a treaty. The Indians must surrender completely, settle down on their reservations, and behave themselves. Otherwise he would send his soldiers to destroy them. The Indians responded meekly and quite differently from their former defiance and impudence. They had no alternative.[14]

The Kiowas and Comanches did not again ride north to attack the settlements and roads. But they frequently raided in Texas and from there deep into Mexico—even as far as Durango. Occasionally they traveled to the land of the Utes and Navahos, and even raided around Fort Sill and their own agency—wherever there were horses, mules, and scalps to be taken. This continued for six years.

During the first week of February, 1869, Custer went with forty soldiers, using Little Robe and his friend Yellow Bear as guides, to the west end of the Wichitas to persuade the Cheyennes and Arapahoes to come to Fort

---

[12] *Ibid.*, 100.
[13] *Ibid.*, 87.
[14] *Ibid.*, 89–93.

Sill or Camp Supply.[15] He readily found Little Raven's village, and the chiefs agreed to move to Fort Sill. They asked for time, saying that their horses were very weak. The Cheyennes, hearing of Custer's approach, fled to the Staked Plains, followed by Custer's guides. Custer felt that Little Robe and Yellow Bear were not truly friendly, and he further heard that John Smith had warned the Cheyennes not to come in, that the soldiers were preparing a trap for them.[16]

Custer returned to Fort Sill, but set forth again on March 2 with the Seventh Cavalry, the Nineteenth Kansas, and a small wagon train, determined to drive the Indians in. After an arduous march, in which the troops at length were reduced to the necessity of eating horses that had dropped dead along the way, Custer found the Indians camped on Sweetwater Creek west of the boundary of what is now the Texas Panhandle. He had a parley with Stone Forehead, whom the whites called Medicine Arrow because he was the custodian of the sacred arrows. Custer learned that the Cheyennes were holding two young white women they had taken in Kansas in August.

Soon after this talk Custer seized four minor chiefs in what the Cheyennes still regard as an act of treachery, violating the laws of hospitality. By threatening to hang them, he forced the tribe to deliver the white women, but he did not release the hostages. The Indians had understood that to be a part of the deal.[17] Two were later killed and another severely wounded in a flare-up while they were in Kansas being transferred from one guard house to another.

The Cheyennes were eager to obtain the release of the women and children captured by Custer at the Battle of the Washita. Also, they were nearly starved, and were eating their animals. The chiefs promised Custer they would go to Camp Supply; therefore, he set forth ahead of them and they promised to follow. Once more the Indians were slow in reporting to the agencies. The Arapahoes arrived at Camp Supply on April 1, but the Cheyennes were much later, and the Dog Soldiers did not come in at all.[18]

Some of the two tribes were still near Fort Sill, and General Hazen had intended to hold them until all bands were assembled before sending them to their own reservation. When he saw that there was no chance in getting them together he sent them piecemeal to Camp Supply. On April 19, Red Moon fled with nearly half of those Cheyennes near the post, and six days

[15] *Ibid.*, 94–95.
[16] Custer, *My Life on the Plains*, 215–30.
[17] *Ibid.*, 231–51.
[18] Sheridan to Sherman, June 2, 1869, "Sheridan Papers," Container 73, 782.

later Little Robe, Minimic, and the rest of the Cheyennes disappeared after one of their braves had killed a teamster.[19]

It has been claimed that in a meeting of all the Cheyennes in May, Little Robe tried to persuade them to surrender at Camp Supply. This is not wholly true. He gave them their choice between surrendering and going north. He told the Dog Soldiers he had lost patience with them because of the trouble they had brought upon the tribe. Nah-to-mah, wife of John Smith, described the stormy meeting as follows:

> During the first week of May, 1869, the Cheyennes held a big talk on the Washita thirty miles upstream from old Fort Cobb, in order to decide what to do next. At the gathering, Little Robe, now the leading chief of the tribe, quarreled with the Dog Soldiers. He told them they had always been the cause of trouble with the whites; and that he, Little Robe, had determined to take his own people back to the reservation and settle down with Little Raven and the Arapahoes.
>
> The Dog Soldiers refused to go with him. Little Robe then ordered them to get out of the country; if they failed to do so he would join with the whites and drive them out. Tall Bull and White Horse of the Dogs replied that they would go north and join the Sioux. They said they would never make any peace that would compel them to settle down, that they had always been a free nation, and would remain so or die.
>
> The Dogs then left Little Robe's camp, and, throwing away any equipment that would impede them, started north. As they left they said they would make a big strike north of the Arkansas.[20]

At this same powwow John Smith delivered to Little Robe Agent Boone's promise that the Cheyenne women and children would be returned if Little Robe and his people came to the reservation and settled down.

Tall Bull's Cheyennes were now off the reservation and subject to attack wherever found. Sheridan had been promoted to lieutenant general and had succeeded Sherman as commander of the Division of the Missouri. He was, nevertheless, still keenly interested in completing the work of driving the five tribes south from the Arkansas River. When he learned of Tall Bull's flight to the Republican River, in Kansas, he ordered the Fifth Cavalry to the Department of the Platte to operate against the runaway Dog Soldiers.

The Fifth Cavalry, under General E. A. Carr, marched again from Fort Lyon, this time heading toward the northwest corner of Kansas.[21] On May

---

[19] Alvord to McKeever, April 24, 1869, "Sheridan Papers," Container 73, 711–13.

[20] Lieutenant Henry Jackson to McKeever, June 6, 1869, "Sheridan Papers," Container 73, 795–97.

[21] Captain George F. Price, *Across the Continent With the Fifth Cavalry*, 134 (hereinafter

13, 1869, as they were preparing to camp on Beaver Creek, the scouts discovered Indian signs. A detachment had followed the trail down the creek five miles, when they sighted a large village ahead. They started back with the news but encountered a party of warriors, who had been hunting buffalo and were returning to the village. The ensuing exchange of shots brought up the main bodies from each side.[22]

The Cheyennes fought a stubborn rear-guard action to cover the withdrawal of the village. At dark they disengaged and joined the women and children, who were in flight toward the Republican. The cavalry bivouacked and waited for their wagon train.

The pursuit was resumed the following day. On May 16, the Indians were overtaken on Spring Creek. Again the Dog Soldiers fought hard to enable their families to escape. Carr drove them vigorously, so that by the time they had reached Beaver Creek they had been forced to abandon much of their camp gear. Nevertheless, they succeeded in escaping.

The cavalry went to Fort McPherson to rest and refit. The Dog Soldiers, as they had promised Little Robe, made a strike on the settlements during May 21–29. They killed thirteen ranchers and kidnapped two young married women who were recent German immigrants, Maria Weichel and Susannah Allerdice.[23] The Seventh Cavalry, which had returned from Indian Territory, was unable to catch the raiders.

Carr was now told to clear the Republican River area of the hostiles. He headed back in that direction on June 9, his column having been reinforced by 150 Pawnee scouts under Major Frank North. Soon a series of encounters demonstrated that the Cheyennes were not intimidated or ready to give up. Twice when the troops appeared to have lost their trail, the hostiles bobbed out to disclose their presence by bold dashes at the cavalry horse herd.[24]

By July 8, General Carr knew that the two captured women were still alive. His Pawnee scouts had seen their shoe prints in the sand along a stream. He wished to rescue the captives before the Cheyennes vanished into the mountains to the northwest. Therefore, he advanced by forced marches on a parallel route in order to get ahead of them, while the Pawnees continued to exert direct pressure.[25]

referred to as Price, *Across the Continent*) ; Report of Major E. A. Carr, "Sheridan Papers," Container 73, 655ff.

[22] Price, *Across the Continent*, 134; Report of Major E. A. Carr, "Sheridan Papers," Container 73, 658.

[23] Price, *Across the Continent*, 136.

[24] *Ibid.*, 135–36.   [25] *Ibid.*, 137.

147

On July 11, the troops came upon the hostile camp near Summit Springs on the South Platte. After a concealed approach, Carr lined up his companies for a charge across level ground. A howling wind covered the noise of his deployment and advance.[26]

Carr had arranged his troops so they would strike the Indian village frontally and on both flanks. One company was assigned to capture the pony herd, off to one flank. It was an exciting charge, reaching almost to the village before the Indians knew it was coming. Captain Sam Sumner, son of the late Major General Edwin S. Sumner, describes what happened:

> The regiment was got together behind a ridge, which completely screened us, the Pawnee scouts on the left, nearest the village, Company D next, Companies C, H, A, G, and K on the right. At the command from the General we all made a rush. The Pawnees on my left had stripped for a fight and went in like red devils. I was ordered to keep up with them. We could not see the village and were riding for the herd, but on reaching the top of the next ridge, there was the village a little to our left and front. You never heard such a shout; the way we rode for it was a caution. Every company tried to get there first but I had the advantage of being the nearest. The Pawnees were with me and seeing themselves supported, pushed right ahead. It was a magnificent sight to see the Regulars rushing ahead at a run.
>
> The Indians we attacked were the Dog Soldiers, the worst rascals on the Plains. They are the same band that General Carr fought in May and the same ones that committed the depredations in Kansas some six weeks ago. They were moving west with their stock and property, and had camped to rest, feeling secure in their out-of-the-way camp. They were taken completely by surprise and did not have time to get anything away but some stock. I expected they would fight for their village, but they made only a feeble effort to stop us.
>
> We rushed through the village and on to the hills after them, about five miles, when we gave up the chase as our horses had given out . . . . We killed 73, captured 17 women and children, 560 head of stock, and their whole outfit. They left their lodges standing with everything in and around them, and this was all accomplished without the loss of a single man on our side.[27]

A more accurate count gave fifty-three Indians dead and over fifty wounded. Tall Bull was killed by Frank North in a ravine. Mrs. Allerdice was found dead and Mrs. Weichel was badly wounded.[28]

---

[26] *Ibid.*, 138.

[27] *Army and Navy Journal*, Vol. VI, (August 7, 1869), 802.

[28] Carr's report indicates that the white women may have been shot in the village, and not necessarily by Tall Bull.

Remnants of Tall Bull's band escaped into the Sioux country. Others turned south, hoping to be forgiven and permitted to rejoin the other Cheyennes around Camp Supply. This privilege was granted them by a committee of the United States Indian Commission, then inspecting conditions on the frontier. Some 150 members of the Dog Soldier band were allowed to come in and ask for peace, stating that they were tired of war.[29]

This marked the virtual end of the military operation initiated by General Sheridan to drive the five Plains tribes south from the Arkansas and into their reservations. There was to be some lingering discontent and intermittent trouble. The Kiowas and Comanches, occasionally accompanied by small groups of Cheyennes, raided each summer in Texas and below the Rio Grande, but there were no major outbreaks until 1874.

[29] Report of the Secretary of the Interior, 41 Cong., 2 sess., *House Exec. Doc. 1414*, 494–97.

16. PEACE NOT YET ATTAINED

When General Grant became President, on March 4, 1869, he put into effect recommendations made by the Society of Friends, who had suggested that Quakers be appointed as Indian agents and superintendents. They proposed to administer Indian affairs with honesty and kindness, which many people thought would be a change for the better. Grant also appointed a full-blooded Indian, Brevet Brigadier General Ely S. Parker, a lawyer who had been on his staff during the war, Commissioner of Indian Affairs. If this combination could not give the Indians sympathetic treatment, nothing could.

While the change-over was taking place, General Hazen remained superintendent of the southern Plains Indians. Albert Gallatin Boone, who had been delayed by illness, finally arrived at Fort Sill to act as interim agent for the Kiowas, Comanches, and Kiowa-Apaches. During the interval when Wynkoop was on terminal leave and Leavenworth's Quaker replacement had not arrived, Captain Henry Alvord served as agent at Forts Cobb and Sill, and the commander at Camp Supply administered Indian affairs there.

Major John H. Page's battalion of the Third Infantry had plenty to do while waiting for the arrival of the Cheyennes and Arapahoes, for the infantrymen were building the post. The men built a stockade of logs set in the ground to enclose Camp Supply where the buildings were not a part of the wall. The ten-foot stockade had a parapet of four feet and was provided with blockhouses at each corner. All the walls were loopholed. Eventually two company barracks were erected, each eighty feet long by eighteen feet wide, also of the palisade-type construction with sod roofs. During the first year and one-half, however, the soldiers lived in dugouts.

Married soldiers and their laundress wives had individual log huts, while the officers were in tents; later officers were given cabins similar to those of the married soldiers. There was a storehouse for supplies and a small hospital. The chief deficiency in the living quarters was the inadequacy of ventilation, for at first there were few glass windows. This meant that, except during the dry season, the dirt floors were generally damp. The first chore in the morning was to harvest the crop of mushrooms and toadstools that had grown up overnight.[1]

By this time, the Regular Army had pulled itself out of the slough of low morale and general inefficiency into which it had fallen after the Civil War and had again established itself on a sound footing. The Third Infantry, part of which garrisoned Camp Supply, was one of the oldest regiments in the army, dating back to the Revolution, and it was proud of its heritage.

The sick rate was low at Camp Supply, the prevalent diseases being, according to the post surgeon, "mild catarrhal affections [Was it wrong to say that they had colds?], intermittent fever, and diarhoea." The doctor thought that the malaria came from "noxious emanations" from the soil. He noticed that it lessened when the wind blew the emanations away, but neither he nor anyone else ever connected it with mosquitoes.[2]

Although the Indians were not yet present to create mischief, several of the same shady white men who had troubled Major Douglass at Fort Dodge were already at Camp Supply and prepared to sell arms, ammunition, and beverages to the Indians. Major Page arrested William Griffenstein and had Fred Jones thrown out of Indian Territory. He also arrested a Dr. Holmes, who had been regarded with disfavor on the Washita and was now in the neighborhood of Camp Supply nosing about for unlicensed mercantile opportunities on the North Canadian.[3]

Little Raven and the Arapahoes arrived from Fort Sill during the first week in May and camped within a few miles of the post. Since everyone agreed that they were friendly, the post commander issued them twelve hundred rations, a bit short of their needs, for there were over thirteen hundred Arapahoes, housed six or more to a lodge.[4] William Soule, who had come from Fort Dodge with Tappan, photographed the scene at Camp Supply when Major Page made this first issue to the Indians.

On May 25, Lieutenant Colonel Anderson D. Nelson, Fifth Infantry, came to Camp Supply. He was accompanied by four more companies of the Tenth Cavalry. Since there were accommodations for only two companies within the post proper, two tent camps were established, one for the Third Infantry and another for the Tenth Cavalry. This was not because of lack of space for one big camp, but on occasion—especially payday nights—there was a certain lack of cordiality between the two units.

[1] Early construction at Camp Supply is covered in the "Medical History, Camp Supply, 6–7; and in *Harper's Weekly Magazine* (February 27, 1869), 140.

[2] "Medical History, Camp Supply," 7.

[3] Page to McKeever, May 27, 1869, "Letter Book, Camp Supply."

[4] "Medical History, Camp Supply," 4.

Nelson should have assumed command of the post by virtue of seniority, but he did not do so until August, when district headquarters reminded him of his responsibilities. Nelson was in his early fifties and an 1841 graduate of the United States Military Academy. He had remained in the Regular Army during the war instead of resigning and re-entering as a Volunteer. Thus he was passed over when the numerous promotions were handed out to state troops by the several governors. Apparently this bothered him a little, surrounded as he was by former juniors who now held high brevet ranks. He was a bit stiff. Indians were not allowed to visit him unless invited, and he would not let them loiter about the officers' quarters with their noses pressed against the windows, staring at the inhabitants. Neither would he permit officers and soldiers to visit the Indian camps where they indulged in horse racing and other sporting enterprises. When he heard that Major Armes was racing against several chiefs, including Big Cow, the noted killer of Major Elliott,[5] he placed the Indian villages off limits. The Indians did not know what to make of this unsociable white man.

There were no Cheyennes at Camp Supply when Colonel Nelson arrived, but Satanta's Kiowas and Taw-Haw's Kiowa-Apaches were there, camped at the point where the Fort Sill–Fort Harker road crossed the Canadian. The chiefs rode into the post to beg for food, complaining that there was nothing at Fort Sill except corn meal, which they could not eat. Nelson curtly refused to issue them rations, saying that they would have to draw supplies at their own agency. They went off scowling and muttering.[6]

Although Nelson had enough troops to justify him in going out and snapping the whip at the laggard Cheyennes, he was not permitted to do so under the new peace policy. He could only hope they would hear of his kindness to the Arapahoes and thus be jollied into coming in for the supplies they needed so badly. He was hopeful, too, that the friendly persuasion of the Quakers would work.[7]

The Cheyennes were suspicious of the whites, partly because of John Smith's warning and, further, because of Custer's treachery. But they were so hungry and generally miserable that, on May 29, Little Robe came in with a few of his kinsmen to scout the situation. Four days later eighty more appeared. The chiefs went to see Colonel Nelson. Their first inquiry

---

[5] *Army and Navy Journal*, Vol. VI (July 17, 1869), 759; "Medical History, Camp Supply," 5.

[6] "Medical History, Camp Supply," 5; Nelson to McKeever, May 28, 1869, "Letter Book, Camp Supply."

[7] Nelson to McKeever, June 2, 1869, "Letter Book, Camp Supply."

after asking for something to eat was about their women and children, who had been captured by Custer.[8]

Nelson wrote to department headquarters:

> They were told that if they all came in and showed they were in earnest for peace . . . a writing would be sent to higher authority . . . asking that their women and children be returned to them. After talking among themselves for a short time they got up and shook hands with me, seeming to agree . . . . They have been deceived several times and are quite suspicious.

> Yesterday the commissary was ordered to issue Little Robe's band double their allowance of rations for five days and the same for four days to the Cheyennes who came in today . . . . Their appreciation of such treatment is not of a very high order, being altogether of a physical character, and among these it is to do nothing and have plenty to eat.[9]

Nelson got quick action from district headquarters on his request for the captive women and children. They were hauled from Fort Hays promptly, arriving on June 22. Nelson at once sent them to their respective camps. This brought Medicine Arrow to see whether it was safe to bring in the rest of the tribe. He even showed Nelson the sacred arrows, and performed a ceremony with them. Nelson was unimpressed, not appreciating that he was being accorded a special honor. Neither did he realize that in coming in at this time the Cheyennes had cut short one of their most important religious activities.

Medicine Arrow asked for permission to go out and fight the Utes. This ancient enemy had recently killed four Cheyennes, and they had to be paid back. Nelson refused.[10] In so doing he was at variance with the more experienced Alfred Sully, who on a similar occasion had remarked that it was not quite the proper thing to interfere too abruptly with the Indians' ancient habits and way of life. If the white men were going to forbid the Indians to fight them, then the whites should occasionally let them fight each other.

On July 1, eight hundred Cheyennes came in.[11] Nelson thought this was all of them, but it was not, for the Dog Soldiers were still out. Minimic rode west and brought in 130 on September 11, but a few still remained far out on the plains.[12]

In the meantime, the new Quaker agent, Brinton Darlington, arrived

[8] *Ibid.*
[9] *Ibid.*
[10] Nelson to McKeever, June 22, 1869, "Letter Book, Camp Supply."
[11] Nelson to Chaflin, July 26, 1869, "Letter Book, Camp Supply."
[12] "Medical History, Camp Supply," 5.

and assumed office. At first he took little notice of Nelson's dealings with the Indians, for he was concerned initially with erecting buildings for the agency. This accomplished, he wanted immediately to start making farmers of his nomadic charges and to get their children in school.[13] The Indians, both young and old, were emphatically disinterested in this.

A more urgent problem finally caught Darlington's attention, as it had already caught Nelson's attention. The Indians disliked their reservation. Too much of it was a barren waste in which both the land and the streams were impregnated with salt or gypsum. Nelson directed Lieutenant Silas Pepoon, Tenth Cavalry, to make an extensive survey to discover better areas. Pepoon's report supported the Indian's views, and recommended several other sites for the agency. General Sheridan disapproved the recommendation, however, on the ground that it would place the Indians too far from Camp Supply.[14]

On August 10, 1869, a sub-committee of the peace commission held a council at Camp Supply with the Cheyennes and Arapahoes. Both sides produced some fine oratory. Felix R. Brunot of the commission gave the keynote address. It reads very much like an Indian speech. Note his opening words:

> The Great Father in Washington has sent us to shake hands with the Arapahoes and Cheyennes. He wants to know how you do. He wants to know if you like your reservation. If you will promise to live on it and do right, you are now his brothers. The white people in Kansas and Texas are his sons and daughters. His brothers must not kill his children. They must not steal their cattle and horses.[15]

Brunot continued in a speech rich in imagery and barren of new or helpful ideas, and the Indians responded in kind. They promised to keep the peace with everyone except the Pawnees and Utes. They expressed an abhorrence of the Osages, too, "who steal our horses," and they stated their desire for food to eat. They were greatly interested in the annuities promised by the Medicine Lodge Treaty, and reminded the frock-coated gentlemen that no presents had been given them since August, 1868. Medicine Arrow slipped in a few pointed remarks about how the soldiers had recently attacked a village of his people in the north and that some of the

---

[13] Report of the Secretary of the Interior, 41 Cong., 2 sess., *House Exec. Doc. 1414, 1869–70*, 824.

[14] Report of Lieutenant Silas Pepoon, July 24, 1869, "Sheridan Papers," Container 73, 844–51.

[15] Report of the Secretary of the Interior, 41 Cong., 2 sess., *House Exec. Doc. 1414*, 495.

latter were still in prison. He would like to have them released, and he would like some ammunition.[16]

The commissioners told him he could not have any.

Little Raven again asked for a pass that would permit him to leave the reservation to kill a few Utes. This expedition was all arranged and was scheduled to leave in a few days.[17]

This was also denied.

Medicine Arrow promised to bring in the rest of the "out" Cheyennes if the commissioners would promise them amnesty and protection. The commissioners promptly agreed to this, and put it in writing.[18]

Before departing, the committee sent a recommendation to Washington that the reservation boundaries be changed in accordance with the request of the Indians. President Grant saw the justice of this, and made the change by an interim executive order, which was later confirmed by the Congress. The commission also recommended that the corn component of the ration be replaced by flour, rice, or soap.[19] The Indians had not asked for these articles. They wanted *Wo-haw*, meaning beef.

Everyone seemed happy over the results of this powwow, but any man who thought the Indians would settle down to farming was simply unacquainted with their background and character.

Medicine Arrow made no attempt to fulfill his promise to bring in the Cheyennes, who had gone north and then drifted back after the Battle of Summit Springs. Nevertheless, some of them did slip into the reservation, a few families at a time. The post commander was aware of this if Darlington was not, and he made no attempt to stop them because he thought it desirable to get all the Indians into their proper reservations.[20]

Darlington's report for 1869 covered only the last five months. He explained that when he arrived, the Indians had just come in from the warpath. Although they desired peace they were full of doubt because in the past they had been promised more than had been delivered. Darlington said their rations were still inadequate and some components were unsuitable. He recommended that the corn be omitted and that the amounts of coffee and sugar be doubled. He thought that the Indians might be getting more beef than they needed, for game was still plentiful.[21]

[16] *Ibid.*, 495–96.
[17] *Ibid.*, 497.
[18] *Ibid.*
[19] *Ibid.*
[20] Berthrong, *The Southern Cheyennes*, 361.
[21] Report of Brinton Darlington, 41 Cong., 2 sess., *House Exec. Doc. 1414*, 824.

The post surgeon observed that the region was a hunter's paradise:

> The country about the post abounds with game of all kinds—black bear, cinnamon bear, raccoon, opposum, badger, weasel, and skunk. Also buffalo, deer, and antelope. Wild fowl abounds: turkey, geese, ducks, several species of grouse, snipe, and plover. Fish in the streams—catfish, buffalo fish, sunfish. In the ponds are black bass. Serpents are numerous—rattlesnake, blacksnake, water moccasins. The insect life is distressingly abundant and varied: scorpions, centipedes, tarantulas head the list which runs through all varieties of spiders, ants, beetles, wasps, hornets, yellow jackets, locusts, and grasshoppers, and ends with horseflies, gnats, and mosquitoes.[22]

He failed to mention mountain lions, wolves, coyotes, rabbits, owls, hawks, pigeons, quail, and many varieties of song birds.

Indian troubles began early in 1870. There were no settlements to attack, no railroad working parties to massacre, no stages or wagon trains to shoot up. However, the Indians did the best they could with what was on hand—trains bringing in their own supplies, teamster camps, and isolated civilians. On January 10, a band of Apaches—the records do not specify what kind—stole 112 horses from Little Robe's camp and 157 from the Arapahoes. Little Robe was refused permission to take the warpath in an effort to recover the stock.[23]

On January 15, Jacob Harshfield, a beef contractor to the agency, was bringing a large herd of cattle from Texas for issue to the Cheyennes and Arapahoes. He was attacked on the North Canadian forty miles downstream from Camp Supply by a band of Kiowas under the jovial Satanta.[24] The Kiowas began shooting arrows into the cattle, apparently just for devilment, and before long some two hundred of the poor beasts were lying dead or wounded on the prairie. The Kiowas also gave some attention to the herders, fourteen of whom were Texans or Mexicans and two Caddo Indians. The Caddoes fought, but the cowboys, who apparently were not the two-gun men typified in film and fiction, did not. According to Harshfield, the Kiowas would have killed them all had not Kicking Bird ridden up with his band and ordered Satanta to stop the fight.[25]

When word of this reached Camp Supply, Major Meredith H. Kidd was sent with four companies of the Tenth Cavalry to rescue the train. Satanta, warned of this by his scouts, disappeared. Kidd followed the raiders for

[22] "Medical History, Camp Supply," 7.
[23] *Ibid.*
[24] Nelson to AAG, Dept. of Mo., January 17, 1870, "Letter Book, Camp Supply."
[25] *Ibid.*

several hours, but when their trail showed they had crossed the Canadian he gave up the chase.[26]

For the next three months the Indians remained relatively quiet, this being the season when their ponies were poor and the women were scraping green buffalo hides. Darlington, convinced that the Indians would be better off if away from the soldiers, was building a new agency one hundred miles down the North Canadian near the present town of El Reno.[27] His consistent kindness to the Indians was having an effect. They were becoming fond of him even though they were unresponsive to his efforts to interest them in farming or stock raising. The Cheyennes, who had been an agricultural people two centuries earlier when they lived in what is now Minnesota, had entirely forgotten this heritage.

Men seeking appointments as traders at the agency or at Camp Supply caused the officials some annoyance. A license to trade with the Indians was an opportunity to get rich quick. The traders were paying the Indians two pounds of coffee or six pounds of sugar for a buffalo robe worth at least ten dollars. Post traders, who sold merchandise to the military personnel, had a monopoly and, even at a small post, made excellent profits. Political pressure was exerted in favor of certain candidates for post traderships, and it has been said that traders who failed to pay tribute to the right officials lost their franchises. One of the most scandalous of such affairs was that involving Secretary of War Belknap who in 1876 was impeached for selling post trader appointments. John Tappan lost his franchise at Fort Dodge, not through knavery, but because someone with more influence snatched it from him. He came to Camp Supply in 1869, bringing Soule, but was unable to obtain an appointment.[28] Benteen claims that Tappan lost out because he would not make a deal with Custer.

The Dog Soldier bands belonging to Medicine Arrow and Bull Bear were either on the reservation or near its western border during the winter, but they did not visit Camp Supply or their agency. Late in the spring of 1870, they disappeared, and Darlington heard that they had gone north to the Platte River and joined the Sioux.[29] There was still dissatisfaction throughout the Cheyenne and Arapaho tribes. Peace had not yet been attained, and not all of the wild Indians had been driven south from the Arkansas.

Because Darlington had selected a site for a new agency, his property and supplies were moved to it by wagon beginning on May 3. Most of the

[26] *Ibid.*
[27] "Medical History, Camp Supply," 8.
[28] Page to McKeever, June 11, 1869, "Letter Book, Camp Supply."
[29] Darlington to Hoag, September 1, 1870, 41 Cong., 3 sess., *House Exec. Doc. 1449.*

Indians located near Camp Supply did not want to go. They said it would make a haul of one hundred more miles for them when they brought buffalo hides to trade, for the buffalo no longer passed near their new agency during their spring and fall migrations. The buffalo were now to be found a little west of Camp Supply. What was worse, some kind of fever, possibly malaria, was prevalent at the new agency, and several Indians had died there.[30]

The chiefs issued an ultimatum: The agency would be moved back to Camp Supply or they would go to war. Darlington was undisturbed, but the military felt certain there would be an outbreak.

They were right. Raiding commenced in the latter part of May. On the twenty-eighth, Little Heart, a minor Kiowa war chief, slipped into one of the camps at Supply during a tumultuous thunderstorm and knifed a man sleeping in one of the officer's tents. The victim was Louis Ortega, an officer's servant. Little Heart later bragged that he had been "looking to kill" an officer but had accepted the Mexican as a substitute.[31]

The same day several Indians took two mules from a gardener employed by Dick Curtis, the post interpreter, at his "ranch" three miles from the post.[32]

The next day a trader named Tracy was engaged to haul supplies to a company of the Third Infantry that was stationed as guards at the new agency. Second Lieutenant Mason M. Maxon, a recent West Point graduate, was sent with ten men of the Tenth Cavalry as escort. When the train was forty miles from Camp Supply, it was attacked by some three hundred Indians. In their first rush the raiders captured all fifty-eight mules, and killed one of the teamsters. Two men got away before the train was completely encircled and made a hard ride back to the post for help. Captain Louis H. Carpenter, Tenth Cavalry, was sent with two companies to rescue the train, taking along enough mules to bring back the wagons. He had not been gone long before Colonel Nelson began to worry that he had not sent a large enough force. He dispatched Captain Nicholas Nolan with more men.[33] Since Carpenter and Nolan had served in the cavalry during the war, Nelson thought that between them they could handle the Indians.

Carpenter found that young Maxon had organized a sound defense and was standing off the Indians. The latter were assembling for another attack

[30] "Medical History, Camp Supply," 8; Nelson to McKeever, May 3, 1869.
[31] "Medical History, Camp Supply," 8.
[32] Nelson to McKeever, June 4, 1870, "Letter Book, Camp Supply."
[33] "Medical History, Camp Supply," 8; Nelson to McKeever, June 12, 1870, "Letter Book, Camp Supply."

when they saw the relief expedition approaching. They hovered about long enough, however, for Carpenter to recognize, because of his scarlet shield and other red trappings, his old friend Satanta.[34]

May 30, was a busy day for the troops at Camp Supply. While Satanta and his braves were entertaining Carpenter and Maxon, other Indians were on the prowl nearer the post. Lee and Reynolds, post traders, missed some of their stock and sent a teamster to search for it. At noon the next day he had not returned. In the meantime large numbers of Indians had been seen on the hills around the post, and cavalry had gone out to drive them away. Since it was suspected that the teamster had been murdered, a sergeant and ten men were ordered to search for him. Three miles from the post they noticed buzzards circling over a draw. There they found the body of the teamster. He was naked, nine arrows had been shot into him, and there was a black bullet hole in his face. Three scalp locks had been cut from his skull.[35]

Also on the thirtieth, Major George Armes arrived from Fort Dodge with an escort. He had been met during the morning by some fifty Indians twenty miles north of the post. Because of his escort, they had offered no threats but had asked for food and tobacco. Some of the soldiers later told Armes that the Indians had two or three fresh scalps and were leading a mule and two horses that were branded and shod—probably taken from the teamster and Curtis' gardener.[36]

Major Kidd, Lieutenant Louis H. Orleman, and fifty cavalrymen had left Camp Supply at eight o'clock that morning, taking ninety-eight condemned horses to Fort Hays, where they were to be sold at auction. When Nelson heard Armes's news he sent Lieutenant Robert G. Smither with twenty-five men north on the Fort Dodge road to meet a train that Armes said had crossed the Arkansas early on the previous morning en route to Camp Supply. It was feared that the train was too weakly guarded. Smither was told to move rapidly, and he was given authority to obtain reinforcements from Kidd.[37]

Smither met the train the following morning two miles north of the Cimarron. They had been visited by fifteen Indians but had not been attacked, probably because they were alert and well armed. The men had not heard of an Indian outbreak.[38]

[34] "Medical History, Camp Supply," 9.

[35] "Medical History, Camp Supply," 8; Nelson to McKeever, June 4, 12, 1870, "Letter Book, Camp Supply."

[36] Nelson to McKeever, June 4, 1870, "Letter Book, Camp Supply."

[37] *Ibid.*

[38] *Ibid.*

159

Except for Carpenter and Maxon, none of the detachment commanders now in the field were certain that the Indians were on the warpath.[39] The savages they met were decked out for it, however, and the absence of women and children was significant.

Although it was not known at Camp Supply until several days later, the Indians who had visited the train near the Cimarron rode from there to a mail station forty-five miles north of Camp Supply. The station was guarded by a sergeant and four privates of the Third Infantry, who had not heard of the outbreak and thus were not alarmed when Indians entered the building and asked for something to eat. They were given food, but the two soldiers in the room sat on sacks containing other rations, to prevent the Indians from snatching them. The men did not have their rifles in hand because they anticipated no trouble. Suddenly the Indians shot and killed them.[40]

The sergeant was outside trying to carry on a conversation with the other Indians, who had dismounted and tied their horses. On hearing the shots, the sergeant rushed inside but was met by a burst of fire and fell with seven wounds. The other two soldiers, who were in the rear cleaning a stable, ran in and attacked the two Indians with their pitchforks before the savages could reload their guns. They would have been killed, however, had not Major Kidd and his troops appeared. In their haste to get away the Indians leaped on their mounts and cut the halter ropes instead of untying them. Kidd went inside the buildings to aid the fallen men. Since the sergeant was still breathing, they loaded him into a light vehicle and started for Fort Dodge, where the surgeon was able to save the man's life.[41]

On June 1, five Indians dashed at a herd of five hundred horses being grazed within a quarter of a mile of Camp Supply. They seized two horses and a mule and galloped on past a party of civilians bivouacked in a grove. The civilians fired at them as they flashed past, causing them to release two of their stolen animals. A small detachment of cavalry went in hot pursuit but succeeded only in injuring several good government horses.[42]

On the afternoon of June 6, several Indians galloped into the herd of a government train that was camped on the Fort Dodge road a thousand yards north of the post. They got nothing, but made two more attempts during the night, one of which netted thirteen head of stock.[43]

[39] *Ibid.*
[40] *Ibid.*
[41] *Ibid.*
[42] *Ibid.*
[43] Nelson to McKeever, June 12, "Letter Book, Camp Supply."

Three days later, Lieutenant Bodamer rescued a long ox train that had been surrounded. Major Page, following the train with a small party, was likewise attacked but drove off the Indians, killing two.[44]

At 3:30 in the afternoon of June 10, two hundred Indians passed within seven hundred yards of the cavalry camp but got only three horses—one of them was Maxon's private mount, and the other two were diseased animals being grazed at a distance from the herd. The Indians then rode to the high ground and favored the post with one of their customary displays of circus-like horsemanship, riding backwards, or standing up, or slung over the side—meanwhile shouting boasts and insults.[45]

Colonel Nelson turned out all the troops this time. He formed the infantry in two lines between the two tent camps, which were six hundred yards apart. When the cavalry was assembled, he sent one force after the Indians who were in the valley of Beaver Creek, and a larger force up Wolf Creek, where most of the Indians were located. Accompanied by two or three orderlies and the surgeon, he then rode to a hill one-half mile from the cavalry camp, from which he had a good view of both valleys. His two cavalry forces were moving deliberately up the valleys, with the Indians falling back slowly in front of them. Soon the action had progressed so far up the divergent streams that the detachments were four miles apart.[46]

Lieutenant Maxon with eighteen men came up the hill and reported to Nelson. Maxon was told to move along the ridge two miles, to its highest point, then turn right and join Captain Nolan's company, which was fighting along Beaver Creek. Nelson, watching through his glass, saw Maxon turn to the right, away from the ridge, and ride at full speed after the hostiles on the opposite slope. Though not visible to Maxon, more Indians were assembling behind trees along the stream and preparing to cut him off. There was a tragedy in the making such as had befallen Elliott on the Washita.

Unlike Custer at the Battle of the Washita, Nelson could see the whole field of action. And he had held out a mobile reserve. He sent Lieutenant Smither with a cavalry company and a howitzer to strike the Indians who were threatening Maxon. This decided the day. The Indians, who did not relish artillery fire, disengaged and soon disappeared.[47]

It was supposed that six Indians had been killed and others wounded, but none were found. The troops suffered no casualties, so it was scarcely a

[44] *Ibid.*
[45] *Ibid.*
[46] *Ibid.*
[47] *Ibid.*

major fight, though quite exciting for a time. Nelson called it a "demonstration."

These small affairs were part of the pattern of the 1870 raiding season. It was a short season, lasting only until July. During the remainder of June three woodchoppers were killed, several trains attacked, and an occasional troop escort exchanged shots with the redskins at a distance.[48]

In no case did the Indians succeed in running off the post herd or even any substantial number of animals, as they had done repeatedly at the posts along the Arkansas. In no instance was there a massacre of teamsters. Part of this was due to increased troop effectiveness. The Regular Army was learning how to march, maneuver, and fight. The leaders in all ranks and grades were getting better, and, in the past year, all personnel had become experienced in taking care of themselves in the field.

[48] "Medical History, Camp Supply," 8.

17. END OF THE FREE LIFE

Camp Supply, established as an advanced supply base for Sheridan's winter campaign of 1868, was retained to protect and supply the Cheyenne and Arapaho agency. Even after the agency was moved to the locality that came to be called Darlington, a garrison was maintained at Camp Supply to guard the supply line running north. The Indian depredations of 1870 caused the commander to fear another full-scale outbreak. He asked for more troops, but Major General John M. Schofield, who succeeded Sheridan as department commander in 1869, refused to furnish them. Agent Darlington scarcely took notice of the raids in his report for 1870. He was confident that the chiefs were sincere in declaring for peace.

When they were not on relief expeditions and warding off attacks on herds and herders near the post, the troops at Camp Supply labored to make their quarters and other facilities more habitable. Since the station had not yet been designated a permanent post, funds and materials were not forthcoming, and the troops had to improvise. Palisade-type buildings were erected to replace the earlier dugouts or tents. The hospital wards had been in three framed tents, but now log cabins were built—one for a dispensary, one for a mess hall, and one for a kitchen. Each company had been baking its bread in homemade ovens; in October, 1870, a post bakery was completed.[1]

The climate was healthy except that during the dry season recurring sand-and-dust storms produced eye, nose, and throat irritation that, according to the surgeon, caused some annoyance. The sick rate was low, however, the chief complaints being dysentery, malaria, and abrasions caused by accidents common to mounted troops.[2] Dysentery plagued the men at the frontier posts just as it had the troops in the Civil War camps.

Under the prodding of their surgeons, and because it was traditional, post commanders kept their installations clean and orderly, but sanitation did not get at the root of the trouble. It was not known in those days that

---

[1] "Medical History, Camp Supply," 9.
[2] *Ibid.*, 10.

dysentery and other intestinal ailments were transmitted by flies or acquired through the use of inadequately sterilized food containers and kitchen equipment.

Garbage and other refuse were dumped in Beaver Creek, which, below its confluence with Wolf Creek, became the North Canadian River. The only reason that drinking water was not obtained from the same source was that it tasted worse than that in Wolf Creek. Both streams were alkaline.[3]

The doctor reported that the meals were well prepared and of good substance.[4] This may have been true for that generation, but by the standards of today the ration was woefully inadequate. Since the nearest settlements were two hundred miles away, no ration supplements could be purchased except from the post trader, the ancestor of the present post exchange, whose prices were astronomical. The adjutant, like the post adjutants along the Arkansas, attempted to start a post garden, but such plants as survived the drought were eaten by jackrabbits, grasshoppers, and locusts.[5]

The Indians abstained from raiding almost entirely during the summer and fall of 1871. Consequently, the men were permitted to go hunting. In their enthusiasm the amateur nimrods managed to shoot someone frequently, either themselves or friends. More soldiers were killed or wounded during the hunting season of 1871 than had been lost in fights with the Indians in 1870.[6] The joy of the chase was little reduced by these bits of carelessness and ineptitude. Grouse and quail were to be found everywhere, ducks and geese stopped over in their migrations when the buffalo wallows were filled with water, and the lordly wild turkey stalked about in huge flocks, feeding on the grasshoppers. At night they roosted in the hackberry trees along the streams, bending the branches with their weight. In November, each company at the post sent out a fowling party who brought in wagonloads of the noble bird. On Thanksgiving Day, every soldier had a whole roast turkey.[7]

Early in 1871, Lieutenant Colonel (Brevet Major General) John W. Davidson, Tenth Cavalry, superseded Colonel Nelson as commander of Camp Supply. This tall, lanky Virginian was more congenial than his predecessor. The Indians were invited to come to his office for talks whenever they felt like it, and this improved relations. Davidson learned in March that the Dog Soldier bands of Medicine Arrow and Bull Bear were

[3] *Ibid.*, 9.
[4] *Ibid.*, 10.
[5] *Ibid.*, 9.
[6] *Ibid.*, 10–16.
[7] *Ibid.*, 16–17.

slowly moving, with governmental approval, from the Platte River back to their reservation. The first small groups arrived late that month and the others straggled in throughout the rest of the year.[8]

The peace of 1871 in the reservation of the Cheyennes and Arapahoes was not matched by the situation in the land of the Kiowas and Comanches. Those redmen had become increasingly obstreperous since Sheridan and Custer had left and a Quaker agent had taken over their affairs. Besides raiding in Texas and Mexico, they killed people around the agency and the military post. They ran off stock from the agency and one night stole all the mules in the quartermaster's corral. They defied the agent and sent impudent messages to Grierson at the post. Kicking Bird of the Kiowas and Tosawi and Horseback of the Comanches were the only leaders who tried to make their young men behave.[9]

An especially outrageous affair was perpetrated in Loving County, Texas, on May 18, 1871, by a large party led by Mamanti, chief medicine man and prominent war leader of the Kiowas. In this grisly triumph, seven teamsters of Warren's wagon train were shot and roasted near the Butterfield Trail west of Jacksboro. General Sherman, on an inspection tour of western posts, had driven past the spot an hour before the attack was made. He learned of the massacre that night when a survivor limped in to Fort Richardson with the story. Sherman ordered Brevet Major General Ranald Slidell Mackenzie (Colonel, Fourth Cavalry) to pursue the Indians. They followed the trail to Red River, but the Indians escaped into their city of refuge on the Fort Sill Reservation.[10]

Sherman arrived at Fort Sill a week later. About this time the Kiowas came to the agency for their rations. Satanta proudly told the agent that he had led the attack against the Warren wagon train. He implicated several other chiefs, including Big Tree and Satank. The agent thought this sounded more like crime than exuberant mischief and notified the post commander.

Sherman immediately called for the Indians to come to the post commander's quarters for a conference. He prepared for the meeting by having the Tenth Cavalry saddle up and remain concealed behind the doors of their stone stables. A detachment with loaded rifles was hidden in the house, ready to shoot from the windows. Because the Indians were not told why they were invited but were always eager to see a big chief, they arrived in

[8] Berthrong, *The Southern Cheyennes*, 359.
[9] Report of Lawrie Tatum, August 12, 1870, 41 Cong., 3 sess., *House Exec. Doc. 1449*; W. S. Nye, *Carbine and Lance*, 106–23.
[10] Nye, *Carbine and Lance*, 132.

large numbers and seated themselves on the ground in front of the quarters. Several of the chiefs were invited to places on the porch.[11]

When Sherman asked about the massacre, Satanta arose and, beating his chest, again bragged that he had been in charge. In spite of efforts by the other chiefs to silence him, he gave other names. At a signal from Sherman the doors were thrown open and the soldiers came out and seized and shackled Satanta, Big Tree, and Satank. This caused an uproar and very nearly a free-for-all. The more courageous warriors wanted to shoot Sherman but were restrained by Kicking Bird.[12] Most of the Indians fled in dismay when they saw the cavalry stables open and the troop columns emerge.

The three prisoners were confined in the cellar of a corner barrack for a few days, then were loaded into wagons to be taken to Texas for trial for murder before a civil court. This was a new departure; heretofore Indians guilty of killings had not been arrested. On the contrary, they were treated as well as the innocent. Usually, the windup of outrages had been a peace council at which the Indians had been given presents in return for their promise to sin no more.

Shortly after leaving the post, old Satank drew a knife he had concealed in his breechcloth and tried to stab one of his guards. He was shot and left dying beside the road.[13] Since his people did not come in to claim the body, he was buried in the post cemetery. The other two chiefs were convicted in a trial held at Jacksboro and sentenced to be hanged. An immediate outcry was raised in the East, and the governor of Texas was prevailed upon to commute the sentences to life imprisonment. Two years later, further pressure induced him to release the pair on parole.[14]

In the meantime, young Kiowas ambitious to win renown in battle visited their Cheyenne brethren and tried to persuade them to join in raids or even in a general war. However, they had little success, owing to the efforts of agent Darlington and friendly chiefs like Little Robe.

One of Darlington's most serious problems was in trying to keep his charges from getting liquor. The commander at Camp Supply was similarly interested, for he too knew that drunken Indians were troublesome. Unfortunately, traders could not be prevented from slipping into the large, unpatrolled expanses of the reservation. The Indian chiefs were unco-

[11] *Ibid.*, 137.
[12] *Ibid.*, 138–42.
[13] *Ibid.*, 142–46.
[14] *Ibid.*, 146, 160, 169–76.

operative. They would give no information as to the identity and locations of the whisky peddlers, for they, as much as their braves, loved alcohol.[15]

In April, 1872, Darlington fell ill with what was diagnosed as "brain fever." He died on May 1, and was succeeded by John D. Miles, former agent for the Kickapoos.[16] Mr. Darlington had not been in office long enough to have made much headway in pacifying or civilizing the Indians, but he at least showed them that not all white men were there to steal their horses, or shoot at them, or sell whisky. In one respect he left a lasting impression. Darlington wore a set of dentures, which he once took from his mouth while conferring with a group of Indians. Their astonishment was so great that he repeated the trick on other occasions for their entertainment. Thereafter, the gesture of removing something from the mouth was a part of the Indian sign language, signifying "agent."[17]

While Darlington was agent, a fairly large number of Quakers joined him as employees. But by the time of his death most of them had returned to their homes, disillusioned by the lack of progress with the Indians and tired of the discomforts of the rude living conditions on the frontier. When Miles took over, the only Quakers at the agency were himself, his wife, and four or five assistants. Miles was an active man with considerable administrative ability. With the able assistance of his wife, he made a success of his incumbency. The Miles family were a credit to their sect and to their calling.[18]

By the fall of 1873, the Indians were getting harder to handle. Part of this was due to their increasing drunkenness. Furthermore, they were becoming more and more disturbed over the inroads of the professional buffalo hunters, who in a few years had killed upwards of seven and one-half million bison. The Indians had begun to realize that the buffalo really could be exterminated, and they knew that this would mean starvation for them. Another cause of unrest came from whites who were infiltrating the reservation and stealing horses. The government was doing nothing about this practice. Perhaps the strongest reason for their bitterness and their desire to restore forcibly the old order was their ingrained distaste for the white man's "road" and the desire to return to the old, free life.

An outbreak finally occurred in the summer of 1874. It started with the Kiowas and Comanches and quickly spread to the Cheyennes. The Arapahoes participated only as individuals and to a minor extent. The first symp-

[15] Berthrong, *The Southern Cheyennes*, 363.
[16] *Ibid.*, 367.
[17] John H. Seger, *Early Days Among the Cheyenne and Arapahoe Indians*, 16–17.
[18] *Ibid.*, 17–20.

toms were an increased sauciness on the part of the disaffected, a series of killings and robberies, and, finally, two big raids. One was an incursion of Kiowas and Comanches into Texas resulting in an affair with the Texas Rangers called the Lost Valley Fight. The other was an attack on a small colony of buffalo hunters at Adobe Walls in the Texas Panhandle.[19] This had been inspired by a Comanche medicine man named Isatai, who promised the Indians that he would make them invulnerable to the white man's bullets. Quanah, a rising young war chief of the Nokonis who fought mostly with the Quohada, was the most prominent leader of an aggregation consisting of warriors from all the tribes. They made a surprise assault on Adobe Walls early on the morning of June 27, 1874. Isatai's medicine proved ineffective. A number of braves were killed, and the attack was repulsed.

When news of the outbreak reached General Sherman in Washington, he telegraphed Sheridan to suggest that a regiment of cavalry be ordered out to "settle matters once and for all."

Sheridan, agreeing heartily, promised quick action and asked Sherman to get him "coverage." A plan was submitted to President Grant under which such Indians as wished to stay out of the impending war would be enrolled in their camps or at their agencies. August 4 was set as the deadline, after which non-registered Indians would be subject to attack. They would be driven in, forced to surrender, disarmed, and dismounted. The ringleaders would be sent to prison.[20]

Grant approved the plan, and the Secretary of the Interior was informed that the military were in control. This was the end of the peace policy.

The Kiowas of Kicking Bird's following were readily enrolled, as were such Comanches as had been consistently friendly. Most of the Kiowa-Apaches and Arapahoes and a small portion of the Cheyenne tribe were also enrolled.[21]

General Sheridan worked out a plan similar to the one he had employed with such marked success in 1868. It was predicted that the Indians would move to their favorite hideouts along the edge of the Staked Plains and the upper reaches of the Washita River and the two forks of Red River. Troop columns would converge on this region from several directions. Brevet

[19] More detailed accounts of the Battle of Adobe Walls are given in: G. Derek West, "The Battle of Adobe Walls," *Panhandle-Plains Historical Review*, Vol. XXXVI (1963), 1–36; Olive K. Dixon, *The Life of Billy Dixon*; the Indian side of the affair is in W. S. Nye, *Bad Medicine and Good*, 178–83.

[20] Sherman to Sheridan, "Sheridan Papers," Box 55, file of telegrams.

[21] Nye, *Carbine and Lance*, 203–204.

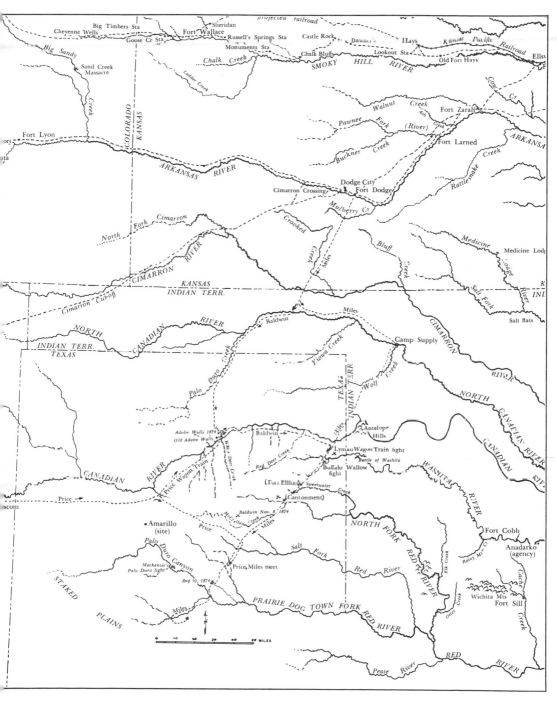

The Campaign of 1874–75, *showing the initial routes of Miles, Baldwin, and Price.*

Major General (Colonel, Fifth Infantry) Nelson A. Miles was to lead a force south from Camp Supply. Colonel Davidson with part of the Tenth Cavalry would move northwest from Fort Sill. Major William Price with a battalion of the Eighth Cavalry would come east from Fort Union, New Mexico. Brevet Major General (Colonel, Fourth Cavalry) Ranald S. Mackenzie would strike north from Fort Concho, Texas. An infantry column under Lieutenant Colonel George P. Buell would operate between Davidson and Mackenzie. The Indians would be kept continually on the run until they were exhausted and ready to surrender.[22]

The Indians enrolled at the Kiowa-Comanche agency, which had been moved sixty miles northeast of Sill to Anadarko, were encamped near Fort Sill, determined to stay out of the war. The hostile portion of the tribe, under Lone Wolf, had just come in from their big raid into Texas and tried to be enrolled, though August 4 had come and passed. Failing in this they went north of the Washita and camped on Cobb Creek.[23]

As late as August 21, Davidson had not started on the campaign. That evening, while relaxing on his veranda, he was notified that the hostiles had gone to the agency for issue day and seemed to be in a troublesome mood. The commander of the troop who was supervising the issue of rations was convinced that there would be trouble. Davidson assembled four troops and made a moonlight march to Anadarko. When he arrived the next morning he found that the non-enrolled Kiowas and Comanches were robbing a store and terrorizing the employees of the agency. He had a squad of soldiers seize a nearby Comanche chief who appeared to be causing some of the commotion. When they tried to disarm him, other Indians in the vicinity started firing. During the morning and most of the afternoon, the troops and Indians continued firing at each other at a distance, producing considerable smoke and noise but not much blood. Finally, the Indians decided they had had enough fun and departed, but not before they had speared and killed four white men who were cutting hay in a meadow two or three miles from the scene and, because of an adverse wind, had not heard the firing.

Although the Indians had been fairly casual about the affair until they rode away, when it grew dark they imagined they were being pursued. Panic built up and soon they were in headlong flight. They did not stop until they reached Elk Creek.[24]

Colonel Davidson and his command returned to Fort Sill, where, without

22 *Ibid.*, 211.
23 *Ibid.*, 203–204.
24 *Ibid.*, 206–210, 213.

any feeling of urgency, they completed their preparations for the campaign. It was a dreadfully hot summer. They did not start their pursuit of the runaways until September 11, when they followed a very cold trail up the Washita. After a week or so, during which they saw no Indians, they returned to Fort Sill for more supplies. They made another scout starting about the middle of October, when the weather was much more pleasant.[25]

The expedition led by General Miles assembled at Fort Dodge in August. The force consisted of eight companies of cavalry, four of infantry, a battery of Gatling guns, and Lieutenant Frank D. Baldwin's thirty-nine-man detachment of Delaware Indian scouts and frontiersmen. On August 14, the expedition marched from near Fort Dodge in a direction about twenty degrees west of south, spread out a bit in parallel columns hoping to intercept any hostile Indians still lingering between Fort Dodge and Camp Supply.[26] When near the site of present Beaver, Oklahoma, Miles and the main column turned east toward Camp Supply while Baldwin and his detachment rode west along the Canadian to Palo Duro Creek.

Baldwin, a vigorous, muscular fellow who had won a Medal of Honor during the Civil War, led his scouts and a cavalry company south along Palo Duro Creek toward Adobe Walls, where it was reported that the buffalo hunters were still brazening out the Indian menace. He arrived just as 150 savages were preparing to make another attack. They withdrew before him, setting fire to the grass. Baldwin then marched east along the Canadian to the mouth of Chicken Creek, where he exchanged shots with another band of elusive Indians. Then he went to a point twelve miles west of Antelope Hills for a prearranged rendezvous with Miles's main column.[27]

While he was on this long loop, Baldwin failed to see any trace of Medicine Arrow's large war party, which had been depredating north and northwest of Camp Supply. On July 4, they had attacked a wagon train on the road from Camp Supply to Fort Dodge, at the present site of Hennessey, Oklahoma. They had tied Pat Hennessey to a wagon wheel and roasted him alive, also killing three of his men. On August 27, they wiped out Short's survey party forty-five miles west of Fort Dodge. Then they went north to the Smoky Hill Road, where, on September 11, they butchered the lonely family of John German, a farmer from Georgia who was moving by wagon to seek a new home in Colorado and did not know that the Indians

[25] *Ibid.*, 212, 225.
[26] Nelson A. Miles, *Personal Recollections and Observations of General Nelson A. Miles,* 163–65; "Medical History, Camp Supply," 28; Final Report of General Miles, dated: Fort Leavenworth, March 4, 1875 (National Archives).
[27] *Ibid.*, 166.

had gone on the warpath. Word of the tragedy did not reach Fort Wallace until October 2, when a detachment of soldiers under Lieutenant C. C. Hewitt, Nineteenth Infantry, went out to investigate. Six miles east of Monument Station they found the remains of four persons, footprints of children in the sand, and a family Bible in which the names of the family of nine had been written. Later it was surmised that the Indians had killed all but four young girls, whom they had captured.[28]

General Miles's force arrived at Camp Supply on August 18 after a hot march through a parched prairie. There had been a severe drought followed by a plague of locusts, and all vegetation was gone.[29]

There were no Indians at Camp Supply; therefore, Miles was spared the embarrassment of shaking hands with people he soon hoped to shoot. The Arapahoes, all enrolled as friendlies, were at the agency one hundred miles to the east. Old Whirlwind of the Cheyennes was there, too, with his immediate family group, as were Little Robe and about 280 others who had slipped away from the hostiles. The villages of the latter were said to be on Sweetwater Creek.

After resting two days and refilling his wagons, Miles started for Antelope Hills. He rendezvoused there with Baldwin and then marched southwest to the Sweetwater, where his guides showed him a trail plainly marked with articles the Indians had discarded. They followed this rapidly until on the thirtieth of August the cap rock along the edge of the Staked Plains loomed ahead. Baldwin, in advance, started through a break in the bluffs and was immediately under attack from Indians on both sides of the canyon.[30]

The scouts lay down among the rocks and opened fire. The cavalry came up at a gallop, formed a line, and charged—although rather slowly on account of having to pick their way over the rough ground. The Indians were driven up into the Staked Plains, which here were badly cut up by gulches. It was rough going for the cavalry, unaccustomed to such difficult terrain. But they pursued the redmen for twenty miles, continuing across the Prairie Dog Town Fork of Red River and up the Tule Creek.

By this time the men were almost fainting from heat and thirst. The horses were trembling, and some had stopped sweating—a bad sign. The

[28] Grace E. Meredith, *Girl Captives of the Cheyennes.* Mrs. Meredith, a niece of one of the German sisters, was my grade school teacher, and told me the story of the sisters many times; General Miles's Final Report, March 4, 1875; Major H. A. Hambright, Fort Wallace, to AAG Dept. of Mo., October 2, 1874; Leavenworth *Daily Commercial*, October 3, 1874.

[29] Miles, *Personal Recollections*, 163–65.

[30] Reports of General Miles, September 1, 1874, March 4, 1875, WDAGO File 2815.

stream bed was dry except for one small stagnant pool covered with green slime. Since there was not enough water for men and animals, Miles made his way back to where he had left his wagons. Here he encamped and sent the train, escorted by Captain Wyllys Lyman's infantry company, back to pick up rations and forage at Camp Supply.[31]

Lyman got as far as Commission Creek, where he met a loaded train coming from Camp Supply. He transferred the supplies to his own wagons and started back to Miles's command. On September 9, he was attacked near the Washita River by several hundred Kiowas and Comanches and forced to corral and dig in. During a siege lasting three days, he lost an assistant wagonmaster and a sergeant killed, and Lieutenant Granville Lewis and three enlisted men wounded. Lewis was permanently disabled.[32]

Major Price's column from Fort Bascom, searching for his supply wagons, which he had expected to meet in the area, came close enough to see the Indians on a distant ridge, but did not go close enough to sight the encircled wagon train. However, the Indians became disturbed over the various bodies of troops they saw in different directions and decided to rejoin their village and leave the area. As they departed, some of them ran into six white men, four soldiers and two civilians, who were acting as couriers between General Miles and Camp Supply. One soldier was killed and four men were wounded. The whites took position in a shallow buffalo wallow, which they deepened with their hands, and stood off the Indians until dark, when most of the savages withdrew. Others stayed in the vicinity and held the men in their hole for two more days. The pit was filling up with bloody water, and the men were suffering greatly from their wounds when they were "rescued" by Price. He left them there, but gave them some food, and kindly notified other troops to pick them up. They were finally succored that evening. This small affair has become famous as The Buffalo Wallow Fight.[33]

The Kiowa village to which the Indians intended to return was on the south bank of the Washita, a little west of an unidentified tributary that may have been the Dry Fork of the Washita. Old men and boys had been left there to defend it. Price, before he crossed the river, approached this camp and skirmished with the defenders. The latter covered the withdrawal of the women and children until they crossed the fork. A sudden

---

[31] *Ibid.*, September 1, 1874.

[32] Ernest R. Archambeau, "The Battle of Lyman's Wagon Train," *Panhandle-Plains Historical Review*, Vol. XXXVI (1963), 89–101.

[33] Miles to AGOWD, September 24, 1874, WDAGO File 2815; "Medical History, Camp Supply," 29.

rainstorm caused it to flood after they had fled eastward, thus cutting off pursuit. The village, which now contained many Comanches in addition to the Kiowas, continued eastward through the stormy night until they reached Elk Creek, about where Elk City, Oklahoma, now stands. In a conference between the chiefs as to where they should go next, the advice of medicine prophet Maman-ti was adopted. His stuffed owl told him they should turn back to the southwest and hide in Palo Duro Canyon, a miniature Grand Canyon located to the southeast of the future site of Amarillo, Texas.[34]

No military scouts saw the Indians as they rode across the Staked Plains and down a narrow trail to the bottom of the canyon. The Kiowas felt safe there, and soon were joined by many Cheyennes and Comanches. But the latter had left a trail to the south edge of the gorge which was being followed by Mackenzie's Tonkawa guides. Early on September 27, Mackenzie and the Fourth Cavalry made a surprise attack on the villages in the floor of the canyon. The Indians abandoned their lodges and scrambled up the sides of the canyon or followed side canyons to the plains above. They lost few killed or captured, but Mackenzie rounded up and shot 1,500 of their ponies. No more serious blow could have been dealt, because without their mounts the Indians were ineffective as fighters and very nearly unable to secure meat.[35]

That night it rained hard. The Indians, having lost their shelters, were thoroughly soaked. In the morning they resumed their flight, the Kiowas going across the arid plains toward an area where they knew cattails grew in shallow ponds or in the mud. Even if the ponds had dried they could quench their thirst by munching the roots of the tules. As they turned south toward the Yellowhouse country (near present Lubbock) they saw the Cheyennes, riding two and three on a horse, still vigorously quirting their ponies though they were now many miles from the battleground.[36]

The Kiowas finally encountered New Mexican militia and Navahos, who pretended to take pity on them in their destitution but at night stole most of their remaining horses. Now realizing that they must return to the reservation, they turned eastward toward the Wichita Mountains and finally straggled in to Fort Sill. They surrendered, were disarmed, and their horses

[34] Statement by Botalye to author, 1935; Nye, *Bad Medicine and Good*, 195–98; Report of Major W. R. Price, September 23, 1874, WDAGO File 2815.
[35] Sherman to Townsend, October 14, 1874, WDAGO File 2815; Robert G. Carter, *On The Border With Mackenzie*, 488–95.
[36] Nye, *Carbine and Lance*, 224.

—any that were left—taken away from them. Other bands came in from time to time and similarly lost their weapons and animals. The chiefs were shackled and thrown into a makeshift prison.[37]

Meanwhile, General Miles remained camped near Red River while waiting for his wagon train to return. A "norther," that weather phenomenon of the western Plains, swooped down following a terrific thunderstorm. In a few hours the temperature plummeted to below freezing and the air was filled with hard-driven needles of ice. Men and animals became as miserable from being wet and cold as they had been from heat and thirst.[38] A day or two later the sun was out, the air was balmy, and the prairie dogs were chirping cheerfully from their warrens.

The soldiers were not chirping, and they were not cheerful. Although their supplies were not gone, the men had been on short rations for a week, and they were hungry. On September 18, Miles decided to double back to meet Lyman. This juncture was accomplished successfully, and after one or two good meals, the soldiers' spirits were revived. The column moved to Miles' previous camp on the Washita. Miles proposed to shuttle supplies from Camp Supply to this point, which was to be used as an advance base.

The Indians were mostly on the Staked Plains where they were hard to find. Detachments kept scouting for them, although without success until October 9, when Colonel Buell's column struck a band between the North and Salt Forks of the Red River, in what is now Greer County, Oklahoma. The Indians abandoned their camp, which Buell destroyed, and fled northward.[39] Four days later Navaho scouts with Price dispersed a group of hostiles between the Canadian and the head of the Washita.[40] On the seventeenth, Captain Adna R. Chaffee of General Miles's force surprised an Indian camp five miles north of the Washita and burned their lodges. The Indians' camp equipment was being whittled down to the vanishing point.[41]

After his first fruitless expedition in September, General Davidson had gone back to Fort Sill for resupply. On October 21, he was again in the saddle and scouting up the Washita toward Rainy Mountain Creek. On October 26, part of his force under Major George W. Schofield, when on Elk Creek, received the surrender of the Comanche bands of Tabananica, White Wolf (Esa Rosa), Red Foot, and Little Crow. The Indians were

[37] *Ibid.*, 224–25, 229.
[38] Miles, *Personal Recollections*, 168, 170.
[39] Drum to Whipple, October 24, 1874, WDAGO File 2815.
[40] Nye, *Carbine and Lance*, 225.
[41] *Ibid.*

taken to Fort Sill as prisoners of war, while Davidson, with the bulk of his force, continued up Elk Creek and cooperated with the other commands.[42]

Miles had consolidated Price's force with his own and put into effect a plan for rounding up the Indians who had fled from Palo Duro Canyon. He left Price on the Washita while he led his force to the vicinity of Adobe Walls. He hoped to get west of the redskins and drive them back into Price's lap. They were flushed out at a point farther to the northeast, however, and made for a northern branch of McClellan Creek.[43]

General Miles learned from his scouts, some of whom, like Ben Clark, had Cheyenne wives, that the four German sisters were still alive and in the Cheyenne camps. Lieutenant Baldwin was given a task force consisting of an infantry company, a cavalry company, a howitzer, and a wagon train, and was told to rescue the girls. On the morning of November 8, he found Gray Beard's camp near the north branch of McClellan Creek, about ten miles south of the site of Pampa, Texas, and charged through it, routing the Indians. The infantry rode standing up in wagons from which the canvas covers had been removed and shot over the backs of the mules. While they mopped up the village, the cavalry pursued the Indians for twelve miles. In their rush to get away, the Indians failed to slaughter their captives. The soldiers found Adelaide and Julia German, aged seven and five, who were alive though scarcely able to talk owing to mistreatment, malnutrition, and prolonged fright. The two older sisters, Sophia and Catherine, were in another village not located by the troops.[44]

On the same date, the Fort Sill column reached the broken country where the head of the North Fork of Red River and its tributary streams cut into the edge of the Staked Plains. Here they found a village of fifty lodges, which they burned, and also buried the body of one of Price's men who had been scalped and mutilated. Colonel Miles came up and saw the Indians in the distance, but he could not follow them on account of the exhausted condition of his horses. Davidson selected 120 of his best horses, mounted good men on them, and sent them in pursuit under Captain Charles D. Viele. The chase was ended by one of those sleet storms that sometimes coats the whole plains country with a thick sheet of ice.[45] The Indians were forced to drop more equipment, but they got away in the opaque storm.

The Cheyennes held out with amazing courage and tenacity for a few

[42] *Ibid.*

[43] *Ibid.*, 226.

[44] Miles to AAG, Dept. of Mo., November 9, 1874, WDAGO File 2815; Miles's Report of Campaign, March 4, 1875, WDAGO 2815.

[45] *Ibid.*, Nye, *Carbine and Lance*, 227.

176

more weeks. Several small groups started to make their way east and tried to slip unnoticed into the villages of Little Robe and other friendlies camped near the agency. But by the end of November only about four hundred had come in, and few more arrived in December.

By January, 1875, Lieutenant Colonel Thomas H. Neill, commander at the Darlington agency, sent word to Stone Calf that he could surrender without punishment if he would bring in the two German sisters, aged seventeen and fifteen, who were in his band.[46] The girls were not brought in until March, probably because the Cheyennes wished to retain them as hostages or else to get more money for them by bargaining.[47] On March 6, Stone Calf, Red Moon, Gray Beard, and several other chiefs brought in their bands, totalling 820 people, and surrendered at the agency.[48] The German sisters were turned over to the military, and in a line-up pointed out the individual Indians who had killed their parents and brothers and sisters and had raped them numerous times. Thirty-one of the guilty men were placed in irons and sent to Fort Marion, Florida, for confinement, together with choice groups from the Kiowas and Comanches. They spent their time in Florida making and selling souvenirs to tourists and were released within a few years.[49] The Cheyennes most guilty of atrocities escaped entirely by going north and joining the Northern Cheyenne and Sioux.

At Fort Sill, the distinguished parole-breaker, Satanta, was returned to the penitentiary in Texas where he committed suicide a few years later by diving from the second story window of the prison hospital to the paved courtyard.[50] His young partner in crime, Big Tree, was pardoned. Eventually he joined the Baptist Church at Rainy Mountain and in his later years taught a Bible class of young Kiowas.[51] Kicking Bird, who had been designated as principal chief of the Kiowas, died suddenly on the day the prisoners were sent off to Fort Marion. Some say he was poisoned, others were convinced that he was prayed to death by Maman-ti, one of the prisoners.[52]

Thus, between 1865 and 1875, the five southwestern Plains tribes were

[46] Letter from Lieutenant Colonel Neill to Catherine and Sophia German, dated January 20, 1875. WDAGO File 2815.

[47] Letters from J. D. Miles and T. H. Neill, January 21, 1875, with indorsement of General John Pope, WDAGO File 2815.

[48] Pope to Whipple, February 26; Neill to Pope, March 6, 1875, WDAGO File 2815.

[49] WDAGO File 2815 contains numerous papers relating to this, including correspondence from Lieutenant Richard H. Pratt, Tenth Cavalry, who was in charge of the Indians at Fort Marion and later was superintendent of the Carlisle Indian School.

[50] Mooney, "Calendar History," 209–10.

[51] Statement of George Hunt, Kiowa historian, to author, 1935.

[52] *Ibid.*

moved south from the Arkansas and subjugated. It had taken much too long. At first there were not enough trained troops, and, when there were, the government could not bring itself to adopt the stern measures needed. In the end it was starvation that brought the Indians to their knees, and it was the loss of their horses that kept them from any further serious outbreaks—although there were one or two occasions when the authorities feared another uprising.[53] At Fort Sill, and possibly in the Cheyenne reservation, 7,500 Indian horses were sold at auction and the proceeds credited to the tribes. A large number were shot, and some that could be identified were turned over to Texans who came to claim them.

The Plains Indian was no longer a free man, able to ride across the sunny prairie and live the life of his fathers. But being subdued did not mean the Indians were civilized. That would be a slow process in which they were to suffer much heartbreak.

[53] George Bird Grinnell, *The Fighting Cheyennes*, 326; Berthrong, *The Southern Cheyennes*, 401–402.

BIBLIOGRAPHY

I. GOVERNMENT DOCUMENTS

A. *Books*

1. *War of the Rebellion: Official Records of the Union and Confederate Armies, Series I.* Washington, Government Printing Office, 1891. This contains reports and correspondence of commanders of units and detachments in the field; of posts, camps, and stations; of district and department commanders and staffs; of the Headquarters Military Division of the Missouri; of the Department of the Army; and in part of the Commissioner of Indian Affairs and his lower agencies; and the correspondence of members of committees and commissions investigating Indian affairs. The pertinent volumes, covering the years 1864–65, until the Volunteer Army was demobilized are: XXXIV, Parts I–IV; XLI, Parts I–III; and XLVIII, Parts I–II.

2. House and Senate Executive Documents for the years 1866–75; annual volumes that contain reports and correspondence of military commanders at all levels; correspondence with officials of the Department of the Interior, including Indian agencies; and correspondence of investigative agencies and peace commissions. The pertinent volumes are:

   a. House Executive Documents—
      39 Cong., 2 sess., Vol. III, Pt. 1
      40 Cong., 2 sess., Vol. II, Pt. 1
      40 Cong., 3 sess., Vol. I, Pt. 1
      40 Cong., 3 sess., Vol. II, Pt. 1
      40 Cong., 3 sess., Vol. III, Pt. 1
      41 Cong., 2 sess., Vol. III

   b. Senate Executive Documents—
      40 Cong., 1 sess., Nos. 1–20
      40 Cong., 1 sess., No. 1308

3. Heitman, Francis B. *Historical Register and Dictionary of the United States Army, 1789–1903.* Vol. I, Washington, GPO, 1903.

4. *Volunteer Army Register, 1861–65.* Washington, AGO.

B. *Post Records*

1. Post Records, File RG 98, "Records of the United States Army Commands," in National Archives. These are the boxes containing the "Letters Sent" and "Post Returns" of each of the posts under consideration; the medical histories of each post; and the Letter Books. The Letter Books contain copies of the letters sent, and they are much easier to read, as the handwriting is generally better and the letters are entered in sequence. The medical histories, written in large ledgers, often contain more information than the correspondence and reports.

2. Records of certain posts, not filed in the National Archives. The partial records of Forts Sill and Arbuckle are in the Library, U.S. Army Artillery and Missile Center, Fort Sill, Oklahoma.

3. Copies in state and university libraries. Microfilm copies of many records are now in state repositories, notably the University of Oklahoma.

C. *War Department Adjutant General's Office File 2815.* Before all such records were transferred to the National Archives, this file was in the old War, State, and Navy Building. It contained all the records, including maps, of the campaign of 1874–75 against the Plains Indians. I have used transcripts that I made in 1935, and which are now in the Fort Sill Library. Perhaps the easiest way to examine this file is to obtain a copy of: Taylor, Joe F., ed. *The Indian Campaign on the Staked Plains, 1874–75, Military Correspondence from War Department Adjutant General's Office File 2815, 1874.* All these documents were assembled into book form and published in 1962 by the Panhandle-Plains Historical Society, Canyon, Texas. A copy of the original map illustrating General Miles's routes is included as a folder. No doubt the original documents are now in the National Archives.

II. Manuscripts

A. Philip H. Sheridan Papers. Manuscript Division, Library of Congress. These papers are well arranged and card-catalogued. The bulk of material covering the years 1868–75 is in containers 72, 73, and in the box of telegrams. Included are many papers written by officers acting as Indian agents, as well as the reports and correspondence of military officials.

B. Letters of General W. T. Sherman. Manuscript Division, Library of Congress. Sherman was a voluminous correspondent, but I used only those letters pertaining to Fort Sill.

C. Correspondence of General B. H. Grierson, University of Illinois Library. There is little in Grierson's correspondence that is of interest to this particular subject.

III. Maps

The maps, prepared by the author, are based on United States Geological Survey maps for topography, with routes and locations from contemporary maps in the National Archives. Additional data were furnished by E. R. Archambeau, Amarillo, Texas, past president of the Panhandle-Plains Historical Society, and E. M. Beougher, president of the Fort Wallace Historical Association. The course of the Santa Fe Trail was checked from information in "The National Survey of Historic Sites and Buildings, *The Santa Fe Trail*," National Park Service Theme XV (manuscript), by W. E. Brown, 1963, and data furnished by Robert M. Utley and Roy Appelman, National Park Service.

IV. Books

Armes, George A. *Ups and Downs of an Army Officer*. Washington, 1900.

Battey, Thomas C. *The Life and Adventures of a Quaker Among the Indians*. Boston, 1889.

Bell, William A. *New Tracks in North America, a Journal of Travel and Adventure Whilst Engaged in A Survey for a Southern Railroad to the Pacific Ocean During 1867–1868*. London, 1869.

Berthrong, Donald J. *The Southern Cheyennes*, Norman, 1963.

Brill, Charles J. *Conquest of the Southwestern Plains*. Oklahoma City, 1938.

Carter, Robert G. *The Old Sergeant's Story*, New York, 1926.

———. *On the Border with Mackenzie*. Washington, 1935.

Clark, William P. *The Indian Sign Language*. Philadelphia, 1885.

Conover, George W. *Sixty Years in Southwest Oklahoma*. Anadarko, 1927.

Corwin, Hugh D. *Comanche and Kiowa Captives in Oklahoma and Texas*. Guthrie, 1959.

———. *The Kiowa Indians*. Guthrie, 1958.

Custer, General George A. *My Life on the Plains; Or Personal Experiences with Indians*. New York, 1876.

Davis, Charles E., Jr. *Three Years in the Army: The Story of the Thirteenth Massachusetts Volunteers*. Boston, Estes and Couriat, 1894.

Dixon, Olive K. *Life of Billy Dixon*. Dallas, 1927.

Ewers, John C. "Hairpipes in Plains Indian Adornments. A Study in Indian and White Ingenuity," *Anthropological Papers No. 50, Bureau of American Ethnology, Bulletin 164*. Washington, 1957.

Forsyth, George A. *Thrilling Days of Army Life*. New York, 1900.

Graham, William A. *The Custer Myth*. Harrisburg, 1953.

Gregg, Josiah. *Commerce of the Prairies*. Philadelphia, 1844.

Grinnell, George Bird. *The Fighting Cheyennes*. Norman, 1966.

————. *The Cheyenne Indians*. 2 vols. New Haven, 1923.

Harrington, John P. "Vocabulary of the Kiowa Language," *Bureau of American Ethnology, Bulletin 84*. Washington, 1928.

Hodge, Frederick W., ed. *Handbook of American Indians North of Mexico*, Bulletin 30, Bureau of American Ethnology. 2 vols. Washington, 1912.

Jones, Douglas C. *The Treaty of Medicine Lodge*. Norman, 1966.

Lowie, Robert H. *Indians of the Plains*. New York, 1954.

Marriott, Alice. *The Ten Grandmothers*. Norman, 1945.

Mayhall, Mildred P. *The Kiowas*. Norman, 1962.

Meredith, Grace E. *Girl Captives of the Cheyennes*. Los Angeles, 1927.

Methvin, J. J. *In the Limelight: History of Anadarko and Vicinity from Earliest Times*. Anadarko, no date.

Miles, Nelson A. *Personal Recollections and Observations of General Nelson A. Miles*. Chicago, 1896.

Mooney, James. "Calendar History of the Kiowa Indians," *Seventeenth Annual Report of the Bureau of American Ethnology*, Pt. I. Washington, 1898.

Nye, Wilbur Sturtevant, *Carbine and Lance: The Story of Old Fort Sill*. 2nd ed., rev. Norman, 1942.

————. *Bad Medicine and Good: Tales of the Kiowas*, Norman, 1962.

————, and Jason Betzinez. *I Fought With Geronimo*. Harrisburg, 1959.

Price, George F. *Across the Continent With the Fifth Cavalry*. New York, 1883.

Prucha, Paul Francis. *Guide to the Military Posts of the United States*. Madison, Wisconsin, 1964.

Richardson, Rupert N. *The Comanche Barrier to Southwest Plains Settlement*. Glendale, California, 1933.

Scott, Hugh L. *Some Memories of a Soldier*. New York, 1928.

Seger, John H. *Early Days Among the Cheyenne and Arapahoe Indians*. Norman, 1934.

Sheridan, Philip H. *Personal Memoirs*. Vol. II. New York, 1888.

Stanley, Henry M. *My Early Travels and Adventures in America and Asia*. New York, 1895.

Taft, Robert. *Photography and the American Scene*.

Tatum, Lawrie. *Our Red Brothers*. Philadelphia, 1899.

Wallace, Ernest, and E. Adamson Hoebel. *The Comanches: Lords of the South Plains.* Norman, 1952.

Wellman, Paul I. *Death on the Prairie.* New York, 1934.

Wheeler, Homer. *The Frontier Trail.* Los Angeles, 1923.

V. Periodicals

Army and Navy Journal, Vols. IV, V, and VI. This unofficial but authoritative gazette of the armed forces published the orders and reports of commanders and headquarters of all pertinent units and posts, the court-martial orders and other orders affecting units and individuals, and letters from correspondents in the field and at posts. It duplicates a good deal of the material in the official files in the National Archives, and contains many eyewitness accounts not in the records. It has been published weekly in Washington since the beginning of the Civil War, today being called the *Journal of the Armed Forces.*

Archambeau, Ernest R. "The Battle of Lyman's Wagon Train," *Panhandle-Plains Historical Review*, Vol. XXXVI (1963).

Davis, Theodore F. "A Stage Ride to Colorado," *Harper's New Monthly Magazine.* Vol. XXXV (July, 1867).

Foreman, Carolyn Thomas. "Col. Jesse Henry Leavenworth," *Chronicles of Oklahoma*, Vol. XIII (March, 1935).

Gibbon, Major General John. "Arms to Fight the Indians," *United Service*, Vol. I (April, 1879).

Harper's Weekly Magazine, for the years 1864–75.

Hazen, General William B. "Some Corrections of 'Life on the Plains,' " *Chronicles of Oklahoma*, Vol. III (December, 1925).

Montgomery, Mrs. Frank C. "Fort Wallace and its Relation to the Frontier," *Kansas Historical Collections*, Vol. XVII (1926–30).

Stinson, M.D., Byron. "Scurvy in the Civil War—A Medical Report" *Civil War Times Illustrated*, Vol. V, No. 5 (August, 1966).

West, G. Derek. "The Battle of Adobe Walls," *Panhandle-Plains Historical Review*, Vol. XXXVI (1963).

Wynkoop, Edward W. "Edward Wanshear Wynkoop," *Kansas Historical Collections*, Vol. XIII (1913–14).

William S. Soule

Photographer of the southwestern Plains Indians, 1867–75.

Lucia A. Soule

Set-tain-te, which means White Bear, was commonly called Satanta by the white men. He was one of the most active raiders of his tribe, although not the principal chief. This photograph must have been made early in the spring of 1867 at Fort Dodge. The chief is wearing a jacket made partly of an army officer's uniform, with the insignia of a captain. In May of that year, General Hancock gave him a major general's coat. He appears to be wearing a Washington medal, but there is no record that he was ever presented with one. Note that his hair is cut off just below the ear on the right side; this was a Kiowa custom.

Smithsonian Institution,
Bureau of American Ethnology

187

This rare photograph by an unknown photographer shows the ill-fated Cheyenne chief, Black Kettle, and a number of his associates at Camp Weld, on the outskirts of Denver. They had assembled there on September 28, 1864, for a peace council with Governor Evans and Colonel John M. Chivington, commander of the District of Colorado. Chivington later attacked their camp in what is known as the Sand Creek massacre.

Some of the identifications of Indians are uncertain. Front row, kneeling, left to right: Major Edward W. Wynkoop, commander at Fort Lyon and later agent for the Cheyennes and Arapahoes; Captain Silas S. Soule, provost marshal, later murdered in Denver. Middle row, seated, left to right: White Antelope (or perhaps White Wolf), Bull Bear, Black Kettle, One Eye, Natame (Arapaho). Back row, standing, left to right: Colorado militiaman, unknown civilian, John H. Smith (interpreter), Heap of Buffalo (Arapaho), Neva (Arapaho), unknown civilian, sentry.

Another identification states that Neva is seated on the left and the Indian next to Smith is White Wolf (Cheyenne).

Library, State Historical
Society of Colorado

189

ROMAN NOSE

This photograph was copied in 1868 from an earlier print by an unknown photographer, possibly Soule, for he had an opportunity to photograph Roman Nose in 1867.

The Indians, left to right, are said to be White Antelope, Man-on-a-Cloud, and Roman Nose. Other photographs (not shown) thought to be of the Cheyenne chief, Roman Nose, were probably of Arapaho or Sioux warriors also called Roman Nose.

Grinnell claimed that Roman Nose was not a chief, but contemporary reports by government officials, interpreters, post commanders, and others refer to him as such. He is named as a chief in the annual reports of the Commissioners of Indian Affairs. In any event, he was a prominent war leader. In this photograph he is shown as a powerfully built man wearing a full war bonnet, uniquely decorated in front with the breast feathers of an eagle. The Cheyennes say it was because he violated a taboo of his war-bonnet medicine that he was killed at the Battle of the Arikaree (Beecher's Island). Note the chief's shirt and leggings, which are fringed with knots of scalp hair. Each knot was thought to represent an enemy killed. This man is also carrying a pipe, which is the symbol of a war chief.

Smithsonian Institution,
Bureau of American Ethnology

This mighty Cheyenne war chief was noted for his outstanding courage; yet at heart he was a man of good will. It shows in his face.

In 1854, during a disastrous encounter between the Cheyennes, Arapahoes, Kiowas, and Comanches on one side, and the Sac and Foxes on the other, Whirlwind was one of the Cheyenne heroes. Bullets clipped his hair, his clothing, and flew all around him. He was saved by his powerful medicine, which consisted of the head of a hawk tied to the front of his war bonnet.

Whirlwind signed the Medicine Lodge Treaty, and he lived up to his word. Thereafter he belonged to the peace faction. In 1874 he moved his band to the agency and kept them out of the war. He was highly thought of by the military people and by the officials at the agency. Mrs. Dyer writes:

Old Whirlwind was always gorgeous in remarkable ornaments, in bright daubs of paint, wearing a pair of cavalry shoulder straps on a vest, moccasins encrusted with beads, while strands composed of beads and shells, and elk teeth hung about his neck. In his time he was one of the most blood-thirsty and daring of the many great fighters, outranking Lone Wolf, Yellow Bull, Satanta . . . .

He was a nephew of Black Kettle. . . . He died in 1895.

Smithsonian Institution,
Bureau of American Ethnology

Little Robe

Little Robe was a prominent Cheyenne chief who usually favored peace. He often tried to persuade the hostiles to come in and settle down, but did not always succeed. He was well liked by the agents and by army officers, and he sincerely tried to keep his young men from raiding.

Smithsonian Institution,
Bureau of American Ethnology

Che'
LITTLE FOX

Daughters of Little Robe

These Cheyenne girls are well dressed, as befits their positions as daughters of a prominent Cheyenne chief. Their hair is neatly combed and braided, they are wearing moccasins decorated with porcupine quills and beads, and the one on the right has an expensive shawl, hair-pipe pendants on her ears, and a necklace of the same material.

*Smithsonian Institution,
Bureau of American Ethnology*

Cheyenne Camp

This small village of ten lodges housed fifty or sixty persons; thus it must have belonged to a family group. The Plains Indians did not often assemble as a tribe except on special occasions such as a sun dance or, in the case of the Cheyennes, the ceremony of renewing the sacred arrows. When the camps were small, it was easier to find game, to obtain good grazing for the ponies, and to find wood and water for the camp.

Note the meat hung out to dry and the two sweat lodges (without covers), or perhaps travois carriers. On the right may be seen the vehicle Soule used for a darkroom and to carry his equipment (partly hidden by a tipi).

Since no horses can be seen and only two persons, it is likely that most of the band are hunting buffalo.

Smithsonian Institution,
Bureau of American Ethnology

Yellow Bear was an Arapaho chief prominent in the wars between his tribe and the Pawnees in 1852–53. In the spring of 1853, he and Little Robe organized a revenge raid against the Pawnees for the killing of a popular Cheyenne named Alights-on-a-Cloud. He was a signer of the Medicine Lodge Treaty, and from that time on he was identified with the peace faction.

Smithsonian Institution,
Bureau of American Ethnology

Newat, or Left Hand, became principal chief of the Cheyennes in later years, after the death of Whirlwind. Photograph by Alexander Gardner, 1872.

Smithsonian Institution,
Bureau of American Ethnology

Big Mouth

Bi-nan-set, or Big Mouth, was an Arapaho chief who signed the first treaty between his tribe and the government in 1851. He also signed the Medicine Lodge Treaty. Like Little Raven, he favored peace with the white men.

*Smithsonian Institution,
Bureau of American Ethnology*

Little Raven

Born about 1820, Little Raven won his chieftainship through prowess in battle. He was one of the war leaders who in 1854 took part in the notable battle with the Sac and Foxes. But like most Arapahoes he was by nature inclined to be friendly and peaceable. He was a signer of the Medicine Lodge Treaty and a consistent member of the peace faction.

Smithsonian Institution,
Bureau of American Ethnology

The man on the left appears to be the same as the man in the photograph labeled Little Bear (the view showing William Bent and Little Raven which follows). The man on the right is said to be Shield, but he does not appear to be the same man as is shown in the next picture. This is typical of the designations given in the Soule albums. There are apparent inconsistencies and errors; it may be that Soule marked these pictures from memory, or that he made the prints somewhat later than the negatives and did not in all cases recall the names.

Note the peculiar scoop-shaped rings worn by the two men in this picture, and the beaded edging of the vest worn by the man on the right. He also has the insignia of a second lieutenant on one shoulder, which is a shoulder strap without bars. In each case the single feather in the hair slants downward. If it were horizontal, the man would be a distinguished warrior. Little Bear is carrying a feather fan, a popular article with Plains Indians and still seen occasionally as late as 1935.

Smithsonian Institution,
Bureau of American Ethnology

Little Raven and William Bent

This photograph is said to have been made at Fort Dodge. It is of interest mainly in that it is a rare picture of the old frontiersman and trader, William Bent. The man on the right is said to be Shield, a son of Little Raven and one of the Indians who started the war in 1868 by committing the atrocities on the Saline. The second man from the right is Little Bear, another of Little Raven's sons. One or both of these men may be nephews rather than sons. The officers on the roof of the adobe are not identified.

Smithsonian Institution,
Bureau of American Ethnology

211

The Kiowa chief Set-angya (Sitting Bear), who was known to the whites as Satank, was an old-time warrior who never absorbed the ways of the white man, although he came in contact with them as early as 1845, when he met an exploring party under Lieutenant J. W. Abert. Satank was a veteran of the wars with the Cheyennes, Pawnees, Utes, and Navahos and a member of the Ko-eet-senko, a warrior order composed of the ten bravest members of the tribe. Notice the leather strap over his shoulder. That was the badge of his order; when he was in battle, he would fix himself to the ground by a medicine lance thrust through a loop in that strap. It was his duty to remain in place until the battle was won, and die, if necessary, to cover the retreat of other warriors.

Satank had two surviving sons—An-pay-kau-te and a smaller boy who was taken East to be educated. The latter returned under the name Joshua Given and worked as an Episcopal missionary to his tribe. His sister, Julia, also educated in the East, became a missionary, too. Her daughter Ioleta Hunt McElheny is now a missionary to the Cheyennes.

Smithsonian Institution,
Bureau of American Ethnology

An-pay-kau-te was known to the whites as Frank Given, probably because the name was conferred on his younger brother and sister when they went to school in the East. His oldest brother was killed while on a raid, and he himself was in raiding parties during 1869–74.

The old warrior inherited his father's Washington medal and one of the tribal medicines called Grandmother Gods. He kept the medal in the pouch which contained the medicine, but removed and wore it for this photograph. It was the first time it had been exposed to view since 1871 when his father was killed.

Wilbur S. Nye Collection

215

KICKING BIRD

His Kiowa name, Tay-nay-an-gopte (phonetic), actually means "Eagle Striking With Talons," but the name was corrupted by the whites to "Kicking Bird," no doubt a mistranslation of the name rendered in the sign language. Born about 1835, he was three-quarters Kiowa, for his paternal grandfather was a Crow captured when a boy and adopted into the tribe. Before he was thirty, Kicking Bird had displayed such outstanding bravery, wisdom, and eloquence that his influence extended well beyond his own band of some two hundred persons. He was a cousin of Stumbling Bear, and his father and grandfather had been noted war chiefs. He was born into the aristocracy of the tribe.

Since he led the peace faction of his tribe and co-operated with the white officials, he was appointed by the agent in 1874 to be principal chief, a position he actually occupied in any event though not formally appointed by the tribal councils. His force of character was so great that he could and did face down Satanta and other older chiefs whenever differences occurred.

Because the officials at Fort Sill asked him to point out men who should be sent to prison in 1875, some malcontents brought about his death by poison or, as some believe, by witchcraft. "I am dying," he said as the end approached. "I have taken the white man's road, and am not sorry. Tell my people to keep the good path." He was forty years old and in the prime of life.

Smithsonian Institution,
Bureau of American Ethnology

His Kiowa name, Set-imkia, is more properly translated: "Bear that is pushing" or "Bear that is shoving you down." He was born in 1832, the year of the "Wolf Creek Sun Dance." He was in the disastrous battle with the Sac and Foxes in 1854, and his bravery there won him a chieftainship at the age of twenty-two. Two years later, he and Big Bow led a raid against the Navahos, and in the winter of 1858–59, he and Satanta led a war party against the Utes. In 1865 he was one of the heroes of the fight with Kit Carson near Adobe Walls, and by this time was a veteran of many battles.

Stumbling Bear joined the peace faction, partly because of the influence of his cousin, Kicking Bird, but also because a doctor at one of the army posts saved the life of his small son who was desperately ill.

Smithsonian Institution,
Bureau of American Ethnology

219

Lone Wolf

Lone Wolf's Kiowa name is Gui-pah-go, which is variously misspelled, sometimes being almost unrecognizable. For example, in one of the contemporary reports he is referred to as "Quiel-parko." Most renditions of his name are phonetic. When old Do-hauson, who had been principal chief for more than thirty years, died, he conferred this title on Lone Wolf; therefore, Lone Wolf must have been an outstanding warrior. He was never quite able to consolidate his claim to the position, being overshadowed by the more spectacular Satanta and the far abler Kicking Bird.

His favorite son, Tau-ankia, was killed while on a raid in Texas in 1873. This made him definitely hostile to the whites, and in 1874 he led the Lost Valley raid that was partly responsible for setting off the outbreak of that fall.

Lone Wolf was one of the Fort Marion prisoners. He died of malaria in 1879, shortly after his return to the reservation, and was buried secretly on the north shoulder of Mount Scott. In 1874 he conferred his chieftainship on a man named Mamay-day-te, who thereupon assumed the name Lone Wolf. Many of the early settlers in Oklahoma knew Mamay-day-te as Chief Lone Wolf.

Smithsonian Institution,
Bureau of American Ethnology

LONE WOLF'S VILLAGE

The Soule label on this picture states that it is Lone Wolf's camp. The album contains another view of the same camp, taken from a different angle, which is labeled "Kicking Bird's village." Whichever it may be, the photograph is a clear view of a Kiowa village near Fort Sill, apparently taken in the winter along Medicine Bluff Creek or near Mount Scott.

Smithsonian Institution,
Bureau of American Ethnology

Zepko-eete was, in his early years as a warrior, one of the most formidable fighters in the Kiowa tribe. Because he lived on the Staked Plains with the Quohada Comanches and did not visit the army posts, he was little known to the white men. He usually went on raids alone or with one or two Mexican captives whom he had adopted. He was a nonconformist with respect to religion, tending to deride the performances of the medicine men. For this reason some of the Kiowas looked at him askance.

Big Bow was born on Elk Creek in 1833, and by 1851 was a recognized war chief. Like other knights of old, he had a way with women. In 1851 he stole the wife of a fellow tribesman.

Big Bow enhanced his fame through expeditions against the Utes and Navahos. Though he was a hostile, Kicking Bird had him enlisted as a U.S. Army scout in 1875 to help bring in the few runaway Indians who had not yet surrendered. In 1886 he led several Kiowas to Antelope Hills, by permission of the agent, to recover stock stolen by some white rustlers. He overtook and killed the thieves and recovered the horses, although he had only a few rounds of ammunition.

Today his grandson, Abel Big Bow, lives near Anadarko, and another descendant, George Tsoodle, is married to Margaret, the daughter of George Hunt.

Smithsonian Institution,
Bureau of American Ethnology

Man-yi-ten was a typical Kiowa war chief. Although he signed the Medicine Lodge Treaty, he was not of the peace party. In the winter of 1868, he remained near Antelope Hills with the hostile Cheyennes. After the Battle of the Washita, he took his band to the vicinity of Sheep Mountain, where he became involved in the Battle of Soldier Spring.

He was one of the hostiles in the 1874 outbreak but soon surrendered. Woman's Heart was one of the Kiowas sent to prison in 1875.

Smithsonian Institution,
Bureau of American Ethnology

White Horse

Tsen-tainte had a reputation among the Kiowas for being a tough, reckless fellow. He was an outstanding horseman and had great physical strength. He gained much notoriety for his raiding during 1870–74, and consequently, he was one of those selected for imprisonment in Fort Marion. He died of a stomach ailment in 1892.

Smithsonian Institution,
Bureau of American Ethnology

Known to the whites as Big Blond and Kiowa Dutch, this captive member of the Kiowa tribe was born in Germany about 1825. He was taken prisoner when about ten years of age near Galveston Bay. He grew up as a Kiowa brave and remained with the tribe until his death.

Note that this man was not as meticulous as a genuine Indian in removing the hair from his face, perhaps because the beard of a white man is heavier and more retentive than that of an Indian. A Kiowa would have been regarded as a man without pride if he let the hair grow on his face. It was all plucked out, mustache, beard, and even the eyebrows. The Indians used brass tweezers for this purpose, and their motive was the same as that of white women today—vanity.

Smithsonian Institution,
Bureau of American Ethnology

231

Ten Bears, an aged Yapparika Comanche chief, signed the Medicine Lodge Treaty, his name being erroneously translated as Ten Elks. At one time he had been a leading war chief, and his memory went back to about 1790. But by the time he became known to the white people, he was already an old man with declining influence in the tribe.

He went on Alvord's junket to Washington in 1872, but the trip was too much for him. When the party arrived back at Fort Sill, the old chief was sick. Since his people had deserted him and would not care for him, the agent gave him a bed in the office. Here Ten Bears died, alone in the midst of an alien people, in an age he did not understand. Once a mighty warrior respected by his tribe, in his old age he had taken the white man's road, and his people cast him off.

Ten Bear's grave may be seen today in the Fort Sill cemetery. This photograph was taken in Washington in 1872 by Alexander Gardner, the former assistant of Matthew Brady.

Smithsonian Institution,
Bureau of American Ethnology

233

Tosawi (Silver Brooch), whose name is sometimes spelled Toshaway or Toshua, was one of the Penateka-Comanche chiefs who generally favored peace with the whites. He co-operated with the authorities from the time that his band was placed on a reservation in Texas through all the succeeding troubles, until peace was finally established in 1875.

This photograph shows him wearing one of the "Jeff Davis" military hats which must have been given to the Indians from surplus military stocks. This hat received its name from the fact that it was designed as a dress hat for the army during the time that Jefferson Davis was secretary of war. When the Civil War broke out, it became unpopular and was not worn by any unit except the famous Iron Brigade commanded by the Quaker general, Meredith. Arthur Woodward, former head of the Department of Ethnology and Anthropology in the Los Angeles County Museum, says that the star worn by the Indian was probably made of cloth rather than metal, for none of them have been found at former camp sites.

Smithsonian Institution,
Bureau of American Ethnology

Pochanaw-quoip, called Buffalo Hump or Bull Hump by the whites, was third-ranking chief of the Penateka Comanches from about 1866–74. His father, of the same name, was one of the leading Comanche chiefs in Texas during the presidency of Sam Houston and his successors. After the cholera epidemic of 1849, the senior Buffalo Hump became principal chief of the Penatekas. He was famous for his large-scale raids in Mexico; sometimes he took parties of nearly one thousand warriors into Chihuahua. His son, pictured here, was also a raider and a troublemaker. He was especially disliked by the personnel at the Fort Cobb agency where, during the Civil War, he was constantly quarreling with the agent and his employees.

Buffalo Hump made the junket to Washington in 1872, where this picture was taken by Alexander Gardner.

Smithsonian Institution,
Bureau of American Ethnology

Comanche. 15ª.

156

A chief of the Nokoni Comanches, but a peaceful Indian, this man's name, Tir-ha-yah-quahip, means Sore-backed Horse, which refers to the fact that the Indian had ridden so far and hard on an expedition that the back of his horse had become sore. The white people shortened this to Horseback.

He signed the Medicine Lodge Treaty and later camped on Chandler Creek near Fort Sill to stay out of trouble. He was suffering from tuberculosis and did not dare leave the reservation to hunt buffalo because he was too sick to fight or run if attacked by troops. The agent did not issue sufficient rations to keep him from starving, and, had it not been for kindhearted officers on the post, he would not have lasted long.

In 1875, Horseback was appointed by the agent as head chief and given the thankless task of choosing the depredators who would be sent to Florida. He was one of the ten chiefs for whom the government built houses in 1879. But he preferred to camp in the yard—"Ho! Heap snakes in house!" He has a number of descendants living near Fort Sill today.

Baldwin Parker, son of Quanah Parker, believes that Horseback is buried in the Fort Sill cemetery or perhaps in a Comanche cemetery on the Fort Sill Military Reservation.

Smithsonian Institution,
Bureau of American Ethnology

Horseback's Son

Little is known concerning Chief Horseback's son except that he was one of the Comanches, supposedly friendly, who attacked Spanish Fort, Texas, on September 1, 1868.

Sarah Pohucsucut said that Horseback had at least two sons, one of whom was named William and the other Ker-tah-duro-co, but I do not know which son is pictured above. William had five children, all living today in the Richards Spur area, where old man Horseback had his camp in the early days.

Smithsonian Institution,
Bureau of American Ethnology

241

HORSEBACK'S VILLAGE

This camp was probably on Cache Creek or Chandler Creek, a few miles north of Fort Sill, and it is likely that Soule took the picture during the winter of 1872–73 when he made the rounds of the villages together with the Evans brothers and Horace Jones. Jones is seen on the left, wrapped in a buffalo robe and posing as an Indian. Note the camp gear piled on a low platform to keep it off the ground during a rainstorm. Two dogs are seen at the right. As is noted in the photographs of all camps, the Indian village is remarkably free from litter. The flaps of the hide tipi are turned back to admit air or to emit smoke. Note how they are blackened from soot.

The Indian standing is probably Horseback or one of his sons.

Smithsonian Institution,
Bureau of American Ethnology

HO-WEA

Ho-wea, whose name means Gap-in-the-Woods, was a chief of the Yap-parika (Root-Eater) band of Comanches. Ho-wea (or Ho-wear) was a familiar figure around Fort Sill in the 1870's. By 1885 he should have been better informed, but so great was his ignorance of the outside world that when he went as a delegate to Washington that year he was badly frightened by the train ride. When the train plunged into a tunnel, he went into convulsions.

Smithsonian Institution,
Bureau of American Ethnology

Tabananica (Hears-the-Sunrise), like Parra-o-coom, was a very large and muscular Indian who was not inclined to adopt the white man's road until forced to do so. He was a Yapparika chief but associated a good deal with the Quohadas. He said at the 1872 peace council, "I would rather stay out on the prairie and eat dung than be penned up on a reservation."

Nevertheless, after the wars were over, he did settle down on a farm or ranch and eventually died of heart failure while running to catch a train at Anadarko, perhaps proving that even an athletic Comanche cannot survive the hazards of modern life.

Tabananica was buried in the Comanche cemetery on the Fort Sill reservation, known as the Otipoby Cemetery.

Wilbur S. Nye Collection

Tahenanikah 1st Comanche Chief
signed treaty with U.S. Goverment Oct....
President
Lonewolf

Quirts-quip, or Chewing Elk, was a Yapparika-Comanche chief who followed the white man's road. He was born in 1827 and died in 1880. This picture was made by Alexander Gardner in Washington in 1872 when Alvord's delegation visited the city. He is remembered for some penetrating comments which he made when he saw white men making money by the bale at a government printing plant.

"I saw big piles of money in Washington," he said. "They could give me some if they wanted to. . . . We have friends in the post at Fort Sill but are not allowed to see them. You must have a big bug or a snake in there."

According to Sarah Pohocsucut, Quirts-quip's name should be written as one word, and his full name was Par-der-yah Kuirts-quiper-nied, which meant Chewing Elk. Quirts-quip was a corruption introduced by the white man, and more closely means Chewed Elk, which is wrong.

Smithsonian Institution,
Bureau of American Ethnology

Interior of Sutler's Store at Fort Dodge

This is a sketch of Tappan's store at Fort Dodge in 1867, in which Soule worked as chief clerk. The man behind the counter on the right appears to be Soule.

Harper's Weekly,
May 25, 1867

SUTLER'S STORE AT FORT DODGE, KANSAS. —[SKETCHED BY THEODORE R. DAVIS.]

William S. Soule and Friend

Miss Lucia Soule presented this photograph to me in 1965, which shows her father (on the right) enjoying a quiet moment with a friend, possibly John Tappan. It is not known where or when this was taken, but it must have been at either Fort Dodge or Fort Sill, not Camp Supply—no stone building had been built there when Soule was at Supply.

Wilbur S. Nye Collection

EDMUND GUERRIER

Guerrier's name appears in nearly all books dealing with the Indian wars of 1864–74. He was the son of a French trader and Cheyenne mother and spent about half his time with the Indians. He often acted as interpreter for agents and post commanders. Considered reliable by the authorities, he was, for many years after the troubled times, a government employee at Fort Reno, near the Darlington Agency. He was called Ned Geary by many, and the town of Geary, Oklahoma is said to have been named for him. It is not certain that this is a Soule photograph.

Wilbur S. Nye Collection

255

This is an Arapaho sun dance, photographed by James Mooney. That of the Kiowas was never photographed.

Smithsonian Institution,
Bureau of American Ethnology

SERGEANT FREDERICK WYLLYAMS

This young Englishman, a member of Troop G, Seventh Cavalry, was killed on June 26, 1867, by the famous Cheyenne warrior Roman Nose or his men during an attack on Fort Wallace, Kansas. A graduate of Eton and a member of a good family, he had been sent to America because of some escapade and had enlisted in the U.S. Army in the hope of winning a commission and thus getting back into the good graces of his family.

While at Fort Wallace, Wyllyams struck up a friendship with a fellow Briton, William A. Bell, who was a photographer with the expedition which was surveying a route west for the Kansas Pacific Railroad.

"On the day on which he was killed," said Bell, "Wyllyams had promised to help me in printing off copies of the photographs which I had taken the day before. I had to print them alone, and to take a photograph of him, poor fellow, as he lay."

Fort Wallace was subsequently abandoned, and the bodies of the men killed in the engagement with Roman Nose were exhumed and reburied in the cemetery at Fort Leavenworth, where they are today marked with a stone pyramid, though not identified individually.

Photographs of mutilated bodies are commonplace today, what with the ghastly atrocities committed almost daily by criminals of all races and in the wartime killings perpetrated in Europe and Asia. But such a photograph taken during the Indian wars is a rarity, all the more since the technique of that day did not permit the making of snapshots. This picture was made soon after the Indians had departed. Indeed, they were said to have been hovering nearby.

Wilbur S. Nye Collection

258

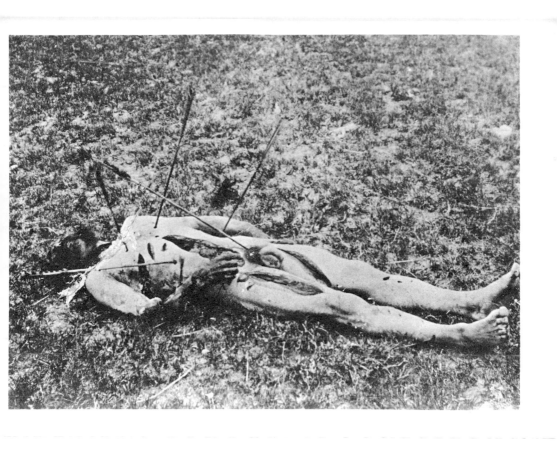

259

Isa-tai was the Comanche medicine man and minor war chief who organized the Indian attack on Adobe Walls in the summer of 1874. This affair touched off the Indian war of 1874–75.

The photograph is not believed to have been made by Soule. It was given to the Panhandle-Plains Historical Society by Isa-tai's descendants who live near Lawton, Oklahoma.

Panhandle-Plains Historical
Society

Medicine Water

Medicine Water is the Cheyenne chief who led the revenge raid after the Battle of Adobe Walls, in the early fall of 1874. His party attacked the German family a few miles east of Fort Wallace, Kansas, killing all except four young girls whom he took captive. These victims were recovered from the Indians after suffering great hardships and lived well into this century. Partly as a result of his guilt in this notorious affair, Medicine Water was one of the Indians selected for confinement in Fort Marion, Florida, from 1875 to 1878.

Smithsonian Institution,
Bureau of American Ethnology

STAGE STATION ON THE SMOKY HILL ROUTE

The men are fighting a prairie fire set by marauding Indians. Note that this redoubt has uncovered trenches, while the ones described in the text had overhead cover, with firing slits. At the left is the stage, waiting to continue the journey as soon as the horses have been replaced and the fire extinguished.

Harper's Weekly,
April 21, 1866

EXTERIOR OF THE ADOBE FORTIFICATION AT SMOKY HILL STATION—FIGHTING THE FIRE.—[Sketched by Theodore R. Davis.]

Soule had ample opportunity to photograph atrocities, many of which occurred near Fort Dodge while he was there. So far as is known, however, this is the only one he made, and it was described by a correspondent of *Harper's*, who wrote:

> The above is probably the only picture ever taken on the plains of the body of a scalped man, photographed within an hour after the deed was done.
>
> On December 7, 1868, Mr. Ralph Morrison, a hunter, was murdered and scalped by Indians within a mile of this post [Fort Dodge.]. [Photographed by] Mr. William S. Soule, chief clerk in Mr. John E. Tappan's trading establishment. . . .
>
> The Indians suffered severely for their bloody act, two being killed by a percussion shell from a Parrott gun belonging to the ordnance at Fort Dodge, served with admirable precision by Ordnance Sergeant Hughes.
>
> The Indians were promptly pursued, and two more of their saddles emptied by our scouts, whose chief, Mr. John O. Austin, is on the right of the picture. The officer is Lieutenant Philip Reade, 3d Infantry. Mr. Austin is one of the most experienced and daring scouts on the plains. He bears upon his person many marks of his adventurous life.

Wilbur S. Nye Collection

Stone Calf was a leading chief of the Cheyennes, who, because of his adherence to the peace policy, was deposed by his people. At the time that the Comanche medicine man Isa-tai was trying to interest the southern Plains tribes in a general war against the whites, Stone Calf advised the Cheyennes to go to the agency and stay out of trouble. Because of his resultant unpopularity at that time, he went on a hunting trip to Mexico with two men who stood by him. Thus he was absent when his son was killed at Adobe Walls and later during the revenge raid in which the German family was attacked. He returned to the tribe late that fall, and at once did all he could for the two oldest German girls, finally getting them released. At the same time he was largely instrumental in persuading the Cheyennes to go to the agency and surrender.

This photograph was probably made by Alexander Gardner, in Washington.

Wilbur S. Nye Collection

The name of this Cheyenne war chief is variously spelled, the English translation being Eagle Head.

Eagle Head was a firm believer in the power of medicine. In 1866 he organized a war party consisting of eighty or more warriors. In order to insure success, he conformed to an old Cheyenne custom of making skin sacrifices. He made a vow to his personal god that every member of the party would permit the medicine man, Big Wolf, to cut a piece of skin from his arm. As they came forward one at a time to make this sacrifice, some of the men indulged in a bit of exhibitionism by offering more than one slice. But Red Moon, when his turn came, objected. He did not see any sense in it. This threw the group into such a turmoil that for a time it looked as if the expedition would have to be cancelled. Finally Eagle Head persuaded Red Moon to conform, explaining that if one man held back, harm would to the party. Let no one doubt the efficacy of a skin sacrifice! Eagle Head's raid was entirely successful.

Like Red Moon, Eagle Head is famous for having renewed the medicine arrows on one or more occasions. Today his daughter, Mrs. Buffalo, lives in Seiling, Oklahoma.

Smithsonian Institution,
Bureau of American Ethnology

RED MOON

A Cheyenne chief, Red Moon, was active in the Indian raids which occurred during the late 1860's and early 1870's.

Wilbur S. Nye Collection

Young Cheyenne

In view of his charm bracelet and somewhat effeminate features and hands, we would not be certain of this Indian's sex were it not for his narrow, braided scalp lock, hair braids wrapped in cloth, and hair-pipe breast-plate. Furthermore, on his left wrist is a bowstring guard or an arm band that would serve as protection against the snap of a bowstring.

The studio props are the customary ones used by Soule: a stump, straw on the carpet, and a painted backdrop. The typical Soule pose—the subject with one hand supporting the head—is not to portray a reflective attitude but to insure immobility while the time exposure is being made.

Note the light diagonal stripes down the cheek. These markings may be paint, scars, or tattooing, probably the former, and were probably used for decoration.

Smithsonian Institution,
Bureau of American Ethnology

Young Cheyenne Woman

This portrait was made by Soule at Camp Supply in 1869. He did not record the name. She may have been one of Custer's captives, for she is plainly dressed and wears no ornaments; the women taken at the Battle of the Washita came away without any of their personal belongings. Ordinarily a woman having her photograph taken would dress up in all her finery.

Cheyenne women were noted for their chastity and their somewhat conservative attitude. They were modest in dress and comportment and industrious in their habits. Though the wife or daughter of a Plains Indian worked hard, she was by no means the downtrodden slave that she is sometimes described as being. In the Cheyenne tribe especially and also in the other southwestern Plains tribes, the women occupied a coequal status with the men. In their own sphere of responsibility, which was the care of the lodge and the upbringing of the children, they had the final word; but they were consulted on other matters, too, including tribal affairs. The women worked hard, but they did not resent this; in fact, they would have been ashamed for their men to have done any of the cooking or housekeeping.

Smithsonian Institution,
Bureau of American Ethnology

Ox Train

An early lithograph, possibly made from a photograph by William A. Bell, of a typical scene along the Arkansas route or the Smoky Hill, where a "bull train" was crossing a tributary. Such spots were often the sites of Indian attacks, because the trains were more vulnerable while fording a stream or camped near a ford.

William A. Bell
New Tracks in America

OLD SIOUX IN VILLAGE DESTROYED BY HANCOCK

This drawing by Theodore R. Davis shows a portion of the Cheyenne village burned by Hancock. Hancock's action initiated a controversy which is still going on about whether Hancock's action started a war. The old Indian had been abandoned by his people when they fled from the village. He later died of cholera at Fort Dodge, as did a young girl who was also abandoned by the Indians.

Harper's Weekly,
May 11, 1867

This illustration was sketched for *Harper's Weekly* by J. Howland who caught the spirit of the occasion, perhaps, but was not too careful about details. Howland claims that the Indians are Kiowas and Comanches, but at that time neither tribe wore feathers in their hair, although a few prominent warriors owned full-length, eagle-feather war bonnets which they put on before going into battle. The leafy arbor, however, is proper. The Indians still use them.

Harper's Weekly,
1868

COUNCIL AT MEDICINE-CREEK LODGE WITH THE KIOWA AND COMANCHE INDIANS.—Sketched by J. Howland.—[See Page 725.]

HANCOCK'S EXPEDITION

General Hancock's brigade camped at Fort Harker on April 2, 1867. Sketch by Philip D. Fisher.

Harper's Weekly,
April 27, 1867

THE INDIAN EXPEDITION—GENERAL HANCOCK'S ENCAMPMENT AT FORT HARKER, KANSAS, APRIL 2, 1867.—SKETCHED BY PHILIP D. FISHER.—[SEE PAGE 270.]

Arapaho Medicine Man Preparing Dinner

The Soule caption states that the medicine man or his wife is preparing a dinner of dog meat for his family. Arapahoes and Cheyennes considered roasted dog a delicacy. They also liked coyote pups. Of the Plains tribes, only the Comanches were disgusted at the idea of eating dogs.

Note the brass bucket, used for carrying water and for boiling food. The Indians obtained such utensils from traders, and they lasted for generations. The Indians did not regularly use them for cooking, for they preferred to roast their meat over an open fire.

Smithsonian Institution,
Bureau of American Ethnology

Four Arapahoes

There are several things to note in this early Soule photograph. It may be seen that all four braves have plucked the hair from their lips, chins, and eyebrows—a universal custom of the Plains Indians. The second man from the right has a "Jeff Davis" military hat with star. This Indian is also wearing a hair-pipe breastplate, silver arm bands and gorget, a ring, and at least two metal or shell discs. His hat is edged with the round metal ornaments seen on other Arapahoes. His hair braids are wrapped in otter fur. In his scalp lock is a bear claw, which means that he killed a grizzly in personal combat, perhaps with a knife. He is a real man, and an Arapaho of substance.

Ralph Whitetail believes that this photograph was taken at Camp Supply.

Smithsonian Institution,
Bureau of American Ethnology

Big Cow, an Arapaho, killed Major Joel H. Elliott at the Battle of the Washita. Since the Indians were defending their village and families against attack, this was an act of war, not of murder. No doubt Big Cow gained a certain amount of honor in his tribe as a result of this exploit.

Smithsonian Institution,
Bureau of American Ethnology

This Penateka-Comanche chief, whose name is sometimes spelled Asa-toyeh, was an "agency" Indian, friendly and co-operative with the authorities. He acted as a guide to Custer in 1868 and helped Grierson locate the site of Fort Sill. Today he is buried in the post cemetery with several other notables. He is shown here wearing an enlisted man's jacket and carrying a Remington or Whitney revolver.

The name Asa-toyet is translated into English as Gray Leggings, the syllable *asa* being pronounced *aesa* (gray) as differentiated from *esa* or *isa*, meaning *wolf*.

Smithsonian Institution,
Bureau of American Ethnology

ESA-ROSA

This Yapparika Comanche, who name means White Wolf, was a lifelong companion and the brother-in-law of the famous chief, Tabananica, and a noted warrior and chief in his own right. He used to have a house northeast of Fort Sill, and a hill in that area is named for him. He has a number of descendants living in Comanche County, Oklahoma, today. J. K. Hillers may have been the photographer.

Smithsonian Institution,
Bureau of American Ethnology

ESA-HAVEY

The name of this Penateka-Comanche subchief has always been spelled Asa-Havey and translated as "Milky Way." But in Indian figure of speech the Milky Way is "The Wolf's Road." Therefore this name should be spelled *Esa*-Havey.

In 1867–69 this man camped with his band near Fort Arbuckle and was helpful to the post commander in visiting the camps of the wild Indians and arranging with them to give up (for a price) the captives they had taken in Texas and Mexico. It was largely through his good offices that the captives taken at the notorious raid on the village of Spanish Fort were recovered. He also was identified with the group of friendly Indians during the time that the agency was at Fort Sill.

Esa-Havey, or Asa-Havey, has frequently been confused with Esa-Habeet, owing to the similarity in the sound of the names. But they were not the same. This photograph was taken in Washington in 1872 by Alexander Gardner.

Smithsonian Institution,
Bureau of American Ethnology

Mow-way

The most dangerous animal on the western Plains was the white man. Next was the grizzly bear which, until about 1860 was plentiful in the plains. The grizzly was a formidable foe—one that would attack without warning. Ti-so-yo, the son of the great war chief Mow-way of the Kotchateka Comanches, tells how his father killed a grizzly with a knife:

> Mow-way with two companions was hunting in eastern New Mexico. They were walking single-file along a dry gulch when suddenly a huge grizzly attacked the rear man. One man fled, but the chief dashed back to help the one being attacked. Badly mauled, this poor fellow was trying to hold the beast's muzzle from his throat. Mow-way stabbed the bear with his knife, which, penetrating a vital spot, killed the beast. Thereafter Mow-way wore as a memento one huge claw tied to his scalplock.

White men thought the name Mow-way (or Mow-wi) meant Shaking Hand or Hand Shaker, but his son says that it means Push Aside. Mow-way, though an associate of the wild Quohada, Parra-o-coom, was friendly to the whites after 1871. He had also signed the Medicine Lodge Treaty.

In 1878, Mow-way abdicated his chieftainship; he wished to spend the rest of his days with his family on a farm south of the agency. He died there of pneumonia in 1886. His family wrapped him in a blanket, took his body three miles east in a wagon to an unmarked grave at the foot of South Arbuckle Hill.

Wilbur S. Nye Collection

Mow-way's Village

In the winter of 1872–73 the Comanche chiefs Mow-way and Parra-o-coom moved their camps from the Staked Plains to the vicinity of the agency, just south of Fort Sill. They stayed there until the late spring or early summer of 1873, while awaiting the return and release of the Quohada women and children who had been captured by Colonel Mackenzie in the fall. Soule visited these camps in the company of Interpreter Horace Jones, and the Evans brothers, post traders, and took a series of photographs of the camps. These pictures give a true concept of the Comanche villages before the Indians had given up any of their primitive ways.

In this view, which is taken along Cache Creek, we see a group of women and children sitting in front of what may be Mow-way's tipi, with Horace Jones seated in the center. To the left is a covered war shield on a tripod. To the right of the group may be seen a large dog, which has moved. It appears to be one of Jones's wolfhounds, not an Indian dog. Note the neat, clean appearance of this camp and the absence of horses. The horse herd of this village must have been very large, but was doubtless grazing at a distance.

Smithsonian Institution,
Bureau of American Ethnology

Parra-o-coom (He Bear) never attended a peace council and never signed a treaty. Head chief of the Quohada Comanches, his principal occupation and pleasure was fighting, preferably hand-to-hand combat. He is the man on the left in the accompanying photograph. Co-hay-yah says of this chief:

> Parra-o-coom was our greatest fighter and our head chief. He was a great bear of a man, with curly hair. He always wanted to have personal fights with the enemy. In the fall of 1872 the soldiers attacked our camps on White River. As soon as he heard the shooting begin at one of the camps farther downstream, Parra-o-coom shouted, "Get all your good horses! Tie up their tails! Mount up! Get ready to fight!"
>
> We rode to where the soldiers were crouching in gullies firing at our camps on the edge of the timber. We could see that it would be hard to get at them with bows and arrows. Then Parra-o-coom made a little talk to encourage us: "When I was a young man like you I met things straight ahead. I fight! I want you young men to do the same. Be brave!"
>
> So we charged right at the firing line. But their bullets cut down at least 20 of us, and we pulled back. Then our women came out with their hands in the air and surrendered.

Smithsonian Institution,
Bureau of American Ethnology

SOULE AND FRIENDS VISIT PARRA-O-COOM

Left to right: Horace P. Jones, post interpreter, Fort Sill; Parra-o-coom, great chief of the Quohada Comanches; Neal Evans, post trader; Jack Evans, post trader; unknown Comanche; William S. Soule (reclining); George Fox, employee of Evans; unknown Comanche. The identification of Soule was by Henry G. Peabody, one of Soule's former associates, or by Soule himself. If the identification is correct, then at that time Soule was wearing a short beard. This appears to be a friendly gathering, undoubtedly made in the winter of 1872–73 when Parra-o-coom was camped near the agency, waiting for the release of the women captured by Mackenzie. He died a year and a half later while west of the mountains, and, so far as is known, this 1873 contact was the only one (other than in battle) he made with the whites. Note the shotguns; Jones and Evans evidently expected to do some bird hunting while on this visit to the Indian camps. Quail, doves, and turkeys were plentiful.

Smithsonian Institution,
Bureau of American Ethnology

WILD HORSE

Kobay-o-burra (Wild Horse), second chief of the Quohadas, took over the principal chieftainship when Parra-o-coom died in 1874. He was a burly fellow and a brave, experienced fighter. A number of his descendants are living in Comanche County today, all respected people. They have a right to be proud of their ancestry, for Wild Horse was one of the finest warriors of his time. However, like most of the Quohadas, he did not come to the notice of the agent and those people who wrote their reminiscences in those days; thus, he is not as well known today as his exploits warrant. This is thought to be a Soule photograph.

When Parra-o-coom died in June, 1874, Wild Horse became first chief of the Quohada Comanches, and Black Horse became second chief. At the time of the fight at Anadarko, Black Horse was with his band in the Staked Plains south of Yellowhouse Canyon. During or just prior to the Palo Duro Canyon affair, this band encountered some of Mackenzie's troops, attacked a few soldiers who were guarding a horse herd, and killed several men. This skirmish occurred south of the site of the Goodnight Ranch.

Black Horse was one of the Comanches sent to prison in Florida. Evidently some of them were permitted to take their families, for in this photograph, taken at Fort Marion in 1875, we see Black Horse with his wife and child.

In June, 1878, when he had just returned from Florida, Black Horse took twenty-five of his people on a buffalo hunt in Texas. Somewhere south of Big Spring they were attacked by seven Texas Rangers. At first the Rangers had the upper hand, but in withdrawing, Black Horse ambushed the Texans, killed one or two and wounded two. He made his way safely back to the reservation. This was the last Comanche fight in Texas. Photograph by Wilson and Havens.

Smithsonian Institution,
Bureau of American Ethnology

Otter Belt was mentioned by Thomas Battey as being a young Comanche who was friendly and helpful. During the winter of 1873–74, he assisted the agent in identifying the hostiles who had killed one of a party of surveyors on the reservation.

The light-colored stripes on the sides of his face are painted there purely for decorative purposes and do not indicate that he was on the warpath. His expression indicates that he was a man of good will.

Smithsonian Institution,
Bureau of American Ethnology

311

COMANCHE WOMEN

Shown here are some of the Comanche women photographed by Soule in 1873 when he visited the camps of Parra-o-coom, Mow-way, and Horse-back. Soule does not give any of their names, but Albert Attocknie said that the one on the left is Cha-wa-ke, or Looking-for-Something-Good.

Smithsonian Institution,
Bureau of American Ethnology

Quanah Parker

After the Indian wars were over, the Nokoni chief Quanah came rapidly to the fore. He had already won great renown as a fighter and was one of the very last to surrender. The son of the white captive Cynthia Ann Parker and a Nokoni chief, Quanah had superior ability and intelligence. It was noticeable that most of the Comanches turned instinctively to him for leadership, for, although he had always lived far out on the plains and had had no contact with the whites, he seemed to know how to deal with them. During the period subsequent to 1875, when large cattle owners were renting grazing privileges on the Indian reservation, Quanah began to acquire a herd of his own and thus laid the foundation for a comfortable income, if not a fortune. He followed the Indian custom of marrying several women and, as a result, has many descendants today, quite a few of whom are influential members of their communities. Quanah Parker has almost founded a tribe of his own, and it is a highly respected clan.

Both Quanah and his mother are buried in the Fort Sill cemetery.

Wilbur S. Nye Collection

Addo-eette, or Big Tree, was born in the winter of 1847. He was an outstanding warrior before he was twenty and a member of most of the war parties that terrorized the Texas border in the spring and summer of 1868. He showed so much dash and courage that, despite his youth, he was recognized as a war chief.

During the famous council with General Sherman, at which he was arrested with Satank and Satanta, he kept quiet, as befits a young man in the presence of his elders. He had nothing to say when Satank was killed, and he did not whine at his trial. He was a model prisoner at Huntsville, and, because of his good behavior and youth, it was felt, after the 1875 outbreak, that he could be rehabilitated. Therefore, he was not returned to prison with Satanta.

In later years Big Tree continued to be of influence in his tribe. He scoffed at the false prophet Poinkia who tried to lead the Kiowas into trouble. Finally he was converted to Christianity and for many years was an elder in the Rainy Mountain Baptist Church. He told George Hunt that he never ceased to regret the many horrible deeds he had committed when a young man on the warpath. He died in 1927.

Smithsonian Institution,
Bureau of American Ethnology

Tau-ankia (Sitting-in-the-Saddle) was the favorite son of Lone Wolf, principal chief of the Kiowas. Since he was the son of a prominent man, he dressed accordingly, and had been given many rich gifts of horses, weapons, and ornaments. He was also a skilled and experienced fighter, having been on many raids prior to the final one in 1873 when he was killed in Texas by Lieutenant Charles Hudson. He and his cousin were popular young men and *on-de*, or members of the highest caste.

This photograph was taken by Soule in his Fort Sill studio in 1872. It shows Tau-ankia dressed similarly to his close friend, Mamay-day-te. Notice his decorated riding crop and his gun, which appears to be a Spencer seven-shot repeating carbine, a weapon used by cavalry.

Smithsonian Institution,
Bureau of American Ethnology

GUI-TAIN

From the dress of this young Kiowa and other internal evidence, this is believed to be Gui-tain (Heart of a Young Wolf), son of Red Otter, and nephew of Chief Lone Wolf. With his cousin Tau-ankia, he was killed in Texas in 1873.

He wears the fur cap which distinguishes the *on-de*. A man was not born an *on-de*; he had to win that honor by his bravery, generosity, and general popularity. It would have been very rare and difficult, however, for a poor boy to become an *on-de*, as he would not have the horses and other property with which to make the necessary rich gifts. Thus while being the son or nephew of a chief did not guarantee that a man would become an *on-de*, it definitely helped.

Smithsonian Institution,
Bureau of American Ethnology

KIOWA BRAVE IN WAR DRESS

This man, Koi-khan-hole, has an unusually large breastplate made of hair pipe, and pendants of the same material hang from at least one of his ears. He also wears beads made of hair pipe attached to his scalp lock. The leather wristlet is to protect his arm at that point from the snap of the bowstring. Around his waist is a fur, evidently from a wolf, and his weapon case appears to be of the same material. Judging from his dress and ornamentation, he was a man of distinction.

Smithsonian Institution,
Bureau of American Ethnology

Another man of distinction, this unidentified brave is also well ornamented, although he does not have as much hair pipe as does the Indian in the preceding photograph. His hair is cut off above the shoulder on his right side, an old-time Kiowa custom, and his bow is somewhat longer than those customarily used by mounted warriors.

Smithsonian Institution,
Bureau of American Ethnology

This young Kiowa, whose name has the musical translation Cry-of-the-Wild-Goose, was the favorite son of Satanta. But although Satanta was regarded as being somewhat of a villain on account of his raiding in Texas, Tsa'l-au-te, or Saloso as he was called by the whites, was a prime favorite at Fort Sill. Evidently he had an attractive personality and was a man of good humor and friendliness. Even though he was a member of Pago-to-goodle's revenge raid for Auto-tainte in 1879, he retained his popularity with the officers at the post. In later years he was a member of Scott's Troop L, Seventh Cavalry, and when he died, he left his father's war shield to Scott. This famous shield, made by Black Horse about 1795 and carried in at least one hundred battles, even as far south as Durango, Mexico, is believed to be in the museum of the University of California.

Smithsonian Institution,
Bureau of American Ethnology

327

Tape-day-ah means Standing-Sweat-House. At the age of fourteen, he went on a three-year raid deep into Mexico with another boy, a grown man named Hone-zep-tai, and several others. After a year of successful horse stealing, they decided to return to their home camps by following the Rocky Mountains. They failed, and during their adventuresome trip Hone-zep-tai was killed, and the two boys, after great hardship, made their way back to Mexico where they were rescued by some Comanches. The experience made a man of Tape-day-ah, and he evidently became quite a warrior, for it is to be noted that he wears the dress of an *on-de*. Maman-ti also selected him to be an apprentice medicine man.

During the period 1870–74, he was a member of every raid made by the Kiowas, but after the wars were over, he enlisted in the troop of U.S. Indian scouts at Fort Sill. He was an older brother of Iseeo.

Smithsonian Institution,
Bureau of American Ethnology

Mooney identifies Bird Chief (Tene-'taide) as a Kiowa warrior who in the summer of 1872 led a small party north on a raid into Kansas. This was over the protests of the other chiefs, who were trying to keep the tribe quiet in hopes of obtaining the release from prison of Satanta and Big Tree. But some of the Indians, especially the Cheyennes, were upset over the appearance in their country of survey parties. They thought that the government was preparing to divide up their land again and parcel it out to the white men or to eastern tribes.

Apparently Bird Chief felt the same grievance. He acquired some Osage recruits shortly after arriving at the Kansas border. Soon thereafter, when near Medicine Lodge Creek, they saw a party of men whom they took to be surveyors. In the skirmish which followed, a Kiowa-Mexican named Biako (Viego) and an Osage were wounded.

Bird Chief is wearing a Jeff Davis hat with an infantry insignia—a bugle. When soldiers wore the hat before the Civil War, they turned the brim up on one side and held it in place with a brass ornament. Also, a large ostrich plume was worn with it.

Smithsonian Institution,
Bureau of American Ethnology

331

Mamay-day-te was an experienced warrior, on whom old Lone Wolf conferred his mantle and name at the conclusion of the Lost Valley fight in July, 1874. The agent did not immediately recognize him as principal chief, but subsequent to 1879, when Lone Wolf died, he slowly rose to that position, or virtually so, for, after the pacification of the Indians, there were few genuine chiefs. In 1886, under the name of Lone Wolf, he was appointed member of a three-man court to try Indians for various offenses. He made several trips to Washington as a tribal delegate, and was one of those who represented his tribe in matters of great importance such as the opening of the reservation to homesteading in 1901. He was converted to Christianity in 1893 and became a member of the Elk Creek Baptist Church. He died in 1923 at the age of eighty and was buried in the Elk Creek cemetery near Hobart, Oklahoma.

It is believed that Soule made this picture about 1870, when Mamay-day-te was a fairly young warrior. His later pictures, mostly made in Washington when he went there from time to time as chief tribal delegate, show that he had changed considerably in appearance.

Smithsonian Institution,
Bureau of American Ethnology

We have no information on this Arapaho dandy, which is unfortunate because he does not appear to be an Indian at all. But whether he is a white captive or the son of a white person is not known. He seems to have light-colored eyes and hair, and his features, especially around the eyes and mouth, certainly suggest Caucasian ancestry. Nevertheless, his dress and trappings and his companions—half-brothers or more likely foster brothers—are definitely Indian.

Smithsonian Institution,
Bureau of American Ethnology

THREE YOUNG ARAPAHOES

The two men on the right appear to be brothers.

Notice the moccasins which show the pattern of the beadwork typical in other photographs of Arapahoes. Shib-o-nes-ter looks even less like an Indian in this view.

Smithsonian Institution,
Bureau of American Ethnology

337

The Soule album identifies this simply as an Arapaho camp. The tipis are in an open, flat, treeless plain. The soil is sandy, and the grass has either been worn away or cropped off by the Indian horse herds. Some firewood must be available nearby, as is seen from the log on which the women are seated.

The Indians are dressed in their best clothes for the picture-making, but the three men on the right are indifferent to the work of the photographer, being absorbed in a gambling game.

Smithsonian Institution,
Bureau of American Ethnology

Arapaho Village

This photograph is said to be of an Arapaho camp near Camp Supply. The picture was taken by Soule in 1870. The band camped here had just completed a successful buffalo hunt, for there is meat hanging to dry, both in the foreground and also just over the head of the man wrapped in the blanket on the left. The reason for the large pile of brush is not known. It may have been built as a wind-break or sun shade, although for the latter purpose an arbor was usually erected, so that the air could circulate.

Smithsonian Institution,
Bureau of American Ethnology

Arapaho Woman

A typical studio shot, employing one of Soule's favorite props—a couch covered with a buffalo robe and the same striped shawl or blanket as is seen in a number of his studio portraits. This young woman, said to be Ba-e-tha or Za-e-tha, is dressed for the occasion. Her dress is made of a good quality trade blanket with a light-colored band around the edge. Her hair is neatly brushed and drawn back to display her earrings. Her belt is decorated with an expensive set of graduated, matched silver discs. In the early days the Indians sometimes beat these from coins, but later they bought silver or German silver discs from the traders. Her moccasins show some good beadwork.

Smithsonian Institution,
Bureau of American Ethnology

This Arapaho chief was in the delegation of his tribe who attended the Medicine Lodge Council. A year later his village was adjacent to that of Black Kettle during the Battle of the Washita. He and Left Hand led the Indians who exterminated Major Elliott's detachment, but Big Cow killed Elliott.

Here we see a proud and successful fighting man who wears a full-length war bonnet and carries a medicine lance tipped with the blade of a saber or bayonet and wrapped in otter fur. His shirt is fringed with scalps, permitted of only the highest caste men of the tribe. His eagle feathers, hair-pipe breastplate, and ceremonial hatchet were costly and denote a man of many horses and high standing as a warrior and leader.

Smithsonian Institution,
Bureau of American Ethnology

Powder Face and Family

Mrs. D. B. Dyer wrote of the Arapaho chief:

He was a finely proportioned, handsome man, with a pleasant expression and dignity of movement. Covered with scars, and celebrated long ago for the many scalps he had taken, he had the right to adopt a dozen names; yet he was known by all the plains tribes and the whites, by the title which was given him from having his face badly burned by an explosion of powder when he was a young man. He has been for years a tried and trusted friend of the government.

His character was all meekness, tempered by becoming firmness. He indulges in no display of his delegated authority; and this noble specimen of his race was a truly good Indian. After greeting you with a few words of English, he would hold up one finger, his face beaming, saying, "He one wife—one wife. Walk."

She went with him everywhere. He would sit for hours, combing her hair, petting and fondling her, this great-hearted man. He had taken several trips East, visiting the large cities, his wife always accompanying him. . . . He loved to tell with signs and broken English, how they went out in a great boat from New York.

There was also a Cheyenne named Powder Face. The man shown in these photographs was identified by Ralph Whitetail—one of the oldest living Cheyennes—as being the Arapaho of that name.

Smithsonian Institution,
Bureau of American Ethnology

Soule took a number of photographs of Arapaho villages, of which we have reproduced several representative ones, illustrative of all the Plains tribes. The one shown above has several interesting features. At first glance this picture contains four adults and a child. However, another person is lying at the feet of the two persons on the left, unless the one nearest the tipi has two right arms. The child is naked, while all the adults are clothed and wrapped in blankets. It was the custom for children below the age of puberty to be unclothed or only partly clothed when in camp.

This tipi is carefully made from closely stitched buffalo hides with the fur or hair side on the interior. Sheets of buffalo meat are drying on a rack, while a hide is staked out on the ground for drying and scraping.

Perhaps one of the most interesting features of this Arapaho village is that it is a Kiowa village. At least that is what Enoch Smoky says.

Smithsonian Institution,
Bureau of American Ethnology

Here we have an excellent illustration of the difficulty in securing the correct names of old-time Indians. Custer gave these three men one set of names. Several Cheyennes and white historians have either followed his lead or have supplied other names. According to Custer, the Cheyennes are (left to right): Curley Head, Fat Bear, and Dull Knife. This is not the Dull Knife who was a leader of the group who tried to join the northern tribes in 1876. In Grinnell the names given these three Indians are (left to right): Young Bear, One Bear, and Island.

They are shown here at Camp Supply shortly after they had been seized on Sweetwater Creek as part of Custer's plan to force the Cheyenne and Arapaho tribes onto a reservation to be established for them with an agency at Camp Supply.

Later, when the Cheyennes arrived at Fort Hays, Kansas, they felt that Custer had violated his promise to release his prisoners if they, the Cheyennes, would come to the agency at Camp Supply and surrender.

At Fort Hays prisoners were confined in a stockade. A few days later it was decided to put the three men in a blockhouse. When a squad of soldiers came in to effect the transfer, the women, thinking their men were being taken away to be executed, tried to attack the guard with their kitchen knives. The soldiers promptly shot Curley Head to death, bayonetted Dull Knife, and clubbed Fat Bear into insensibility.

Smithsonian Institution,
Bureau of American Ethnology

Soul.

Issue Day at Camp Supply

This is probably the first issue of rations and annuities at Camp Supply. For years this photograph was believed to have been made at Fort Sill, but more recent information places Camp Supply as the site. This identification comes from Morgan Otis, a construction engineer and a descendant of the Fort Marion Kiowa prisoner, Zotom (Zontam), and of Pacer, the Kiowa-Apache chief. Mr. Otis is married to a descendant of Yellow Bear and Spotted Wolf—Arapahoes. This illustrates how modern Indians are sometimes the offspring of intertribal marriages. Frequently the parents met at school.

The agency ration issues initially were flour, sugar, coffee, dried fruit, and desiccated vegetables. Beef was issued later after the buffalo had become scarce.

Wilbur S. Nye Collection

SUN BOY

Pai-talyi (Sun Boy) was another prominent chief of the Kiowas. He visited Washington in 1872 as a member of the delegation escorted by Henry Alvord. The Kiowa calendar shows that during the sun dance in 1876, some Mexican traders stole all of Pai-talyi's horses. Two years later he took his band on a buffalo hunt under troop escort. One of the band, Au-to-tainte, was killed by Texas Rangers when he chased a deer across Red River. This set off the revenge raid by Pago-to-goodle the following year.

Sun Boy died in 1888 in a camp northwest of Mount Scott.

Smithsonian Institution,
Bureau of American Ethnology

Whenever old Kiowas got together for some storytelling, the name of Pago-to-goodle (Lone Young Man) was sure to come up. He was a member of almost every warlike expedition launched by the Kiowas in the sixties and seventies, and was the leader of many of them. Apparently he was somewhat like Maman-ti in that he shunned publicity, for his name does not appear in written history. Nevertheless, he was one of the bravest and most experienced fighters the tribe ever produced, and he bore a magic name. His grandfather or great-grandfather, of the same name, was also famous in the annals of the tribe, having had a wonderful adventure in warfare against the Comanches in about the year 1790. As might be expected, Pago-to-goodle was a member of the Ko-eetsenko.

Pago-to-goodle, who was a brother of Sun Boy, led the last raid ever made by the Kiowas—a revenge raid made in 1878 for the killing by Texans of another brother, Au-to-tainte, the heir to Satanta's medicine lance. The party went to the site of Quanah, Texas, and killed a man named Joe Earle.

Pago-to-goodle later enlisted in Troop L, Seventh Cavalry, where he served faithfully, sometimes running down outlaw Indians. In 1898 he went to Washington as a tribal delegate, and it was on that occasion that Mooney made the accompanying photograph.

Smithsonian Institution,
Bureau of American Ethnology

Eonah-pah and Wife

Eonah-pah (Trailing-the-Enemy) was the only Kiowa who was in the Battle of the Washita; he had been spending the night in Black Kettle's camp when Custer attacked. He was a very active warrior, taking part in most of the better-known Kiowa expeditions against the Utes, Texans, and Mexicans. He married two of Satanta's daughters, one of whom is shown here with him. This woman, Alma, who was still living in 1935, was then a big, jolly person, very friendly and well liked. Notice the large number of elk teeth on her dress. Each of these was worth several dollars. It is to be noted also that she bears a resemblance to her famous father.

Eonah-pah became a member of Troop L, Seventh Cavalry, during the eighties and nineties, serving faithfully for a number of years.

Smithsonian Institution,
Bureau of American Ethnology

358

359

Poor Buffalo, or more accurately Lean Buffalo or Lean Bull, was a minor Kiowa chief and a member of many war expeditions in the sixties and seventies. He was in the last group to surrender in February, 1875. His descendants furnished the author with much valuable information, especially concerning the very early history of the tribe—in the days before peace was made with the Comanches.

Gillett Griswold obtained the following identifications from descendants: Poor Buffalo (center), Odl-kaun't-say-hah, Kaw-tom-te, Haun-goon-pau, A'tah-ladte.

Smithsonian Institution,
Bureau of American Ethnology

Ah-peah-tone (Feathered Lance) was famous mainly for his part in the Ghost Dance excitement in 1890–91. In order that the Kiowas might be informed as to the authenticity of the Indian messiah who had started the Ghost Dance, Ah-peah-tone made a pilgrimage to Utah to see the messiah for himself. But he found only an ordinary Indian without stigmata or any other evidence that he was what he claimed to be. Greatly disillusioned, Ah-peah-tone returned to his tribe and made a report that was largely responsible for the Ghost Dance dying out among the Kiowas.

As may be seen, Ah-peah-tone is richly dressed. Note the long fringes on his doeskin shirt and the 1889 medal bearing a likeness of President Benjamin Harrison. This photograph, by an unknown photographer, was made in 1894 when Ah-peah-tone was a delegate to Washington from his tribe.

After Lone Wolf died in 1879, part of the tribe recognized Ah-peah-tone as principal chief.

Ah-peah-tone's grandson, Taft Hainta, is president of the Kiowa Gourd Dance Clan.

Smithsonian Institution,
Bureau of American Ethnology

DO-HAUSON (TO-HAUSON)

The principal chief of the Kiowas from 1834 to 1866 was a mighty man named Do-hauson (Little Mountain), who bore a hereditary name but who won his chieftainship through ability. On his death the principal chieftainship passed to Lone Wolf. The man pictured here was a nephew of the old chief. This nephew was an able warrior and participant in many of the important raids and battles staged by the Kiowas. He was a member of the 1872 delegation to Washington, and he was in the Lost Valley fight and the siege of Lyman's wagon train in 1874. This Do-hauson was one of the last warriors to surrender in February, 1875. The photograph of him and his wife Ankima was taken by James Mooney in 1893. It shows Do-hauson dressed in a war shirt trimmed with ermine tails and Navaho scalps.

Ermine tails, a symbol of alertness, were obtained from northern tribes and from traders. The channel of trade was indeed a strange one. About 1800, according to Woodward, the Kwakiutl on the Northwest coast began to obtain ermine from traders who bought it from the great fur center of Leipzig, Germany.

Smithsonian Institution,
Bureau of American Ethnology

Maman-ti means Sky-Walker, or Man-Who-Walks-on-the-Clouds. There is no known photograph of Maman-ti, the powerful Kiowa medicine man, prophet, and war chief. This photograph, made by an unknown photographer, is of Maman-ti's son Rainy Mountain Charley. Hoodle-tau-goodle, Maman-ti's daughter, says that the son looks exactly like his father.

Maman-ti organized and led many raids, including the Warren wagon train massacre, but he let Satanta take the credit. He was a somewhat sinister character and is supposed to have prayed Kicking Bird to death, but in so doing he forfeited his own life. He was one of the Fort Marion prisoners, and was reported by Pratt to have died of dysentery. It is doubtful if he ever came to Fort Sill except as a prisoner.

Hugh D. Corwin Collection

Hoodle-tau-goodle (Red Dress) was a daughter of the Kiowa medicine man, war chief, and owl prophet—Maman-ti.

She was also a foster sister of Tehan, the captive Texan member of the tribe who disappeared after the wagon train fight in 1874. Some Kiowas think he was killed by Big Bow. A man named Joe Griffis came to Anadarko in later years, claiming to be Tehan. But Hoodle-tau-goodle says he is not the Tehan she knew.

Wilbur S. Nye Collection

TROTTING WOLF AND WIFE

Trotting Wolf was one of Kicking Bird's assistants. The first schoolteacher among the Kiowas, Thomas Battey, mentioned him several times as being hospitable, friendly, and very helpful. On a number of occasions he protected Battey against several Kiowas who were attempting to bully or frighten the Quaker teacher. Trotting Wolf's wife often prepared Battey's meals. Her apparent beard in this picture is a flaw in the negative, but it is obvious that she was no beauty.

The name Trotting Wolf was used by Battey, and Soule probably got it from him. Enoch Smoky says a better translation would be Walking Coyote.

Smithsonian Institution,
Bureau of American Ethnology

371

ENOCH SMOKY

Enoch Smoky is notable mainly because he was one of John P. Harrington's chief assistants at the time Mr. Harrington was gathering data for his book *The Vocabulary of the Kiowa Language, Bureau of American Ethnology, Bulletin 84*. This photograph was made by Soule when Enoch was a small boy, and was labeled, probably as a joke, "Kiowa Warrior."

He is one of the oldest living Kiowas.

Wilbur S. Nye Collection

Dego or Pacer

Generally known as Pacer, a corruption of an Apache word meaning Iron Sack, this man was head chief of the Kiowa-Apaches. He had considerable ability and was a consistent advocate of friendly relations with the white people. Like Kicking Bird of the Kiowas, he was appointed by the agent and post commander to act as contact man between the authorities and his people. His tribe camped between Fort Sill and Fort Cobb, and a number of them, including Pacer, made a real effort to become farmers.

Pacer died five days after Kicking Bird, the cause again unknown. At the request of his family, he was given a civilized burial in the post cemetery. Tennyson Berry, a prominent member of the tribe, states that Pacer's line has died out.

Mooney lists the following men as subchiefs of the Kiowa-Apaches: Gonkow, Daha, Gray Eagle, Dauveko, and White Man. Gray Eagle was one of Pacer's sons. White Man was second chief. Dauveko, a subchief, has several living descendants, among them Stewart and Virginia Klinkole and Henry Witseline.

Smithsonian Institution,
Bureau of American Ethnology

Mount Scott is seen in the background. Two or three war shields on their tripods are visible in this photograph by Soule, thought to have been made in 1873.

Smithsonian Institution,
Bureau of American Ethnology

Pacer's Son

The name of this young man is not given, but Soule took him in two poses which are almost identical. He has a rather arrogant appearance and is richly dressed. Notice the hair-pipe breastplate, brass hatchet, silver beads, silver chain tied to his scalp lock, and beaver or otter fur wrapped around one braid.

Smithsonian Institution,
Bureau of American Ethnology

No doubt these cousins were "partners," it being a custom among the Plains Indians to operate in pairs, usually brothers or cousins. This was like the "buddy system" tried out in the U.S. Army during World War II.

Note the neckpiece made of short pieces of hair pipe. John C. Ewers states that this type of ornament, actually made of conch shell, was a rarity.

Smithsonian Institution,
Bureau of American Ethnology

381

BLACK HAWK

It is unfortunate that nothing is known today concerning this Kiowa-Apache, for he is a fine-looking man and his face shows much character. He had a reputation for being friendly and co-operative. He is wearing some expensive ornamentation and a Washington medal, and has the shoulder insignia of a major or lieutnant colonel.

One wonders if this might be Black Eagle, a Kiowa who signed the Medicine Lodge Treaty.

Smithsonian Institution,
Bureau of American Ethnology

383

Taw-haw was a Kiowa-Apache minor chief, as indicated in the records of Camp Supply, wherein it is told that Colonel Nelson, on arrival at that station, had to order Taw-haw and Satanta back to their own agency. They had come from Fort Sill to draw rations, saying that they were given only corn at Sill.

During the Ghost Dance excitement, Taw-haw became one of the priests of that movement.

Wilbur S. Nye Collection

Caddo George once told trader Jack Evans that he had killed his father with an ax. The provocation, he explained, was that his father was a witch who was trying to cast an evil spell over him. Lizzie Borden-like, he had given his father forty whacks, then had chopped his body into small pieces to insure that it remained harmless.

In August, 1861, Caddo George espoused the cause of the Confederacy, although most of his tribe went north with the Wichitas. Under his Indian name, Showetat (Little Boy), he raised and commanded a battalion of Indian scouts which served with the Confederate forces west of the Mississippi.

At the end of the war, Caddo George switched his allegiance quickly to the United States and began to loiter around the frontier posts of Fort Arbuckle and Fort Cobb. When the Caddo-Wichita agency was placed at Anadarko, he settled there and ran what the Indians called a "store." He bootlegged firearms to the wild Indians and liquor for certain white men in the area who sold it to the Indians. He must have obtained some Spencer carbines, possibly from war surplus sales, for several Indians say that most of the arms used in the Warren wagon train massacre came from Caddo George.

In this Soule photograph, Caddo George is dressed as befits his position as a Caddo chief. His pants may be a trifle long, but otherwise he is right in style.

Smithsonian Institution,
Bureau of American Ethnology

387

Soule took a number of good photographs of Medicine Bluff Creek and the four bluffs, probably during the winter of 1868–69 when the troops first came from Fort Cobb to establish Fort Sill. The mounted men shown here appear to be Colonel Benjamin Grierson and some of his officers. Grierson was famous during the Civil War as a cavalry leader, being then a major general. After the war, he commanded the Tenth Cavalry.

The Indians held Medicine Bluff in veneration for centuries before the white man came. Prior to the establishment of the military post nearby, they used to go there to fast and pray for their god to confer "power" upon them. This usually took the form of a dream or hallucination in which they were instructed about what their own private medicine should consist of.

Smithsonian Institution,
Bureau of American Ethnology

Hunting Scene

The man on the right is Horace P. Jones, post interpreter at Fort Sill. He had been an interpreter of Comanche at various posts since before the Civil War. The third man from the right is W. H. Quinette, long-time post trader at Fort Sill, later a pioneer banker in Lawton.

Wilbur S. Nye Collection

GROUP AT CAMP SUPPLY

This 1870 Soule photograph was taken in front of a typical sod house at Camp Supply. An authentic replica of one of these pioneer dwellings may be seen today in the Old Stone Corral section of the Fort Sill Museum. This picture shows several army officers from the Third Infantry and Tenth Cavalry, together with sutlers, Arapaho Indians, and unidentified whites.

Smithsonian Institution,
Bureau of American Ethnology

Esadowa (or Isadowa) was chief of the Wichita village adjacent to the Comanche camp attacked by Van Dorn in 1858. In 1861, Esadowa led his people north to Kansas, then in 1865 brought them back to Indian Territory. On June 14, 1873, Esadowa was killed by Osages while he was hunting buffalo.

Esadowa's quizzical expression does not stem from a sense of humor. He was a victim of Bell's Palsy, a mild form of facial paralysis which afflicts quite a few of the southern Plains Indians even to this day. Pe-at-mah, one-time wife of Hunting Horse, had it in 1935. When she was not cured at the government Indian hospital at Lawton, she applied to Silverhorn, a skilled Kiowa medicine man, for relief. As nearly as I was able to understand from the story she gave me in sign language, the treatment was as follows: The medicine man, using a piece of broken beer bottle, made several gashes in the skin of her temple and back of the ear on the affected side of the head. Then he squeezed out the "bad blood," which he said was causing the trouble. Finally, he knocked out one or two of her back molars, using a bone tool and a rock for a mallet. The operation, which was entirely successful, was accompanied by singing, prayer, and the shaking of a gourd rattle. One is reminded that in the not too distant past white doctors extracted teeth for many ailments. Without, of course, the music.

Smithsonian Institution,
Bureau of American Ethnology

Miss Lucia A. Soule presented this photograph to me in 1965, the last picture she had discovered of her father's collection. It appears to be "Tawakoni Jim," chief of the Tawakoni tribe.

Wilbur S. Nye Collection

WICHITA GRASS HOUSE

The Wichitas made a permanent lodge by covering a pole frame with rush thatching. The only opening was the door, so that the interior was dark and sooty. Lodges of this pattern were seen by Coronado in 1541 when he visited the "Kingdom of Quivira." The Wichita village seen by the Dragoon expedition in 1834 on the North Fork of Red River and the one near the Comanche camp attacked by Van Dorn in 1858 contained grass houses identical to those shown here. Later the Wichitas built a few grass houses in their village near Anadarko, but gradually these came to be used as outbuildings for the storage of farm implements and produce, since these Indians were acquiring houses. Today a replica of a grass house may be seen in the Old Stone Corral annex to the Fort Sill Museum.

Wilbur S. Nye Collection

The Caddo lodges, although similar to those of the Wichitas, differ in that they have vertical walls, sometimes boarded up instead of thatched. Archeological evidence indicates that Caddoan prehistoric lodges had low earthen walls, but they probably had thatched roofs. This photograph was taken near Anadarko.

Smithsonian Institution,
Bureau of American Ethnology

The Wichitas used a tipi similar to that of the other Plains tribes when they were away from their permanent grass-house villages, for instance, when on a buffalo hunt. Also, they used tipis during the Civil War when they were refugees in Kansas; in 1868 when at Fort Cobb; and in 1869–70 when camped near Fort Sill. This picture was probably taken at Fort Sill before the Wichitas were moved to their own agency near Anadarko. Notice that many of the tipis are made of canvas rather than buffalo hides. These Indians had not had opportunity after the war to acquire buffalo hides, but their agent furnished canvas, perhaps from salvaged military tentage. The darkening at the top of the lodges is caused by smoke and soot from the fires built on the ground inside.

Smithsonian Institution,
Bureau of American Ethnology

WICHITA WOMEN

"Wichita women were well dressed from the waist down." The women of the other southern Plains tribes—Cheyenne, Arapaho, Comanche, Kiowa— were by present-day standards excessively modest in their dress. The Wichitas at first constituted an exception, but the Quaker agents and the missionaries soon brought them into line. Before these women learned that it was wrong to appear in public partly nude, Soule obtained a series of photographs which undoubtedly sold well at Fort Sill as prairie pin-ups.

Smithsonian Institution,
Bureau of American Ethnology

Soule's duty as post photographer was to take pictures, for the quartermaster, of the buildings while under construction. This is one of a series, which shows the work in progress on the officer's quarters. The work was done by Negro troopers of the Tenth Cavalry under the supervision of civilian foremen. Some of the wood was cut locally, and the stone was quarried at Quarry Hill, east of the old post.

The view here is of the east line. The last building on the right was reserved for the post quartermaster. In 1890 that officer was Captain Hugh L. Scott, a great friend of the Indians. My family and I occupied it in 1935, and here we talked to many of the old warriors who came to the post for visits. They were always ready to recall the exciting days of old and to get some wo-haw (meat) and "some of that good Army bread."

Wilbur S. Nye Collection

INDEX

23, 29, 36, 38, 66, 69, 79, 95, 106, 107, 114ff., 122, 127, 128, 133; first occupied, 3; permanent post started, 4; exposed to attack, 7; buildings of, 8; horses stolen from, 9–11; Curtis' expedition to, 12; ammunition shortage at, 16; receives first regular troops, 40; as site of Hancock's conference with Indians, 76ff.

Fort Leavenworth, Kansas: 6, 9, 11, 13, 53, 95

Fort Lyon, Colorado: 3, 7ff., 79, 130, 141, 146

Fort Reno, I.T.: 124

Fort Riley, Kansas: 3ff., 11, 15, 16, 23, 29, 38

Fort Sill, I.T.: 114, 142ff., 150, 165, 170, 171, 176

Fort Wallace, Kansas: 50ff., 95, 96, 124, 126, 130, 171; established, 45; site of changed, 46–47; early construction of, 47; visited by Indians, 48; Indian attacks near, 83–84; threatened, 85; attacked, 86–87, 90; construction of resumed, 93; cholera at, 97; facilities of, 98

Fort Zarah, Kansas: 9, 12, 13, 16, 18, 23, 29, 40, 50, 58, 62, 76, 79, 88, 111

Forsyth, Maj. (Bvt. Col.) George A.: 124, 125

Foster, L. S.: 25

Fourth U.S. Artillery: 68

Fourth U.S. Cavalry: 165, 174

Freight trains: 53–54

"Galvanized Yankees": *see* U.S. Volunteers

German, John: 171–72

German sisters in captivity: 172, 176, 177

Getty, Col. (Bvt. Maj. Gen.) George W.: 142

Gibbs, Maj. (Bvt. Maj. Gen.) A. M.: 43, 44, 69

Goose Creek Station, Kansas: 83, 84, 86, 93

Gordon, Capt. G. A.: 42

Gordon, Capt. James J.: 45ff.

Graham, Capt. George W.: 125, 126

Grant, Gen. Ulysses S.: 30, 34, 129, 150, 155, 168

Gray Beard (Cheyenne): 176, 177

Gray Head (Cheyenne): 110

Greenwood (surveyor): 93

Grierson, Col. (Bvt. Maj. Gen.) Benjamin F.: 96, 142, 165

Griffenstein, William ("Dutch Bill"): 133, 135, 151

Grover, Abner S. ("Sharp"): 121, 124

Grover, Col. (Bvt. Maj. Gen.) Cuvier: 40

Guerrier, Edmund ("Ed Geary"): 53, 67, 122

Habby-wake (Comanche): 141

Hale, Lt. Joseph C.: 50, 76, 83, 88ff., 133

Halleck, Maj. Gen. Henry W.: 24, 25

Hamilton, Capt. Louis H.: 137

Hammer, Capt. Elisha: 30

Hancock, Maj. Gen. Winfield S.: 49, 51, 62, 66, 86, 89, 92ff., 105; makes plans for expedition, 52; expedition of, 68ff.; background of, 68–69; in council at Ft. Larned, 69–70; with Roman Nose, 71; burns village, 72; visits Ft. Dodge, 73; derided by historians, 74; offers to enlist Indians, 75; in council at Ft. Larned, 76ff.; gives Satanta a coat, 78; ends campaign, 79

Harker, Brig. Gen. Charles G.: 43

Harlan (secretary of the interior): 27

Harney, Maj. Gen. William S.: 38, 105

Harris, Cyrus: 113

Harshfield, Jacob: 156

Hays, Brig. Gen. Alexander: 78

Hazen, Col. (Bvt. Maj. Gen.) William B.: 120, 127, 128, 135, 138, 145, 150

Heap of Bears (Kiowa): 37, 110, 116, 121

Helliwell, Lt. Albert: 18

Henderson, John B.: 105